GOOD COMPANY

THE STORY OF
SCRIPPS HEALTH
AND ITS PEOPLE

SARITA EASTMAN

FOREWORD BY CHRIS VAN GORDER

SCRIPPS HEALTH
4275 Campus Point Court
San Diego, CA 92121
scripps.org

Author: Sarita Eastman
Art Direction and Design: Christina Barrila

Library of Congress Control Number: 2012935224
ISBN: 9780985208806

First Published by Scripps Health, Marketing and Communications, May 5, 2012

Printed in the United States of America.

Scripps

for Brent

Contents

Foreword

The story of Scripps Health is also the story of San Diego. San Diego would not be what it is today without Mother Mary Michael Cummings, Ellen Browning Scripps, Mercy Hospital, Scripps Memorial Hospitals, Scripps Clinic, The Scripps Research Institute, and other organizations that have evolved from the contribution these visionary women made to San Diego. From their initial contributions, San Diego has become an international hub for health care, biotech, research, and education. From the day I first walked through the doors of Scripps more than a decade ago, I have been inspired by the Scripps legacy that dates back to the early days of the city this health system serves. I have been inspired as well by the thousands of physicians, staff, volunteers, and donors who have made Scripps Health what it is today.

It is a privilege to lead an organization with such a rich history. Each of the countless stories I've been told over the past decade is compelling, but when woven together with the chronology Dr. Sarita Eastman has researched and authored—one can truly appreciate the Scripps legacy. And that is why I commissioned this book. I feared that we may lose these stories if they were not documented soon. We are at a rare place in the history of Scripps when many of the individuals mentioned in these pages are still able to be interviewed by the author. A few have passed since the project started, but we were fortunate to be able to capture their stories in time.

Our story begins with the vision of two strong, intelligent, and determined women—Ellen Browning Scripps and Mother Mary Michael Cummings. Their commitment to provide for the health care needs of a growing community has resulted in the Scripps Health of today, a nationally recognized health care system with hospitals and clinics throughout the San Diego region. Yet the story of Scripps is not about bricks and mortar, it's about people. *Good Company* tells the story of the many leaders who followed Miss Ellen and Mother Mary Michael to create this health care system.

As San Diego grew, so did Scripps. And we were instrumental at some of the critical moments in this city's history. In 1905, San Diego experienced the worst peacetime disaster in U.S. Naval history when the USS Bennington suffered an explosion in San Diego harbor. The Sisters of Mercy were there to care for the injured, and San Diego rallied to support the Navy. The response inspired the military's decision to make San Diego its West Coast base, including establishing the Naval Medical Center San Diego, which was the largest hospital in the world during World War II.

Both Scripps Mercy and Scripps Clinic have long traditions in academic medicine and research, decades before a medical school was established in San Diego. Miss Ellen's founding of a metabolic clinic and hospital in La Jolla in 1924 resulted in not just Scripps Health, but also the Scripps Clinic Medical Group and The Scripps Research Institute. As I have already noted, these three institutions evolved as the cornerstones of today's biotech and clinical research hub in Southern California. Miss Ellen could not have dreamed that in the twenty-first century, Scripps would be leading research in cardiovascular, cancer, orthopedics and diabetes care, genomic and translational medicine, and wireless health.

As hospitals in Encinitas and Chula Vista were added, and clinics from Oceanside to Eastlake, Scripps continued its mission to meet the health care needs of the community—and provide high-quality jobs. Today, Scripps Health is recognized as one of the nation's best employers. After the government, the largest employers in San Diego are health systems, making a significant economic contribution to the community.

I want to thank Dr. Sarita Eastman, whose own family history played an important role in the history of Scripps. She is the daughter of Dr. William Doyle, 1964 chief of staff at Scripps Memorial Hospital La Jolla, and of pioneering surgeon Dr. Anita Figueredo, whose history Dr. Eastman recounted in her first book, *A Trail of Light: The Very Full Life of Dr. Anita Figueredo*. A pediatrician with Scripps during her medical career, Sarita Eastman is the wife of Dr. A. Brent Eastman, distinguished trauma surgeon, chief medical officer of Scripps Health, N. Paul Whittier Chair of Trauma at Scripps La Jolla, and a founder of San Diego County's internationally recognized trauma system.

Writing this book was a labor of love for Sarita, and the story of Scripps could not have been in better hands. I thank her for her generosity of spirit and her dedication to the research and storytelling. Her personal and professional history made her the perfect author to share the Scripps story with the rest of the world.

I also want to acknowledge and thank the publishing team at Scripps who supported the author in completing this book. Christina Barrila, Shannon Strybel, Christine Clay, and Catherine Hooper provided countless hours of research, copyediting, and graphic design.

Scripps today is facing many challenges and, like many times in our history, is undergoing significant change. The stories in this book should serve as inspiration to the thousands of Scripps employees, physicians, and volunteers who work daily to continue the vision and mission of our founders. Indeed, I would hope that Scripps and the legacy of Miss Ellen and Mother Mary Michael could be an inspiration for our entire community.

I often ask myself, "Would Miss Ellen and Mother Mary Michael be proud of Scripps today? Are we living the legacy they began?" After reading *Good Company*, I have no doubt that the answer to both is an emphatic *yes*.

I hope you enjoy the book.

Chris Van Gorder, FACHE
President & CEO, Scripps Health
2012

Preface

Without social history, economic history is barren
and political history is unintelligible.

Truth is the criterion of historical study;
but its impelling motive is poetic.

> G. M. Trevelyan, *English Social History*[1]

This is a work of social history and, I hope, of poetry as well.

In *Good Company*, it has been my pleasure to tell the history of Scripps Health through other people's eyes as a way of bringing the whole great narrative to life. I have always known it was a wonderful story.

My reaction, when Chris Van Gorder first asked me to take this on, was a mixture of relish and apprehension, a sense of the great honor, and a thundering responsibility. Like all of us at Scripps, I knew a fair amount about my own "home"—Scripps La Jolla—but little enough about everyone else's, including the Clinic which sat directly behind the house in which I grew up. I knew less about the epic history of Mercy than did my own parents — my mother who operated there for a time under the all-seeing eye of Sister Alexine, and my father who cared for children at Guadalupe Clinic who had nowhere else to go.

Fortunately, I am a natural denizen of archives. And, having spent much of my medical life just listening, I learned to pay close attention to nuances of speech and what makes a memorable story. My method in assembling this rich history was to read and to listen: to read every primary and secondary source I could find and to interview key figures from our own time who could tell us what *really* went on before. All these sources and what amounted to hundreds of hours of interviews are recorded in the endnotes. The complete interview transcripts, along with priceless photographs, scrapbooks, letters, newspaper clippings, and other ephemera uncovered during the last two years will be housed in a permanent archive for curious browsers and historians of the future.

But the numbers of persons and sheer span of years demanded a cohesive story line, and medically that became the great arc of cardiology. Cardiology, as the number one clinical care line today and for many decades, is a metaphor for the evolution of medicine from the nineteenth to the twenty-first centuries. A subplot is the drama of emergency care. And every person identified by name is a spokesman for many hundreds of others who are not named, but have done great things.

In all of this, I am much indebted to those who have gone before me, beginning with Prof. Molly McClain of the University of San Diego, whose monograph on *Why the Scripps Family Came to San Diego*[2] allowed me to place our founders on the San Diego stage together at nearly the same moment in time, and who sent me to the Ella Strong Denison Library at Scripps College in Claremont, California, which holds eighty cubic feet of *The Ellen Browning Scripps Papers* housed in a small room crafted especially to hold them and part of Miss Ellen's personal library as well. The historical societies of our city and public library history rooms yielded treasures and *are* treasures. I salute my physician-friends devoted to preserving our common history, especially Dr. Clifford Colwell, who organized and led several key interviews; also Drs. John Carson, David M. Roseman, and Ralph Ocampo; as well as Robert H. Smith, former Development Director of Scripps Clinic, who presented me two years ago his trove of Scripps materials several inches thick and effectively launched this book. And I have sent many grateful thoughts heavenward toward the anonymous Sister *annalists* who so diligently preserved the history of Mercy that might otherwise have been lost.

My wonderful in-house publishing team, introduced by name in Chris's foreword, has prepared a beautiful book for us and for posterity. I hope you enjoy *Good Company.*

Sarita Eastman

Ellen Browning Scripps, c. 1891
courtesy of Ella Strong Denison Library, Scripps College

Mother Mary Michael Cummings, c. 1890s
courtesy of Scripps Health

CHAPTER ONE
Beginnings
1890 AND BEFORE

THE STORY OF SCRIPPS HEALTH is first of all the story of two single women from Illinois who grew up on farms a hundred miles apart and made their separate ways west to San Diego in the unpromising year of 1890. Ellen Browning Scripps and Mother Mary Michael Cummings never met in this life, but they were linked in myriad ways and more alike than most observers would have guessed.

"Miss Ellen" Scripps, founder of the first hospital and clinic to bear her name, and Mother Mary Michael, founder of the hospital of the Sisters of Mercy, were a short generation apart—seventeen years—but were both in middle age when they arrived in a dusty, waterfront town with a perfect Mediterranean climate and not much else to recommend it. The two women who would establish a new standard of health care for their neighbors were accustomed to personal hardship and indifferent to their own comfort. They were both hands-on nurses in an era when illness of all kinds was rampant and effective medicine scarce. It was their habit to put the interests of others first. But they were also strong-willed, determined to make a difference, and adept at converting men with power and money to their cause.

Ellen Browning Scripps explored the serene coast of La Jolla on a visit to San Diego in 1890. Seven years later, Miss Ellen would build her first home in the seaside colony. *courtesy of La Jolla Historical Society*

Their paths nearly crossed, but Ellen Scripps set foot in San Diego first.[1] On February 15, 1890, she and her rheumatic brother Fred took rooms at Horton House on Fourth and D Streets (or Broadway, where the US Grant now stands).[2] This would have been a short walk away from the little dispensary over a clothing store at Sixth and H Streets—four blocks south, two east—when opened by Mother Mary Michael in July of 1890,[3] but that was five months off.

Ellen and Fred Scripps had come to California in the first place to comfort an ailing sister in Alameda and—when that situation seemed acceptable, at least—continued on down the coast to visit cousins in San Diego[4] and explore. They ferried over for a look at the glossy new Hotel del Coronado, built to be "the talk of the Western world" and already attracting titled guests.[5] They made their way to the little colony of La Jolla, protruding into the sea at the northern edge of the city, and walked the beach and tide pools, then undertook a horse-and-carriage tour of the whole terrain west to Point Loma, south to the new border town of Tijuana,[6] and north to Fallbrook. They were introduced to important San Diegans (among them Father Antonio Ubach,[7] the Catholic pastor of San Diego, who was romanticized in the immensely popular 1884 novel *Ramona* and would shortly interact with the Sisters of Mercy). Overall, Miss Ellen's first visit to San Diego lasted about three weeks and, before leaving again for the house in Detroit she shared with her brother James, she agreed in principle to invest in a parcel of land because her brother Fred felt so much better in the sun.

Ellen Browning Scripps was wealthy by 1890, but not an heiress as one might suppose. In fact, she was an extraordinarily self-made woman. Born in the Mayfair district of London, England, in 1836, young Ellen was the fifth of thirteen children born to bookbinder James Mogg Scripps and three successive wives. The little girl was named for her mother, Ellen Saunders, who died in 1841 after bearing three more children in as many years and after a "long and painful struggle with breast cancer," and for an obscure preacher, the Reverend J.N. Browning, who baptized the baby at Hope Chapel, Hotwells in Bristol[8] (so not the English poet who was a decade away from eloping into fame with Elizabeth Barrett).

James Mogg Scripps, father of Ellen Browning Scripps

courtesy of E.W. Scripps Archive, Mahn Center for Archives and Special Collections, Ohio University Libraries

Though they lived in a district with many fine homes and some neighbors among the gentry, the London Scripps were "one step up from working class,"[9] and their fortunes rose and fell. Ellen's grandfather, William Armiger Scripps, was the most prosperous of his generation (and, in fact, all William's own siblings went off to America in search of a better life, while he stayed on in London to publish the *London Daily Sun* and the *Literary Gazette)*. But the grandfather had too many progeny himself[10] to keep them all afloat through hard times, and his middle son, James Mogg, father of Ellen, eventually found himself "twice-widowed and twice-bankrupt"[11] and was urged by his father to make his way west to the New World.

Thus, in 1844, after the death of Ellen's mother and two siblings, the surviving family sailed for America and settled on a family farm in Rushville, Illinois, near the earlier wave of cousins, with a new stepmother and a succession of new brothers and sisters. Although by all accounts, James Mogg had been a good bookbinder, he was not a farmer, and every child in the family was required to work hard. Among a lot of outsize personalities, Ellen was the peacemaker at home and in the wider world. As one biographer wrote:

> Miss Ellen's vast influence, now almost totally obscured by her charities, derived from her relationship to a very complex genealogy which still can be confusing, even to current generations of the Scripps family.
>
> [Her] outstanding career was based upon a simple fact: she could handle the male members of her large family and tranquilize them, when internecine strife threatened to collapse the fabulous early successes in newspaper publishing which built all the Scripps' fortunes.[12]

The Scripps family gathered for this group portrait in spring 1900 at Miramar Ranch, built by E.W. Scripps for the extended family. In the 1970s, the area became a residential development named Scripps Ranch. From left, seated, are Eliza Virginia Scripps; Ellen Browning Scripps; Frederick T. Scripps (above); E.W. Scripps and his son, Robert Paine; unidentified boy; Nackie H. Scripps (wife of E,W.), Harriet Scripps (wife of James E. Scripps); and Elizabeth Mary Scripps Sharp, in the rocking chair. From left, standing, are Katherine Pierce Scripps (wife of William Scripps), William A. Scripps, and James E. Scripps. *courtesy of E.W. Scripps Archive, Mahn Center for Archives and Special Collections, Ohio University Libraries*

Ellen Browning Scripps as a young woman, c. 1850.

courtesy of E.W. Scripps Archive, Mahn Center for Archives and Special Collections, Ohio University Libraries

Eleven Scripps children survived infancy, but Ellen was the only sister who was both physically well and agreeable. The elder Elizabeth was deaf and "cantankerous;" Julia Anne, though gentle, suffered debilitating arthritis; and the youngest girl, Eliza Virginia (a high-spirited La Jolla "character" in her later years) was "continually upsetting the household" with an abrasive personality once described as a "…cross between a barbed wire fence and a coyote…"[13] The brothers were mostly—except for the hapless Fred—clever with money, belligerent, and left home as soon as they could. That left Ellen as caretaker, peacemaker, and endlessly called-upon family nurse.

Fortunately for her family and the hospital system which would eventually bear her name, Ellen Scripps was up to the constant demands and was bright, as well as patient and reliable. She was voraciously curious, a constant reader and writer, and the only member of the family to go to college (Knox College, Galesburg, Illinois) at a time when women in college were extremely rare, and where the "outstanding event of her college years" was the Lincoln-Douglas debate of 1858.[14]

Ellen Browning Scripps
Her Siblings and Their Parents

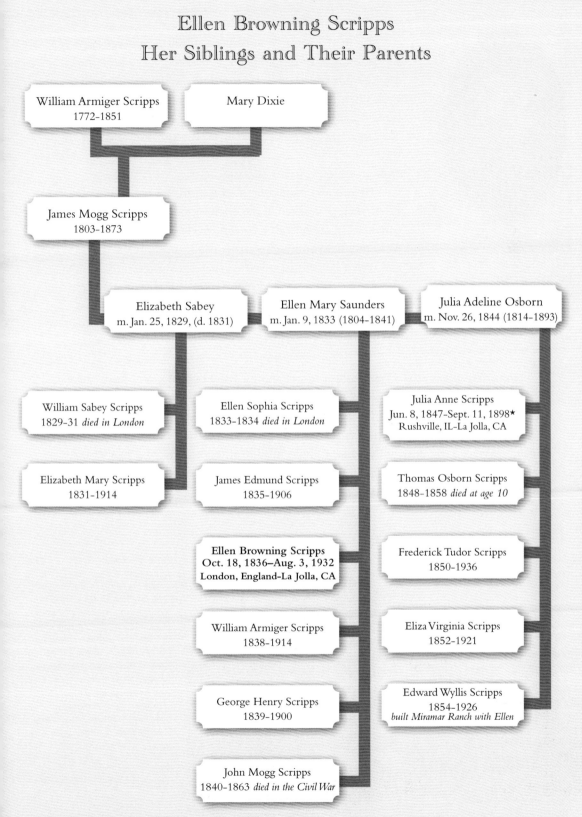

William Armiger Scripps 1772-1851	**Mary Dixie**

James Mogg Scripps 1803-1873

Elizabeth Sabey m. Jan. 25, 1829, (d. 1831)	**Ellen Mary Saunders** m. Jan. 9, 1833 (1804-1841)	**Julia Adeline Osborn** m. Nov. 26, 1844 (1814-1893)

William Sabey Scripps 1829-31 *died in London*	**Ellen Sophia Scripps** 1833-1834 *died in London*	**Julia Anne Scripps** Jun. 8, 1847–Sept. 11, 1898★ Rushville, IL–La Jolla, CA
Elizabeth Mary Scripps 1831-1914	**James Edmund Scripps** 1835-1906	**Thomas Osborn Scripps** 1848-1858 *died at age 10*
	Ellen Browning Scripps Oct. 18, 1836–Aug. 3, 1932 London, England–La Jolla, CA	**Frederick Tudor Scripps** 1850-1936
	William Armiger Scripps 1838-1914	**Eliza Virginia Scripps** 1852-1921
	George Henry Scripps 1839-1900	**Edward Wyllis Scripps** 1854-1926 *built Miramar Ranch with Ellen*
	John Mogg Scripps 1840-1863 *died in the Civil War*	

★Scripps Memorial Hospital is named for Julia Anne Scripps, "Annie"

In 1873 Ellen Browning Scripps pooled her money with her brother, James E. Scripps (above, c. 1870) to found the *Detroit News*.

courtesy of E.W. Scripps Archive, Mahn Center for Archives and Special Collections, Ohio University Libraries

She had a strong constitution, ate little, worked hard inside and out of the house, and walked everywhere she could. Thin and plain, with tightly-arranged hair and big eyes, Ellen seems never to have had a romance. Instead she nursed, carried food to, counseled, and provided shelter for her large and complicated clan, and in the end outlived all but one.

Before and after college, and until the age of thirty, Ellen Scripps worked at "women's jobs," mostly teaching for miniscule pay. She and a cousin Marie opened the Scripps Academy for young scholars in 1860, and four years later she wrote her brother George that she was earning less than the woman who washed her clothes.[15] But prosperity was on the horizon. The oldest brother, James, had found his way onto a newspaper in Detroit and was about to change all their lives.

James, like Ellen, was a "scrupulous saver" and by 1859 owned part of one share of the *Detroit Advertiser*. But within a year, he was able to parlay that small stake into an ownership position on the *Detroit Tribune*, where he soon became convinced that the future was in low-priced papers for the common man. When nobody else on the *Tribune* embraced the new faith, James called on his brothers to join him in Detroit. George asked Ellen's opinion as the family mentor; she "welcomed the idea of a family enterprise," joined her brothers in Detroit, and they were off.[16]

Rolls of newsprint are delivered to the first *Detroit News* building in downtown Detroit. The Scripps family, including James, E.W., and Ellen Browning Scripps worked tirelessly to publish the first penny papers in the United States, including the *Detroit News*. "Miss Ellen," as she was affectionately known, pioneered the concept of the feature article and wrote a widely distributed daily newspaper column.

courtesy of The Detroit News Archives

There were fits and starts for Ellen the journalist. From 1867-71, she was a reporter and proofreader on the *Detroit Tribune*. Then she was called home to Rushville to nurse her father through a protracted last illness until released by his death. But finally, in 1873, the siblings were together in the newsroom of the *Tribune*: nearly all the Scripps brothers who had survived both childhood and the Civil War[17]—James, Will, George, and Ed ("E.W.," the headstrong youngest, age 19)—and Ellen, who was thirty-six years old. Ellen would make her primary home with James for nearly two decades, while devoting herself to her trade.

> On James' paper Ellen was proof reader and head of the copy desk by day, and her evenings were devoted to clipping and rewriting articles from other papers for the next day's issue. This was the beginning of her famous *Miscellany*. Under her hands dull items acquired life and meaning with historical or literary allusions, the elusive news behind the news.[18]

But there was more. Within months of her second arrival in Detroit (after the death of their father) Ellen and James had pooled their money and founded the *Detroit News*,[19] and Ellen had begun building her fortune.

When Ellen joined the staff as proofreader, she invested her savings from several years of teaching and later received two shares in the business.[20] Her brother George invested more and would eventually will some of his shares to Ellen, ballooning her funds for the philanthropy of her later life in La Jolla.[21] But before all that, the younger Ellen roomed at James's house and helped with domestic tasks, working sixteen hours a day. She edited and wrote copy, including her groundbreaking column, and did anything else on the paper that needed to be done.

Meanwhile, the Scripps brothers founded in Cleveland a new kind of paper for the working man called *The Penny Press*. It was an inexpensive four-page sheet with simple, punchy prose and was a runaway success. From Detroit, Ellen sent her *Miscellany* to *The Press* as well as to the *News*. We are informed that "Ellen continued her grueling work and it paid off. By 1879, the annual profits of the *News* were over $50,000." [22]

All told, Ellen worked for the family papers for seven years. Then, in 1881, when she was 44, Ellen began traveling, and she traveled for most of a decade. The first trip began, like everything else in Ellen's life, as a help to someone else–in this case, accompanying her wildly excessive brother, Ed, on a journey to regain his health from too much liquor, work, cigars, and unwise romantic attachments.[24] As they made their way along a grand tour of England, the "Continent," and North Africa, Ellen transformed herself into a foreign correspondent, writing travel letters home for the family papers, and also into something of a new Ellen—learning to ride horseback and galloping down the sands of Cairo, the Bosporus, Jerusalem, and Algiers, to the amazement of onlookers. In the Adriatic port city of Trieste, Ellen and Ed were taken by what a modern-day writer describes as:

> ...the brilliantly situated Castle Miramare...a gleaming white fairy tale vision floating just above the waves...and looking impossibly romantic.[25]

The brother and sister would remember the castle and the name when creating their own vast estate, with the barest glimpse of sea, in the sage and chaparral of San Diego.

They made their way home after eighteen months abroad in the spring of 1883, and Ellen returned to Detroit to live with James, but not to the paper. A few months later she was wintering in Cuba, then again in Mexico, and by 1887—when James' doctor said he, too, needed a change—Ellen was off again with James and a half-dozen other relations for another two years in Europe.

While they were away, the unregenerate Ed stirred up great trouble at the *Detroit Evening News* by seizing control from the man hand-selected by James, a "nefarious" act which resulted in a complete rupture between the brothers on James' return in 1889. It seemed a good time for Ed and the long-suffering Ellen to visit their ailing sister, Julia Anne, in Alameda, California, where she had gone in search of a cure. But, as it happened, Ed's young wife fell ill with diphtheria, so Ellen took the ten-day train ride from Chicago west to the Golden State with Fred, while Ed stayed home with his wife.

E.W. Scripps launched his first paper, *The Penny Press*, in Cleveland, Ohio, in 1878, after working with his sister Ellen Browning Scripps and his brothers at their Detroit papers. E.W. would build a publishing conglomerate, including 25 newspapers and a newspaper syndication service, before his death in 1917. In 1890, he and Miss Ellen resolved to move to California, where they could devote themselves to philanthropy.

courtesy of E.W. Scripps Archive, Mahn Center for Archives and Special Collections, Ohio University Libraries

The details of the long illness and treatment of the woman for whom Scripps Memorial Hospital would be named are a window into the state of medicine at the time. [26]

Julia Anne, called "Annie," was the first of James Mogg's third set of children—the five born to James and his American wife Julia Osborn—and ten years younger than Ellen. Annie was certainly one of Ellen's favorites: in a letter to E.W. from Alameda, Ellen described her as "very gentle, patient….. religious…and the ablest of the lot." Annie's arthritis was disabling enough by the time she was in her twenties that she was seeking help at far-flung places, such as Dansville New York.[27] By the time Ellen came to visit in January of 1890, Annie had been living at the Remedial Institute and School of Philosophy in Alameda for more than two years.

Ellen Browning Scripps would name Scripps Memorial Hospital after her beloved half-sister, Julia Anne Scripps, or Annie, shown here, c. 1860. In 1890, Miss Ellen visited her half-sister at the Remedial Institute in Northern California, where Annie lived for two years in search of a cure for her debilitating arthritis.

courtesy of E.W. Scripps Archive, Mahn Center for Archives and Special Collections, Ohio University Libraries

The history of the Remedial Institute sheds light on utopian communities and the pull of spiritualism in American life and health care of the late nineteenth century. The institute's director, Dr. Horace Bowen, was a homeopathic physician who provided a community of brotherly love for invalids like Annie, who might convert her "weakness," as she wrote, into "further development of my soul."[28] In addition to love, practitioners provided such alternative therapies as "magnetism, massage, mind-cure, electricity, and electrovapor baths."[29] Though skeptical themselves, Ellen and E.W. Scripps supported Annie's treatment financially because their sister seemed more comfortable at the Remedial Institute than anywhere else and also because the state of medical care in America was so generally perilous at the time. The reality for invalids everywhere was that:

> In 1890, physicians in America…were rarely able to alter the course of disease or prolong life. Standard practices for medical training were absent [and] ignorance was rampant…Bright spots of progress appeared sporadically, but largely, the state of the art was abysmal.[30]

After her first brief visit to San Diego later that year, Ellen Scripps was committed to buying land and returned home to Detroit to plan the purchase of a farm for Fred— though soon she would agree to partner in the building of a great house with her youngest brother. Years later, when Miss Ellen came to found a health care system for the twentieth century and to name it for Annie, the era of medical science had truly begun. But meanwhile, at a time when the touch of a competent nurse might be the best medicine of all, the Sisters of Mercy had arrived in San Diego.

SAN DIEGO, JUNE 5, 1890

We confirm the appointment of Sister M. Michael as Mother Superior

of the community of Sisters of Mercy in this city,

and give permission to said community

to build a hospital with their own means in or near said city.

Francis Mora, Bishop of Monterey and Los Angeles[1]

CHAPTER TWO

The Sisters of Mercy in San Diego

1890-1924

ON JULY 6, 1890, the day after her thirty-seventh birthday and presumably while she was still getting used to her new authority, the former Sister Mary Michael Cummings opened her first health care center in downtown San Diego and called it St. Joseph's Dispensary. She was now Mother Superior of a community of two, and would soon lose her one companion who "grew weary of the heavy persistent troubles" and went home.[2] And no wonder. The task facing the two "friendless and almost penniless" nuns was enormous.[3] The bishop had asked the Sisters of Mercy to build a Catholic hospital in a city of the stranded and out-of-work and his blessing was the sum total of his support.

There were hospitals in the city serving the poor to a minimum standard when the Sisters arrived. By the time of the *First Annual Report of the San Diego County Hospital and Poor Farm to the Board of Supervisors for 1889,* the count included The Hospital of the Good Samaritan with sixteen beds on the corner of Cedar and Union Streets (now Little Italy), a "free Receiving Hospital for the care of the indigent sick and injured," and the County Hospital built for more chronic cases in 1880 in Mission Valley.[4] But there was no place providing skilled nurses twenty-four hours a day for anyone—well-off with private physicians, or destitute and friendless—who could reach their doors.

Fifth Avenue (above) in Hillcrest was the first street to be extended downtown onto the San Diego mesa. By the end of 1891, the Sisters of Mercy opened a three-story hospital in the area. *courtesy of San Diego History Center*

San Diego in that summer of 1890 was a ramshackle port nearly flattened by the collapse of a boom touched off by a rate war between the California Southern Railroad and its rival, the Southern Pacific Railroad. The idea was that California Southern would run a line from National City north to what is now Barstow, where it would connect to the Atlantic and Pacific line. But construction was interfered with repeatedly by Southern Pacific with strategically stalled locomotives and armed men, and the rate war began. Beginning in 1886:

> For a short time one could travel from the Mississippi to Southern California for as little as one dollar. Streams of people poured into southern California, some with land options attached to their RR tickets. Property values skyrocketed and people made fortunes on paper. [But] by the late spring of 1888, it had all ended.[5]

The bust was bad, but the boom, with its influx of 30,000 people within two years, had brought its own troubles, including "filthy streets and offensive odors along its bay…Foul smells from garbage heaps, open cesspools and sewers…"[6] And the health officer in 1888 had this to say:

> Many of the older buildings in this city were, during the "boom," enlarged by the addition of more rooms and extra stories, without the least regard to either light or ventilation; and, in consequence, we have to-day many buildings that are a disgrace to our city. Many cases of colds, coughs, lung diseases and even death were due to those dark, close, chilly and unhealthy rooms.[7]

Now, in 1890, half those new people were gone, but many who remained were indigent and ill—partly because of the unpleasantness described above, but also because of local boosterism promoting San Diego as the "healthiest climate imaginable" and claims by local physicians that "the San Diego Bay region is the most healthy spot in the United States, perhaps in the world,"[8] which brought invalids to the city in the first place.

A common diagnosis of these health seekers was tuberculosis, called "consumption" or "phthisis" when it produced a progressive wasting away. Whatever the diagnosis, some of the afflicted could pay for treatment in private "sanitaria," but others could not and when desperately ill became the responsibility of the County Hospital or languished untreated at home.

Roman Catholic Bishop Francis Mora, whose vast territorial responsibility stretched 500 miles from Monterey to the Mexican border, and Father Antonio Ubach, pastor of San Diego, had studied possible sites for a hospital and recommended that the sisters purchase a ten-acre plot at the crest of a hill (Hillcrest) on the north end of town. It had been Father Ubach, doggedly rebuilding a Catholic community after the retreat of Spanish friars and Mexican governors, who had "applied repeatedly" to the Sisters of Mercy in San Francisco to open a Catholic hospital in his territory and was now "exultant to have secured Sisters of Mercy at long last."[9] However, the Sisters could not yet afford the hospital on the hill (although, astonishingly, Mother Mary Michael would manage to buy that very site and erect a three-story building by the end of the following year).

But meanwhile St. Joseph's Dispensary, rented with a fifty dollar gift from Father Ubach,[10] was at least convenient to all comers, in a direct line from the wharf and in the heart of the business district.

The Sisters of Mercy gathered in 1899 for this photo. Nine years earlier, led by Sister Mary Michael Cummings, they opened St. Joseph's Dispensary.

courtesy of Scripps Health

Mercy Hospital originated as St. Joseph's Dispensary, located above a men's clothing store at the corner of Sixth Avenue and H Street (later renamed Market Street), and leased for fifty dollars. Left, the middle two windows on the third floor housed the small dispensary.

courtesy of Scripps Health

Mother Mary Michael Cummings and Sister Mary Alphonsus Fitzpatrick[11] leased the two upper floors of the Grand Central Block with "sixty or more rooms"—telling a reporter for *The San Diego Weekly Union* that they wouldn't try to furnish all the rooms at once but only enough to begin with[12]—and set up what they called a *dispensary.* The term *dispensary* ordinarily referred to a peculiarly nineteenth century institution. An outpatient center, "created in the hope of providing an alternative to the hospital for the urban poor,"[13] it dispensed soothing ministrations and prescriptions with an eye toward returning the patient home. Almost certainly, the Sisters set up an acute care clinic for the poor who could not afford to visit any of the myriad private doctors' offices in town. The *MercyShield Centennial Edition* says "the dispensary soon served dozens of patients a week,"[14] though no outpatient record survives. Yet, regardless of the name, St. Joseph's was a hospital from the start.

The first patient admitted within hours of opening on July 9, 1890, was John O'Connell[15] with malaria, who stayed thirteen days and survived, who returned three times with relapsing malaria in February, May, and December of 1891, and who walked out the doors again each time. He paid his bills in full and became a devoted supporter of the Sisters of Mercy:

> I have the proud distinction of being the first patient admitted and I am proud to say that Sisters' gentle and unremitting care nursed me back to health when I was given up by the doctors. Not being a Catholic, I entered their hospital when every other place was closed to me, not without some misgivings, but I found the Sisters always the same: intelligent, kind and tender nurses. I saw them minister to the unfortunate consumed with fever, soothe the hopeless consumptive and wipe the perspiration from the cold and clammy brow of the dying. Never will I hear the Sisters of Mercy mentioned without giving testimony to their pure, unselfish purpose and truly compassionate nature.[16]

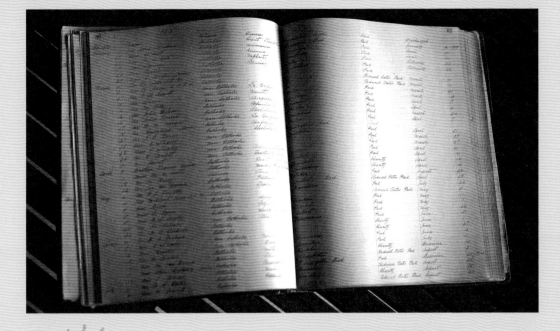

Mother Mary Michael's big red-and-black ledger of admissions, *St. Joseph's 1890-1913* (twenty-three years in one book!), is a goldmine of information about turn-of-the-century disease and medicine in San Diego and about the running of a self-supporting hospital on a shoestring. A special delight of the ledger is Mother Mary Michael's recording of "Religion" alongside Name, Date and Diagnosis, Physician, Payment, and Date of Discharge. Nobody escaped a designation—there was none of the modern "declines to state"—and the choices were *Catholic and Baptized* (chiefly newborns and the mortally ill), *Non-Catholic, Greek Catholic, Jew and Pagan, Heathen,* and *Infidel.*[17]

The Sisters kept a ledger with patient names, dates, diagnoses, physicians, payments, religion, and dates of discharge in Mother Mary Michael Cumming's big red-and-black ledger of admissions. Above is the ledger from 1890-1913.

courtesy of Scripps Health

The first month, St. Joseph's Dispensary admitted seven patients, including two with phthisis, one of whom died in a day and the other who was discharged after more than two months; the average stay for the seven was eighteen days. As the year progressed, the number of new admissions remained within a relatively narrow range of four to twelve patients per month who generally stayed a long time, an average three to six weeks—not counting one man with an amputated limb who settled in for three years. The physicians of San Diego embraced the dispensary from the start: in a town of 16,000 people[18], twenty-four different physicians admitted patients before the end of 1890, including both current and former city health officers, Drs. David Gochenauer and Daniel Northrup; the county physician, Dr. LeFevre; female doctor Maria Averill; and most members of the board of health.

And the physicians brought private patients who could pay, outnumbering those needing "reduced rates" or "charity" at a rate of five to one. The phenomenon of "free enterprise and resourcefulness as an American success story" is described by nursing historian Sioban Nelson in *Say Little, Do Much: Nursing Nuns and Hospitals in the Nineteenth Century* (in which she refers to religious sisters as "vowed women"):

> In the second half of the nineteenth century Catholic hospitals, owned by communities of vowed Catholic women, were playing a major role in hospital foundation in the United States...Throughout the country the sisters were able to provide the best value for money in the care of the indigent sick, attracting excellent doctors [and] their private patients...By the end of the century patient fees were what supported Catholic hospitals. The success of the sisters' nursing work...is the story of the sisters coming to understand the particularities of the American political and economic climate to run the best businesses in the market. America respected that.[19]

The Sisters of Mercy never turned away a patient. Careful records were kept of patient diagnoses, from pleurisy to alcoholism.

courtesy of San Diego History Center

The girl who would be Mother Mary Michael was born Rose Anna Cummings in 1853 on a farm in Madonnaville,[20] an intensely Catholic hamlet of Monroe County, Illinois, near St. Louis.[21] She was the youngest of seven children of parents from Galway, Ireland, and had a childhood of much farm life and just enough Catholic education to make her First Holy Communion, which is to say she left school at age twelve. Rose Anna was a good-natured child, thought by her mother to be "a born nurse," as evidenced by her care of sick and injured animals about the farm.[22] Her attraction to nursing and the religious life seemed intensified by the death from consumption of her older sister Margaret, a young nun in St. Joseph's Convent of Mercy in St. Louis. When Rose Anna was seventeen (October 5, 1870) she entered the same convent to take up the unfinished work her sister had just begun.[23]

Mother Mary Michael Cummings in 1892

courtesy of Scripps Health

When Rose Anna Cummings entered the Sisters of Mercy, the order was still young, having been founded in Dublin, Ireland, in 1831, by the extraordinary Catherine McAuley (1778-1841), who was fifty-three years old at the time.[24] In middle age, after a quiet single life tending to those around her, Catherine inherited the vast sum of 25,000 pounds and spent her money and the rest of her life "tending to Christ's poor," especially in the "visitation and care of the sick." [25] This was then an unusual rule among Catholic orders of nuns, who were more commonly teachers or contemplatives (devoted to a cloistered life of prayer). A biographer comments:

> The question remains [as to] where Mother McAuley acquired her interest and gained her experience in caring for the sick. There were no nursing schools in her age and the professional nurse as the term is used today did not exist.[26]

It appears that Catherine McAuley learned by doing, just as Ellen Browning Scripps did: by offering herself to the invalid, by looking and listening with affectionate regard, and concentrating on cleanliness, food and drink, and the emotions of the sufferer. She wrote:

> [The nurse] should act with great tenderness to relieve distress, and to endeavor in every practical way to promote cleanliness, ease and comfort of the sick person [and] to show compassion.[27]

Regarding the poor, whom to Mother McAuley meant *anyone with a need*, what she most communicated to the young women who joined her order was:

> There are things the poor prize more highly than gold, though they cost [us] nothing; among these are the kind word, the gentle, compassionate look, and the patient hearing of their sorrows.[28]

By 1843, the first Sisters of Mercy arrived in the United States from Ireland, settling at Pittsburgh and at St. Louis by 1856,[29] so that Rose Anna Cummings was among the first generation of novices in her city. After receiving her religious habit and name in November, 1871, the new Sister Mary Michael spent the next nine years nursing the poor and sick of St. Louis in the hospital, in their homes and in the city jails.

Moving west in response to calls from pioneering bishops, she went to the aid of miners in Colorado and incidental invalids seeking cures in the mountain air and mineral springs of Durango and Ouray. From Colorado, Sister Mary Michael pushed on to California, briefly to Salinas, and finally made her way to San Diego after nineteen years in the trenches, well-tested for the work ahead.

St. Joseph's Dispensary downtown was always meant to be a temporary setting, and when Mother Mary Michael began planning a permanent hospital, she realized there would be no help from foundering banks and began soliciting funds from relatives and friends. *The Annals of the Sisters of Mercy in San Diego* refer to "the vexations which beset the Convent of Mercy in San Diego and well nigh broke the spirit" and of "Mother Michael's darkest hour,"[30] and yet the speed with which great things were done is astonishing. Within a year, the Sisters (that is, Mother Mary Michael and a devoted new novice, Sister Mary Josephine Smith)[31] had enough money to buy the ten-acre site originally favored by their priests, on University Avenue between Sixth and Eighth Avenues—right on the grade where Sixth Avenue runs down to Mission Valley—and less than half a mile from where Scripps Mercy San Diego now stands. By the end of 1891, the three-story building called St. Joseph's Sanitarium was "finished and blessed"[32] and opened to the public.

At the turn of the new year, 1895, *The San Diego Union* was reporting on "the remarkable progress of St. Joseph's Hospital and Sanitarium...which has so far surpassed the most sanguine expectations of the sisters that they have been unable to supply the increasing demand for admittance, hence the extensive additional buildings now almost completed." The paper also commented on "the regular staff of visiting physicians and surgeons, comprising the most eminent and successful of San Diego's medical practitioners" and "the appointment of a resident physician in constant attendance at the hospital"–the first hospitalist–"whose services are free of charge to all patients."[33]

By the end of 1891, the Sisters of Mercy opened a three-story medical facility called St. Joseph's Sanitarium on University Avenue in Hillcrest. The new hospital replaced the tiny St. Joseph's Dispensary, which was always meant to be temporary.

St. Joseph's Sanitarium sat on ten acres in beautifully landscaped grounds, including a deep canyon, with fruit and shade trees, flowers, arbors, and seats for rest and contemplation. Patient rooms offered tranquil retreats for the chronically ill.

courtesy of Scripps Health

By the turn of the new century, 1900, Mother Mary Michael could have instructed the populace on how to take a loan of fifty dollars, some rented rooms downtown and end up with a three-story hospital on ten acres, with operating rooms, a pharmacy, a laboratory, physician apartments, a large sunny dining room, a kitchen, a reading room, homes for the aged and working girls of good character, a convent for a rapidly growing community of nuns, and a chapel seating 300 persons in beautifully-landscaped grounds, including a terraced deep canyon with fruit and shade trees, flowers, arbors and seats for rest and contemplation—all within a decade. [34]

The name *sanitarium,* which would also be used by Ellen Browning Scripps for her first small hospital in La Jolla, derives from the Latin term *sanitas,* meaning *health*, and generally referred to a medical facility for long-term illness—when, before the era of antibiotics, antipsychotics and chemotherapy for cancer, the best regimens offered were mostly kindness, rest and good nutrition over time. The diagnoses and lengths of stay of patients admitted to St. Joseph's Sanitarium reflect this.

In May, 1910, for instance, forty-two new patients were registered in Mother Mary Michael's ledger (seventeen Catholics, twenty-one non-Catholics, four pagans) with diagnoses such as syphilis, pleurisy, and septicemia, with fewer than half discharged the same month, and one with phthisis confined to bed for 165 days. Patients were admitted with insanity, nervousness and alcoholism. La Grippe (influenza) filled beds in winter. Women and men with carcinoma likely received what we would recognize today as the best hospice care and often lived months in the sun-filled rooms and arbors of St. Joseph's.

In 1899, the Sisters of Mercy acquired a thousand-acre spread they named Mount Carmel Ranch. Over time, they would build a thriving farm that supplied dairy products and produce for the hospital. For the hardworking sisters, Mount Carmel was a cherished retreat that offered respite from daily duties. Above, Sisters Regis and Teresa enjoy the peace and tranquility.
courtesy of Scripps Health

And then there was Mount Carmel Ranch—a thousand-acre spread which the Sisters bought in 1899 and named for a ridge along the southern perimeter that bears a striking resemblance to the holy mount in Israel.[35] How the Sisters happened to acquire the ranch from the homesteading McGonigle family is a fluid tale, as described in a *Historic Architectural Survey on Mt. Carmel Ranch:*

> By one account, the McGonigles were unable to meet the mortgage payment on this land and, rather than go through foreclosure, sold it to the Sisters of Mercy for payment of the balance. In another account, the Sisters were treating ill members of the family at the time and the favorable terms of the sale were a reflection of their gratitude…It is possible that both accounts are correct. In any event, the property was sold to the Sisters of Mercy on January 17, 1899.[36]

For a few years, the acreage was undeveloped. Then, around 1905, the Big House was built on a general plan developed by Mother Mary Michael: a two-story gabled redwood house with a basement kitchen and two dining rooms—one for the Sisters and one for the hired hands—common areas, a chapel on the first floor, and a large number of small bedrooms in the second story and attic. (Less grand, perhaps, than *Miramar*, the 47-room castle of Scripps Ranch, ten miles east, but comfortable, none-the-less.) Outbuildings included a milking barn, a hay barn, silos, and a cemetery serving both residents and neighbors in their turn.

Mount Carmel Ranch was inhabited by the Sisters for three eventful decades until 1935—through the First World War, the building of the new Mercy Hospital in 1924, the Roaring 20s, and the Depression—and, throughout most of that time, served three important functions for the Sisters and their patients: providing dairy products and produce for the Hospital; as a "haven of much needed peace and refreshment,"[37] for the nursing Sisters, and as a home for the homeless, mostly the aged before World War I and, for a short period afterward, some twenty-two neglected and orphaned children.

Mount Carmel Ranch, the peaceful retreat for the Sisters of Mercy, served as a home for orphaned children after World War II.
courtesy of Scripps Health

The sisters grew vegetables, raised hogs and cows, and made daily deliveries of milk to the hospital. About a half-dozen nuns were permanent residents at the ranch, supervising the agricultural operation. *courtesy of Scripps Health*

Although for the majority of the Sisters of Mercy, Mount Carmel was a cherished retreat, about a half-dozen Sisters were permanent residents at the ranch to supervise the agricultural operation—forty to fifty head of cattle, a dozen mules, and ten to fifteen breeding sows—and to care for the homeless. A vegetable garden was maintained by a Chinese gardener who lived on the ranch. Trucks daily carried milk and vegetables the twenty miles to Mercy Hospital and brought garbage back for hogs.[38] The Sisters sold the Ranch in 1945, and the property now straddles highway 56; the Big House still stands to the south, as City of San Diego Historical Landmark No. 391, between the exits for Carmel Creek and Carmel Country Roads. Across the freeway the Old Cemetery has become St. Therese of Carmel, an acre-and-a-half of peaceful separation of Catholics and Protestants, buried on opposite sides. And the whole of what was once McGonigle Canyon is Carmel Valley.

Meanwhile, back at the Hillcrest campus in 1904, Mother Mary Michael had opened San Diego's first training school for nurses in order "to provide the best scientific professional nursing" in the city. [39] This seems an astonishing feat, considering that the tireless Superior was creating the ranch at the same time, along with the latest new wing at St. Joseph's for a total of 220 rooms. Miss Kate Sullivan, a graduate of the first Mercy Hospital in Pittsburgh, was hired as director and produced the first ten graduate nurses—all Sisters—in 1906. Mercy School of Nursing would continue to train highly-regarded nurses in San Diego for three generations—1,550 nurses in all—before closing its doors in 1970.[40] With the founding of the Nursing School, the Sanitarium became officially, as well as in the eyes of the public, St. Joseph's Hospital.

Despite the up-to-date nursing and the building-out of the whole campus at St. Joseph's, Mother Mary Michael was always looking to the future. Her original community of two Sisters had burgeoned to forty[41] when a gift of land in 1916—six acres on Washington Street and Fifth Avenue bequeathed by philanthropist Anson Stephens—set the stage for an even bigger and better hospital. On New Year's Day, 1917, a special edition of *The San Diego Union* announced a fund drive by the Sisters of Mercy for the new hospital, complete with architectural drawings, statistics about their non-sectarian charity, and testimonials from city fathers. Several sizable contributions were received, including $5,000 from E. W. Scripps. But the clouds of World War I had finally gathered over the United States, and uneasiness about the war apparently kept most people's wallets closed; the money taken in ($22,000) was only enough to build a surgery and nursing-school annex at the existing site.[42]

Finally, five years later—after the end of the war and the raging influenza pandemic that caught up the Sisters afterwards—the 1922 New Year's edition of the *Union* carried the announcement that the Sisters of Mercy had once again asked architects to provide plans for a new hospital which would be fireproof, after a blaze in the convent in 1919 nearly ignited St. Joseph's. This time the citizenry was disposed to give and a bank prepared to loan, but Mother Mary Michael did not live to see it. Her great heart gave out, literally, on October 6, 1922,[43] just after she had called her architect and before he arrived at her bedside with their latest plans.[44] She was sixty-nine and had given nearly half her life to the people of San Diego.

Mercy School of Nursing trained three generations of nurses before closing its doors in 1970.
courtesy of Scripps Health

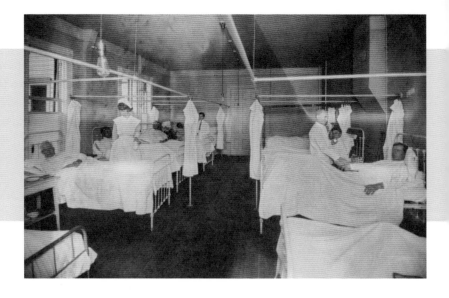

Patients at St. Joseph's Sanitarium often suffered from long-term illness. The best regimen of the era was kindness, rest, and good nutrition.

courtesy of San Diego History Center

After the death of Mother Mary Michael, the new hospital did rise on Washington Street, and it fell to a new superior with the odd religious name of an Italian bishop saint to get it done. Sister Mary Liguori McNamara—who had incidentally nursed American soldiers at Matanzas, Cuba, in the Spanish-American War[45]—gathered up all the deeds to:

> …several large and valuable pieces of property [belonging to the Sisters of Mercy] some of which had been purchased at a nominal figure in the pioneer days of San Diego, and other parcels being gifts to the Sisters from grateful patients who were glad to offer, in lieu of money, the property which they owned. All this property was mortgaged to the Hibernia Bank and a loan of $700,000 was raised. [46]

The loan was enough to get construction under way in 1923, but more money was needed for equipment and for a new convent, nurses' residence and old people's home. This time the donor angel was John D. Spreckels, son of the Hawaiian sugar baron and "the richest man in San Diego,"[47] who guaranteed the funds required.

In May 1924, while the new hospital was still under construction, Sister M. Liguori officially changed the corporate title of St. Joseph's to Mercy Hospital. And on November 15, 1924, the new hospital on Fifth and Washington Avenues opened its doors, and "the Sisters, nurses and patients bid a final adieu to the old St. Joseph's. Moving began at noon and by 6 PM the patients were resting comfortably in their new surroundings."[48] After thirty-four years, the first private hospital in San Diego was facing the future from a high hill and head-on.

Meanwhile, just two months earlier and a dozen miles north, Ellen Browning Scripps had created a hospital for the little village of La Jolla and was about to open a metabolic clinic next door.

The new six-story hospital, now called Mercy Hospital, opened its doors in 1924 on Fifth and Washington Avenues in Hillcrest. Families could visit in the parlor, and many patients had private rooms.

courtesy of Scripps Health

In 1906, what is now Torrey Pines Road in La Jolla was an open field. *courtesy of La Jolla Historical Society*

CHAPTER THREE

Miss Ellen and Her Family

1890-1924
SCRIPPS MEMORIAL HOSPITAL

AFTER HER FIRST THREE WEEKS IN SAN DIEGO in the winter of 1890, Ellen Scripps was never happy living in the Midwest again. Detroit was a vigorous industrial city of 200,000 people and about to become the motor car capital of the world,[1] but Miss Ellen was done with making money. She and her brother, E.W., had read a life-changing novel called *Looking Backward, 2000-1887*,[2] "the third-largest best-seller of its time, after *Uncle Tom's Cabin* and *Ben Hur*"[3] and "one of the most remarkable books every published in America."[4] The book's protagonist falls asleep at the end of the nineteenth century and awakens on the eve of the twenty-first to find a brave new world—a utopia in which greed is abolished along with the whole industrial system that viewed men as "beasts of prey." The new era brings an end to poverty, but also to great wealth.

Ellen and E.W. Scripps considered that the policies of their own newspapers may have created "poor widows and orphans…who are such because our companies have been too mean to furnish healthful work rooms and …salaries sufficient to feed and clothe them properly" and they asked one another, "Did you not feel…justly attacked for your selfishness and your folly?"[5] They resolved to move permanently to California, where there was the possibility of building a different kind of city and of devoting themselves to philanthropy. However, the first order of business was to improve the society of their own fractious family, which is how they came to build the great estate at what is now Scripps Ranch.

At the end of 1890, E.W. Scripps came out to see San Diego for himself and liked what he saw. He and Ellen together bought 400 acres of treeless land an hour's drive ("with a good horse")[6] north of San Diego for a total of $5,500 and the idea that their brother, Fred, would somehow succeed at creating a ranch. Of all the Scripps siblings, Fred seemed the least able to stay out of trouble and giving Fred a new start was part of a more ambitious plan to build a secure home for the ill, elderly, and feckless of the family who—up to now—had been moving about the country from one temporary haven to another. By August 1891, E.W. and his brothers began building the ranch house which, in its earliest pictures, looks like the set for a western movie—one story, flat roof, buckboard in the dusty courtyard—but by 1898 was a forty- seven room castle named *Miramar* consisting of three-and-a-half wings with crenellated towers at the corners, "Renaissance breakfronts and chests, Louis Phillipe china, Gobelin tapestries, stained-glass windows, Genoese marble and Italian and Dutch tile."[7] All seventeen bedrooms had a fireplace and there were thirteen bathrooms,[8] as well as a gymnasium, barbershop and dentist chair, a thirty-two room bunkhouse for servants, and 300 different types of eucalyptus trees planted on the 700 additional acres bought by E.W. in the interim.[9]

E.W. and Ellen Browning Scripps purchased 400 acres in what is now Scripps Ranch. Eventually, the ranch house became a forty-seven room castle, called Miramar, with seventeen bedrooms, thirteen bathrooms, and a gymnasium.

courtesy of E.W. Scripps Archive, Mahn Center for Archives and Special Collections, Ohio University Libraries

Eucalyptus trees became a "craze" in Southern California after the Gold Rush. E.W. Scripps planted 300 varieties at Miramar. *courtesy of La Jolla Historical Society*

These great stands of trees—which would come to symbolize the modern community of Scripps Ranch—were part of an enormous eucalyptus "craze" that began after the Gold Rush, when Australian miners took in California's "barren hills and valleys [and] could visualize how their lofty and majestic eucalyptus could change such a bleak picture."[10]

Back home in Australia,

> the whole eucalyptus tree could be used from its roots to its crown, from its bark to its foliage. It not only provided fuel, windbreaks, medicine, shade and beauty, it also was lumber for implements, nectar for bees, pulp for paper... When cut down, the eucalyptus would resprout providing yet another crop of products within a few years. It appeared to be a miracle tree only limited by one's imagination.[11]

What's more, the eucalyptus seed is tiny and a small sack holding several thousand seeds, on one ship from Australia to the gold fields, was all that was needed to start a forest and an industry.

In the late 1870s, the Central Pacific Railroad decided that the eucalyptus was the answer to its constant need for ties, poles, posts, and firewood, and ultimately planted one million trees for the purpose. But the great miscalculation was in attributing the virtues of centuries- old Australian trees to raw, unseasoned timber, and the new wood promptly warped, shrank and split, would not hold a spike, and easily rotted away. Strange to say, this information was not uncovered by the Santa Fe Railroad, which repeated the experiment decades later in Rancho Santa Fe.

Scripps siblings, left to right: William Armiger, James Edmund, George Henry, and Miss Ellen gathered at Miramar in 1900 to be with George in his final illness. George's health was never strong after his stint as a soldier in the Civil War, and he died in April 1900.

courtesy of La Jolla Historical Society

The various members of the clan did come to Miramar, at least temporarily: E.W.'s own wife and children; Annie; Virginia; their mother, Julia Osborne Scripps; and the brothers, Fred and Will and briefly George, who died there in 1900.[12] E.W. hoped and expected that Ellen would make Miramar her permanent home and gave her a room "sacred to her use, a tower room on the second floor."[13] But by the time Miramar was finished, Ellen was longing for a place of her own and had rediscovered La Jolla.

As might be expected, Miramar Ranch did not cure the Scripps family members of their various plagues of illness and unhappiness, nor even serve as a permanent home for most. The final irony was that E.W., the eccentric old master of the house himself, eventually left both castle and family after a partial stroke in 1917 and took to the sea, where he died "of apoplexy" aboard his yacht, *Ohio,* in 1926, off the coast of Liberia.[14]

Decades of slow decline ensued for Miramar. Ultimately too expensive to maintain, the house was sold to developers in 1968, and most furnishings and artwork removed by family. What remained was stripped by thieves in 1972, down to the doorknobs and the marble on the carved wood paneling. The developers' original plan to create another tourist attraction similar to Hearst Castle in San Simeon came to naught. The San Diego Historical Site Board refused acquisition, saying that "the time is past when practical preservation of the building might be possible," and Miramar Ranch House was leveled in June of 1973.[15]

All that remained was a good road from Miramar to La Jolla built by E.W. for Ellen.[16] (Most of E.W.'s highway is still in use. One lasting curve is at the original front door and first address of Scripps Memorial Hospital on the mesa, before the construction of interstate 5 and Genesee.[17] What was once 3770 Miramar Road is now Voigt Drive, dividing Scripps from the University of California, San Diego.)

Left, Ellen Browning Scripps built her first redwood home in La Jolla on Prospect Street in 1897. Right, Miss Ellen built an elegant second home in La Jolla of concrete and stucco when her redwood cottage burned down.   *courtesy of La Jolla Historical Society*

By 1924, Ellen Browning Scripps had been living in her own home in La Jolla for more than a quarter-century and was a clear-headed eighty-eight years old. She'd built her first redwood house on Prospect Street in 1897 and, when that was burned down by a disgruntled gardener, built the elegantly modern concrete and stucco replacement by Irving Gill—now the San Diego Museum of Contemporary Art—in 1916.[18]

Miss Ellen's lively interest in the village seemed boundless. She encouraged all sorts of cultural and social endeavors and was already a major donor to the Scripps Institution of Oceanography, The Bishop's School, Torrey Pines State Reserve, and the La Jolla Woman's Club, La Jolla Library, and La Jolla Recreation Center and Playground, to give an incomplete list. But within a year of moving into the new house, "it was apparent to Miss Ellen that a growing La Jolla needed better hospital facilities."[19]

There were 2,000 people in La Jolla in 1924,[20] and before Miss Ellen got involved the only health care facility was the wood frame Kline House (1904), which was one of the largest homes in town and had the particular virtue of sitting up high in the 400 block of Prospect Street, overlooking the ocean. In 1916, Mrs. Kline's house was converted to a six-bed sanitarium by Dr. and Mrs. Samuel Gillispie, recent arrivals from Kansas.

The first health care facility in La Jolla was in the wood-frame Kline House, which was converted to the six-bed La Jolla Sanitarium in 1916 by Dr. Samuel Gillispie and his wife, Ada.

courtesy of La Jolla Historical Society

The La Jolla Woman's Club honored their benefactress at a luncheon in March 1915. Ellen Browning Scripps, seated right, donated her time and money to countless San Diego institutions, including the La Jolla Woman's Club. *courtesy of San Diego History Center*

Ada Gillispie was a nurse and her husband one of the town's first physicians, after Martha Dunn Corey (1906) and Truman Parker (1914).[21] The first "La Jolla Sanitarium," so-called, was presumably better than nothing—or at least more convenient than the long, uncomfortable drive by railway or Model T along the coast road into Hillcrest and the Sisters of Mercy. But when Miss Ellen's personal secretary was admitted to the Sanitarium for treatment, Ada Gillispie was quick to tell her visiting employer about the need for a larger facility.[22]

Miss Ellen was persuaded and in 1917 agreed to build her first La Jolla hospital. In all subsequent correspondence, she was very clear about her intention, despite the fact that the new structure would continue the name "La Jolla Sanitarium." (Several years later when she began building the hospital to be called Scripps Memorial, it was referred to in letters as the Addition to the La Jolla Sanitarium.) Miss Ellen explained to her attorney, Jacob Harper, on June 14, 1917:

> Beginning for about a year Mrs. S.T. Gillispie has been conducting a hospital or sanitarium in the Cline [sic] House in La Jolla. It has been demonstrated that there is local need for such an institution. The Cline House is altogether unsuited for the work.[23]

Six months later, after the turn of the New Year 1918, land adjacent to the Kline House had been purchased, and Miss Ellen gave specific instructions to proceed:

> Referring to the document which I signed addressed to you dated June 14th, 1917 concerning Mrs. Gillispie and the La Jolla Hospital Project: the purchase of lots 43, 44, and 45 in block 17, La Jolla Park, has been completed, and I paid the total consideration amounting to fifty eight hundred dollars. Plans are being prepared by Mr. W. S. Hebbard for the erection of a building thereon in accordance with Mrs. Gillespie's ideas.
>
> I authorize you to spend in and about the erection of said building the sum of twenty five thousand dollars.

As with all her philanthropic building, Miss Ellen insisted on both beauty and function. This time though, despite the fact that Irving Gill designed nearly every other space she gave to the people of La Jolla, the project was given to his former partner, Will Hebbard. Jacob Harper explained the decision:

> You may ask why I did not entrust the work to Gill. For the reason there is a widespread feeling in the village that the Gills do work in a very expensive way and Mrs. Gillispie had a vital interest in keeping down the cost; so I let her select the architect.[24]

The architect began work quickly, and, within days of Miss Ellen's instructions to Jacob Harper, Will Hebbard wrote the attorney on January 23, 1918:

> Confirming our conversation of today in regard of the proposed La Jolla Hospital, I wish to state that I am proceeding with the working drawings. My fee for the working drawings and specifications will be 4% on twelve thousand dollars ($480), of which amount $120 has been paid.

Left to right, Ellen Browning Scripps, Ada Gillispie, Captain Wesley Crandall, and Fred Higgins stand in front of the first Scripps Memorial Hospital ambulance.   *courtesy of Scripps Health*

Ellen Browning Scripps underwrote a new La Jolla Sanitarium, realizing that a growing La Jolla needed an expanded hospital. The eight-patient facility opened its doors in 1918 on Prospect Street, next door to the Kline House.

courtesy of La Jolla Historical Society

Mr. Hebbard disagreed with Irving Gill's increasingly rigid belief that ornament had no function or importance,[25] and his design was inviting:

> The front facing on Prospect Street will be one story, but at the rear, where the grade falls off to the ocean, there will be practically three stories. Entrance will be gained through an artistic pergola leading to the reception room and the living rooms of Dr. and Mrs. Gillispie. The first floor will contain eight patients' rooms and three nurses' rooms…all on the south side will open onto a porch through French windows.[26]

There would be a solarium and a flat roof fitted up with awnings, cots and other furnishings so that convalescents might take the sun and ocean air. On the floor below was to be a direct entrance for autos into the hallway so that patients could be brought in on stretchers "without being exposed to the elements."[27]

But the actual construction nearly foundered on attempts to keep costs to the specified $25,000. At this stage, Ada Gillispie was thinking of the small hospital as her project and a business arrangement with Ellen Scripps. Two months after the plans were submitted for bids, Mrs. Gillispie wrote Jacob Harper a harried letter about trying to keep costs down:

> I have not written you sooner concerning the hospital as there seemed to be nothing definite to say. I have spent these weeks making and remaking the plans with Mr. Hebbard, cutting out many things and trying to reduce in every possible way the cost of the building….[Yet] the lowest bid was much in excess ..

Patients at the La Jolla Sanitarium could take advantage of the sun and ocean air on the south-facing porch.

courtesy of La Jolla Historical Society

Hardly knowing what steps to take, I talked the matter over with Miss Scripps, who assures me that she expects us to go ahead with our plans for the hospital… doing all we can to bring the cost down to the sum we had agreed upon.

…the last few weeks have proven more than ever before that we do need a hospital, and Miss Scripps tells me that I must go ahead with it by all means. This, of course, means that we must attempt to make reductions someplace…as I know how you feel about what the building will cost.

I cannot now see just where any more can be cut out.[28]

And she added,

I certainly do not feel that I am asking Miss Scripps to *give* the money for a hospital. I assuredly believe she will receive interest on every cent invested. And you surely know I hope to someday call it mine because I will have actually paid for it.

J.C. Harper, left, served as attorney to both E.W. and Ellen Browning Scripps. Mr. Harper was instrumental in helping Miss Ellen build Scripps Memorial Hospital and Scripps Clinic. Here, Mr. Harper talks with Harry Smithton, who was chief aide to E.W. Scripps until E.W.'s death in 1926.

courtesy of E.W. Scripps Archive, Mahn Center for Archives and Special Collections, Ohio University Libraries

The winter of 1918 was wartime in the United States, and Jacob Harper was engaged in government business that was sapping his strength. He had been shuttling 500 miles each way by train between Cincinnati, Ohio, and Washington, D.C. and was exhausted. On March 14, 1918, he sent a Western Union Night Letter from Cincinnati to Ada Gillispie in La Jolla:

> Am engaged on important government matters requiring continuous attention until completed. Am dangerously near nervous breakdown and cannot act on your matter now. I wrote Miss Scripps yesterday.[29]

And Mr. Harper elaborated in a letter to Mrs. Gillispie the next day:

> For a long time now I have been working under pressure that is not fair to either myself or my family. I reached Cincinnati one night and was hustled out the next for a long and arduous trip. I had cleared up the more urgent matters which had accumulated during my absence and was getting started on the work which brought me to Cincinnati when I was called by wire back to Washington…I simply must concentrate on that work until it is finished. My old enemies, insomnia and indigestion are again on the ascendant.
>
> Your [letter] indicates unwillingness to consider any other plan that the one you have set your mind on…[30]

After a three-week silence, Mrs. Gillispie ventured to write again:

> Knowing the pressure under which you were working and your threatened breakdown, I promised myself not to annoy you again with the project of "hospital" even though [it] meant anxiety for me. But the time has come when I just must have a word from you…
>
> I am disappointed that these plans did not come nearer to the figure we had in mind but I do believe that we have gotten in a "lot of hospital" for that sum…I feel we have cut out everything that can be cut out, and likely building will never be any cheaper during the time I shall be interested in hospitals.
>
> There is a growing need for such a place in La Jolla. We have never been so busy as the past six weeks.
>
> Coming to the point, will you kindly send me a line telling me if you plan to go on with the building when you return?[31]

This was not the end of the tense correspondence between Ellen Scripps' attorney and the strong-willed nurse-manager, who was wrestling her hospital into being. But finally on June 4, 1918, Miss Scripps wrote Jacob Harper (who was at last back in La Jolla):

It has been found that the cost of the proposed work will be greater than I had expected when I fixed twenty-five thousand dollars as the limit of expenditure. I regard the construction and operation of the hospital as a War necessity.

I direct you to go ahead and enter into a contract for the construction and equipment of the building even though the total expenditure may exceed twenty-five thousand dollars.[32]

Ellen Browning Scripps, seated, holds a flag-raising ceremony on Draper Street in La Jolla. The flag was raised to signal a quarantine during the influenza epidemic of 1918.

courtesy of La Jolla Historical Society

Building then proceeded quickly and, a few weeks before the sanitarium was ready to receive patients, Miss Scripps clarified legally for the first time that this was more than a business arrangement. On October 23, 1918, Ellen Browning Scripps created with Jacob Harper a perpetual trust in which she declared her desire:

to promote the public welfare by founding, endowing and by having maintained within the State of California a hospital for the relief of the sick …

and more particularly a general hospital or sanitarium for the care of sick, invalid or disabled persons, including surgical and obstetrical cases, and a general school for the education and training of nurses.

The name by which said hospital and school for nurses shall be known is "La Jolla Sanitarium."[33]

By the first of November 1918, Mrs. Gillispie had moved her operation out of the old sanitarium and into the new, which had facilities for ten adult patients and two infants.[34] The little hospital opened its doors in the midst of the ferocious influenza pandemic which struck San Diego that fall and again the following spring.[35] Ellen Scripps spoke approvingly of Ada Gillispie as "a level-headed businesswoman,"[36] and, for some years, the new Sanitarium was called the most modern hospital in its time and was thought to have brought complete medical care to La Jolla.

A few weeks after the opening, Dr. Robert Pollock, personal physician to Ellen Scripps, "was visiting a patient in the La Jolla Sanitarium and was both surprised and pleased with the building and its conduct," Miss Ellen wrote her brother, and added (curiously), "It seems one of the few successful public ventures I have indulged in."[37]

However, in January 1922, Miss Ellen—who liked to care for herself—slipped on the concrete floor of her sleeping porch, "while putting her room to rights" and broke her hip.[38] Miss Ellen insisted on being taken to the Sanitarium down the street so as not to be a burden upon anyone. Her chauffeur Fred Higgins, who drove Miss Ellen's first car—the big Pierce-Arrow her brother E. W. gave her for her 80th birthday[39]—told an interviewer:

> The poor soul had been laying on her porch for probably two hours before anybody discovered her. The housekeeper thought it was a coyote howling…My brother and I carried her [the two blocks] down to the La Jolla Sanitarium on a stretcher with blankets over her to keep her warm. They called Dr. Thomas Burger who was one of our leading surgeons at that time and he came out and operated in the La Jolla Sanitarium.[40]

It was the first time she had ever been a patient[41] and she did not care for the role:

> I can't go where I would or do what I like. I have to submit to be mauled around by alien hands…the whole performance being punctuated by my howls and screeches.[42]

Ellen Browning Scripps was a fixture in La Jolla from the time she moved there in 1897 until her death in 1932. Her extraordinary generosity lives on through her myriad philanthropic endeavors.

courtesy of Scripps Health

Howls and screeches aside, considering that modern fixation of hip fractures was years in the future with the development of aseptic technique and antibiotics, and that Ellen Scripps was 85, her recovery was surprisingly rapid. The initial X-ray report is lost, but a three-month follow-up by Dr. Lyell C. Kinney showed that Miss Ellen's left femur had fractured through the trochanter and been treated with a cast,[43] presumably (since this was 1922) a spica cast which would include at least one leg and a body component as high as mid-chest.[44]

The April X-ray showed "bony union" and by June 1922 Miss Ellen was reported to be standing on the dock to greet her brother E. W. when he returned from a long ocean voyage. However, she was under medical care for several months and had time to converse with her doctor about the changing face of medical science and the need for still another bigger and better hospital.

La Jollans with serious illnesses were by that time traveling as far as Los Angeles, to the Good Samaritan Hospital, for care.[45] Again to E. W., Miss

Ellen wrote:

> My latest adventure will have to be, I think, a new hospital building
> which is sadly needed. For I suppose accidents and appendicitis and
> babies and other ailments will continue for a few more generations
> of humanity – in spite of Psycho-analysis. You know we own nearly
> 100 feet adjoining the present sanitarium to the south, on which a
> building of sufficient size to last for many years can be erected.[46]

Ellen Scripps' personal physician, Dr. Robert Pollock,[47] was scientifically-minded. He was also active in medical politics at the local, regional and state level, including a stint as President of the Southern California Medical Society with headquarters in Los Angeles. Dr. Pollock began appearing in the *California State Journal of Medicine* in 1915 and remained a regular contributor through at least 1923. As associate editor of the *Journal* representing the San Diego County Medical Society, he reported on San Diego medical affairs— including frequent admiring updates on the Sisters of Mercy and St. Joseph Hospital.

Over the long months of her recuperation at the Sanitarium, Miss Scripps would almost certainly have heard from Dr. Pollock about the findings of *The Hospital Betterment Movement in California,* published in the *Journal* in 1920 and 1921:

> The minimum requirement for a modern hospital is that it shall be
> constructed, equipped, organized and personelled to supply all the
> complex requirements of modern medicine, both preventive and
> curative…and at the same time to constantly train new workers in
> the many special fields….[48]

> The aim of every good hospital is the same. It is sympathetic,
> courteous, efficient care of the sick; intelligent co-operation in the
> program of public health, and an earnest part in the education of
> physicians, nurses…and all specialists necessary to administer to the
> health of our citizens.[49]

By April 1923, Jacob Harper was writing to Ellen Scripps' banker in Cincinnati:

> You are already aware, I believe, of Miss Scripps' purpose to build
> *a fireproof addition to the La Jolla Sanitarium.* Plans have been in
> preparation for many months…I am opening a new account in the
> La Jolla Bank called Sanitarium Building Fund.[50]

And in November, the banker received this update:

> Last week, under written authorization from Miss Scripps, I
> employed Mr. J.H. Nicholson as contractor [for] the building and
> work is already underway. The total cost of the building, excluding
> equipment will probably be in the neighborhood of a hundred and
> seventy-five thousand dollars.[51]

Dr. Charlotte Baker left, San Diego's first female doctor, was an early advocate of women's rights who delivered more than 1,000 babies in San Diego. Ellen Browning Scripps turned to her friend, Dr. Baker, for advice about staff and building needs for Scripps Memorial Hospital.

courtesy of San Diego History Center

In Ellen Scripps' philanthropy she appears to have formed friendships and partnerships with other women whom she called upon for advice, including two women physicians: Dr. Mary Ritter, wife of the first director of the Scripps Institution of Oceanography, and Dr. Charlotte Baker who, with her physician husband, Fred, had been an early supporter of Mother Mary Michael Cummings at St. Joseph's Sanitarium, and the first woman president of the San Diego County Medical Society (1898).[52]

> When Miss Scripps decided to build the La Jolla Women's Club, she got Mary Ritter to supervise the construction. When Miss Scripps decided to fund a hospital, she discussed building needs and staff with Charlotte Baker... Charlotte Baker or her well-connected husband could make quiet inquiries about...the cost of hospital equipment without attracting public attention. This was often the research that preceded a gift from Miss Scripps.[53]

For her architect, Miss Ellen turned this time to Louis John Gill, who was Irving Gill's nephew and chief draftsman on her second home. Louis Gill was more open than his uncle to various architectural streams and chose the "Spanish Eclectic" style of the great 1915 Exposition Buildings in Balboa Park. Next door to the Sanitarium ("next south"), the new hospital began rising in November 1923—but only after the hard-pressed Jacob Harper recorded this Memorandum on November 17, 1923:

> For sometime past Miss Scripps has expressed impatience that the erection of the new hospital building was not under way. She has asked me several times when work would begin. The preparation of plans has consumed vastly more time than I had anticipated. The variety and complexity of questions to be considered have been a revelation to me. I have visited a number of hospitals *in this and other states*. The mistakes that have been made in these buildings caused me to feel that it was very desirable to take extraordinary precautions to avoid them in this work as far as it is humanly possible to do so.
>
> About a week ago I submitted to Miss Scripps a set of new full sized floor plans. We went over them in detail. She expressed herself as gratified...
>
> The actual moving of dirt began on the 20th.[54]

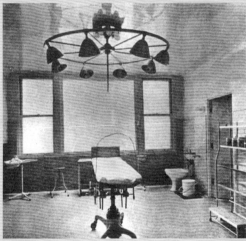

Top, staff at the new Scripps Memorial Hospital had access to obstetrical and surgical departments, which had one operating room, left. Of the fifty-seven patient rooms half were private, right, and patients were welcomed in an inviting and spacious lobby, bottom left.

courtesy of Scripps Health

The total cost of building, equipment and furnishings was $275,000, which was the "largest single gift" Miss Scripps had made so far.[55]

A few months before the hospital was finished, Miss Ellen "had not been well for some time and finally gave out"[56] and was admitted one last time to the old sanitarium (five years old) after which, under doctor's orders, she sailed for Hawaii. But she was home in time for the grand opening.

Scripps Memorial Hospital opened September 1924 at 464 Prospect Street and was named for the gentle Julia Anne who moved from Miramar Ranch to La Jolla the last year of her life—slipping into her sister's new redwood house even before Miss Ellen installed herself—and died there in 1898, aged 51.

The new hospital was grand for La Jolla, with 57 beds, half of them private rooms and the rest two-and four-bed wards, besides the nursery and children's wards. Sickrooms had wooden sash windows open to the salt air, with views of the ocean or of grass and green vines; they were furnished with "dark or creamy" bedsteads and dressers, and bentwood rockers like a fine hotel. There were medical, obstetrical and surgical departments—a single operating room painted "warm grey" instead of the usual white[57]—laboratory, X-ray, physiotherapy and a sun porch on the roof. The pleasing Prospect Street façade had [and still does have as City of San Diego Historical Site 234] a low sweeping mansard roof of Spanish tile with wide overhangs, recessive arched entries, red tiled porch, and a wooden arched door with cross-panes and carved plaster door surrounds.[58]

In charge of operations and continuing on as superintendent for the next five years was the redoubtable Ada Gillispie.[59]

Two months later, when the local press had scarcely finished celebrating the new Hospital, they were invited back to Prospect Street to admire the former La Jolla Sanitarium in its brand new incarnation as the Scripps Metabolic Clinic.

Scripps Memorial Hospital opened in 1924 on Prospect Street in La Jolla with 57 beds, a nursery, and children's wards.

courtesy of La Jolla Historical Society

Staff at Scripps Metabolic Clinic worked together to ensure patients were comfortable and received the best care possible. Dr. James Sherrill is the tallest man in last row, right of center.

courtesy of Scripps Health

CHAPTER FOUR
Scripps Metabolic Clinic
1924-1955

IT SO HAPPENED THAT MISS ELLEN'S PHYSICIAN had an overriding interest in what was then called "metabolic disease"—a turn-of-the-century term for diabetes, as well as for anemia, high blood pressure, obesity, and nephritis. The art of treating metabolic disease was called "physiatrics,"[1] though it has a different definition today.[2] Dr. Robert Pollock gave lectures on "Diabetes" (and also on "Hyperchlorhydria," on "The Influence of Metabolism on Tooth Structure," and one wonderfully inscrutable title called "The Slowly Elaborating Stomach").[3]

The great scientific advance of 1922, which essentially ushered in a new era of medicine, was the discovery of insulin for the treatment of diabetes by the dogged and irascible Canadian Frederick Banting and his beleaguered medical student, Charles Best. Prior to insulin, patients with diabetes either died rapidly, or—if they had funds—wasted away over months or years on starvation diets in places such as The New York Physiatric Institute, run by Dr. Frederick Madison Allen, who was the world's authority on starvation, until sinking into oblivion overnight. The timing of the explosive publicity about insulin, late summer and fall of 1922,[4] helps explain why Ellen Scripps decided to fund two new institutions, a Hospital and a Metabolic Clinic, nearly simultaneously.

Dr. James W. Sherrill was the first director of the Scripps Metabolic Clinic. Dr. Sherrill served as a United States Army medical officer in Panama.

courtesy of Scripps Health

In 1923, shortly before groundbreaking for Scripps Hospital, Dr. Pollock convened a meeting of San Diego physicians at the University Club to discuss the urgent building of an institution for diabetes, modeled after the highly regarded Potter Metabolic Clinic at Santa Barbara Cottage Hospital. One attentive listener was Jacob Harper, Miss Scripps' faithful attorney and facilitator of all her philanthropy; when Mr. Harper advised that the cause was worthy, Miss Ellen pledged her support.[5]

Dr. Nelson Janney, director of the Potter Clinic, was consulted in January 1924 by Dr. Pollock and Jacob Harper. Dr. Janney was enthusiastic about a facility south of Los Angeles and set out the ideal criteria for the director, which were that he have both general medical and specialized training, but not yet a national reputation (because the salary for a "star" would be prohibitive), and a keen interest in research and the ability to carry it out. He said:

> The vital thing was a Director who would be interested in and capable of conducting research work; that such a man would not only have regular medical training but also special training that would represent in all, thirteen years; and that he did not believe that such a man could be procured at less than $5,000 a year.[6]

Dr. Janney went on to say that:

> To conduct research was absolutely necessary not only for the sake of enlarging the scope of knowledge, but also to bring the clinic to the favorable notice of the profession; that the clinic should not depend upon local patronage but should draw patients from all over the country; and that the director should be a man who could present the work of the clinic to national, state and local medical associations.[7]

When the next day, Mr. Harper reported to Miss Scripps the conference with Dr. Janney:

> She stated that she was [even] more interested in research work than in the treatment of individual patients; that she looked upon the project favorably and believed that she had the money to provide.[8]

The man selected as the first director, Dr. James W. Sherrill, Sr. (1890–1955), was a native Texan and a graduate of Baylor University and Johns Hopkins University Medical School (1917). After serving his internship as a United States Army medical officer in Panama (1918), Dr. Sherrill joined Dr. Allen in New York City on E 51st Street at his private sanitarium for the treatment and study of diabetes.[9] Dr. Allen was said to have a heavy brass paperweight on his desk inscribed: "The less food, the more life," and the bible of care in 1919 was a manual entitled *The Starvation (Allen) Treatment of Diabetes.*[10] The following year, Dr. Allen moved his operation to a large, lush estate "with an Italianate mansion of magnificent proportions" in Morristown, New Jersey—though he continued to call it the New York Physiatric Institute.

Dr. James W. Sherrill, Jr., son and namesake of the first director, gives this account of how his father won the job:

> My father was working with Frederick Allen at the Institute where all the people in America who could afford it went for treatment of their diabetes. When insulin was discovered, Dr. Allen sent my father up to Toronto to work with Banting and Best. There was another gentleman there named E. Foster Copp, who was a Canadian. They were the four of them working together. So my father learned about insulin and went back to New Jersey and was in charge of the insulin.
>
> And somewhere along the line, at about 1924, Ellen Browning Scripps decided she wanted to build a clinic in La Jolla and sent for some men to be interviewed as director. People from around the country, I suppose half a dozen, got on trains and came out.[11]

By June of 1924, an advisory board assembled by Jacob Harper, including Drs. Pollock and Janney, as well as "Dr. Parker in San Francisco, Dr. Owens at the Naval Base Hospital and Dr. Thornton in the Electric Building" had interviewed several candidates and voted unanimously for Dr. Sherrill.[12] Significant in the choice, Dr. Janney said, was:

> that it would be a decided advantage to our clinic to start with a man who had secured eastern recognition. The fact that his medical research and clinical work had been carried on chiefly in the east and particularly under a man of such note as Dr. Allen, would have a standing that a man from the coast would not have.
>
> At the same time, it was good to find that Dr. Sherrill was born in Texas and therefore likely to have the western spirit rather than the spirit which you are likely to encounter in New England men.

On June 28 1924, Miss Scripps approved the choice of Dr. Sherrill and the going forward of the clinic organization, and Jacob Harper wired Dr. Sherrill the news.[13]

The younger Dr. Sherrill said:

> And so my dad proposed to my mother, Lucy Heath, after dating her
> for years. They got married, got on a train and came out here, lived in
> a little house right above the Cove which is still there. And she, Miss
> Scripps, of course, bought the property for the Clinic, paid for it, built
> it. I presume my father helped plan it. And then he started working
> and running it. About a year later he needed some help; they were
> getting very, very busy, so he called up Dr. Copp in Canada, and Copp
> came down to assist.[14]

And Lucy Heath Sherrill reminisced:

> I remember on our arrival in La Jolla, August 15, 1924, that the town
> was filled—then, as now. My husband, Dr. Sherrill, was busy getting
> plans ready for the establishment of the Scripps Clinic and set me to
> house hunting.
>
> After a week of contacting estate agents, I found two of the size
> suitable for a young couple just starting out. Upon asking to see the
> bath in the first one, I was told by the occupant, "There isn't one – we
> swim in the ocean!"
>
> The owner of the second house demanded that I sign an agreement
> to vacate on two weeks notice as this was a guesthouse. I did, and
> we lived there four-and –a-half years, until we built our present
> home. The owner said he liked us better than he did his guests.[15]

Never one to waste time or money, Ellen Scripps simply transformed the now-empty La Jolla Sanitarium, Will Hebbard's pretty little building with the artistic pergola, into the Scripps Metabolic Clinic with twenty beds. Doors opened four months after Dr. Sherrill arrived, on December 11, 1924. Since the patients arriving for treatment were not usually acutely ill, the décor more resembled a comfortable home than a hospital.[16]

The professional staff consisted of two physicians, and the first year of operation two-thirds of the beds were filled.[17] Miss Ellen wrote with satisfaction in January, 1925, "The newly established Metabolic Clinic has transcended the predictions of its most enthusiastic supporters."[18]

At the end of the year 1925, Miss Scripps built a third building on the Prospect Street campus as a Nurses Home.[19] The word soon got out that La Jolla, California, was an attractive place for a young nurse on her own; the following excerpt is from a prize-winning essay entitled "My Love Affair with a Village," by a Miss Verna Brooks:

The Nurses Home became part of the Scripps Prospect Street campus in 1925. Nurses could relax in the spacious living room and cook meals in the kitchen. *courtesy of San Diego History Center*

> The woman at the nurses' registry in Los Angeles had told me, "I have two openings: one in the desert and one in La Jolla. I would advise you to check out the one in La Jolla first, although the other job pays better." So here I was riding south on a bus along the bright blue Pacific with its white-crested waves beating endlessly against the shore. Arriving in La Jolla, I looked around me in awe and thought, "This must be Shangri-La!" Flowers were blooming everywhere, roses, camellias, hibiscus...
>
> It was November and I had recently left Pittsburgh where the temperature was -7 degrees... I had an appointment with Lucille Stevens, Directress of Nurses at Scripps Metabolic Clinic...and I was walking along a sun-drenched street lined with giant palm trees, wearing a full-length Hudson seal fur coat.[20]

All three buildings had been planned in the original Articles of Incorporation for Scripps Memorial Hospital (September 25, 1924), which gave the purpose of the corporation as "to establish and maintain:"[21]

1. a general hospital in La Jolla, in the city of San Diego,
2. clinics and laboratories for conducting medical research, and
3. a training school for nurses.

The same Articles added for emphasis: "It is one of the principal purposes of this corporation to carry on medical research and to that end the Scripps Metabolic Clinic has already been established." And finally, an amendment of March, 1925, left no doubt, in case anyone still wondered, as to Ellen Scripps' intentions about research:

The Prospect Street campus became home to three medical facilities: Scripps Memorial Hospital, Scripps Metabolic Clinic, and a home for nurses. *courtesy of Scripps Health*

> The primary and permanent purpose of this hospital is to zealously promote and protect the health of this community…by advancing the medical education and science of those that serve therein…[Only thus] will take its place as *a modern temple of health*.

In 1928, Dr. Sherrill established a dietetic school and hired his first director of research, Dr. Eaton MacKay, who had a particular interest in diabetes and the kidney. (Apparently Dr. MacKay was both a good researcher and a memorable personality; along with Dr. Arne Wick, he made one of the major contributions to the understanding of diabetic ketoacidosis in the early 1940s.[22] He lasted twenty-two years at the Clinic until he resigned "after a quarrel with Dr. Sherrill and the Board" in 1950—but only after threatening to quit several times previously. Dr. MacKay's daughter married Charles Scripps, who succeeded to the chair of the newspaper chain; her mother-in-law, who was a member of the 1950 Board of Scripps Metabolic Clinic, urged her colleagues to accept the resignation).[23]

In 1928, the front section of the original La Jolla Sanitarium was replaced with a Spanish-style façade so that it would coordinate with the Scripps Memorial Hospital.

courtesy of La Jolla Historical Society

Also in 1928, the front section of the original Sanitarium was removed and replaced with a Spanish-style façade to coordinate with the Hospital next door. Behind the new façade, the rear portion of the 1918 building remained, and it stayed there through "a great many" alterations and enlargements of the Clinic—hiding out of sight of the bulldozers, so to speak—until the last of the Sanitarium was finally razed in 1951.[24]

Rapid expansion was assumed to be unstoppable during the 1920s. But with the crashing onset of the Depression through the end of World War II, the Metabolic Clinic "stagnated."[25] For its part, the Hospital, which had a robust list of 156 admitting physicians in 1932, lost 70 percent of its doctors in a decade to the economy and the war, and was down to a skeletal forty-eight in 1942.[26]

Nurses were in desperately short supply. Obviously, citizens continued to be sick and injured, requiring that the Clinic's doctors be pressed into service at the Hospital and research projects scaled down—all of which aggravated the stress that had been present from the start because of the differing priorities of the two institutions.

The war kept Hospital and Clinic together as increasingly unwilling bedfellows, but no sooner was the Armistice signed than they sued for divorce. On October 10, 1946, an "action" was filed in Superior Court of San Diego by Scripps Metabolic Clinic seeking separation from Scripps Memorial Hospital and asking for transfer of certain assets. Two weeks later, the Board of Directors of Scripps Memorial Hospital voted to explore the possibility of creating two completely separate legal corporations with their own individual boards and operations. Eighteen months later, on May 15, 1947, the final legal separation of Hospital and Clinic was complete.[27]

For another eight years after the divorce, Dr. Sherrill continued building the reputation of the Scripps Metabolic Clinic as *the* medical destination in Southern California for the optimal management of diabetes and related complications, such as heart and kidney disease. His own laboratory research had been done mostly before coming to La Jolla.[28] He recruited physicians (all men at the time) with national reputations. After the initial cohort of the 1920s was assembled—Drs. E.F.F. Copp[29] and Dr. MacKay, along with radiologist Dr. A. B. Smith and cardiologist Dr. Francis Smith—there was a second wave: Dr. Arthur Marlow in hematology, endocrinologist Dr. Thomas Lambert and Drs. James Calloway, J.T. Cole, and William Bethard. Drs. Arne Wick and Grant Bartlett were "the research department"[30] after the departure of Dr. MacKay.

Dr. Sherrill was also first in a line of very socially astute directors of Scripps Clinic. His son reminisced:

> Our house was always busy socially with people that were coming to the Clinic and some were fairly famous: J Edgar Hoover, who summered in La Jolla every year with his friend Clyde Tolson; and Gene Tunney, Al Jolson, the actor Charles Correll from *Amos 'n' Andy*. They would come up to the house for dinner, and we'd even go up to Los Angeles to some of their houses.

Dr. James Sherrill, Sr.'s career as director of the Clinic lasted thirty years, from 1924 until 1955. During his tenure, Scripps Metabolic Clinic treated many well-known individuals, including J. Edgar Hoover and Jack Dempsey.

courtesy of Scripps Health

> I remember walking into my dad's home office one afternoon as a
> boy, and here's this guy who was huge. And my dad said, "Do you
> know who this is?" And I said, "No, sir." (You said "sir" in my house,
> you know.) That was Jack Dempsey. He shook my hand and my hand
> disappeared.[31]

Dr. Sherrill's career as director of the Clinic lasted for thirty years, from the summer of 1924 until his death from a third myocardial infarction on January 4, 1955, at the age of 64. He had been in poor health since the first attack and had just resumed part of his duties at the Clinic after an absence of many months. Tributes included this letter to Mrs. Sherrill from Dr. Henry J. John, a colleague from the early days at Dr. Allen's Physiatric Institute:

> I can't tell you how sorry I am about James. To say nothing about his
> outstanding medical knowledge, he was such a fine fellow, always a
> gentleman…The world has lost in him a good friend.[32]

The loss of the first director of Scripps Clinic without a succession plan threw the choice of a new director into the hands of the 1955 Chairman of the Board of Trustees, William Scripps Kellogg,[33] a grandnephew of Miss Ellen. Mr. Kellogg was at that time manager of La Jolla Beach and Tennis Club, for his widowed mother Florence Kellogg, [34] and had a friend and neighbor on Spindrift Drive, right next to the Marine Room, who was allergist Dr. Edmund Keeney.

Dr. Edmund Ludlow Keeney (1908-2000)[35] was a product of Shelbyville, Indiana, and Indiana University (1930), and a graduate of Dr. Sherrill's alma mater, Johns Hopkins University Medical School (1934). The young Dr. Keeney contracted tuberculosis during his internship at Baltimore City Hospital, recovered and completed his internship in 1937—then went on as instructor in medicine at Johns Hopkins and director of the Johns Hopkins Mycology Laboratory where he oversaw the development of adrenalin for asthma..He married and had two children, but—when his first marriage ended in divorce—moved from Baltimore to La Jolla in 1948.

Dr. Keeney's mother had vacationed in La Jolla for years and owned a home on Avenida Cresta, which her son occupied in his first months in town. He first opened a clinical practice in allergy in downtown San Diego with Dr. Charles Moore ("an exceptionally warm and amiable person")[36]; and, after a time, Drs. Keeney and Moore moved up to La Jolla to an office just west of Scripps Clinic. The allergy practice was notably successful. Dr. Keeney joined the research staff at the Clinic in 1949 and authored a textbook and many articles in the fields of allergy, immunology, and mycology. He was also handsome, well-spoken, and engaging, and made many friends—including William Scripps Kellogg, who named him director of Scripps Metabolic Clinic in 1955 out of a field of many contenders for the post.

CHAPTER FIVE
Scripps Memorial Hospital
1924-1964

THE LEGAL DIVORCE BETWEEN Scripps Hospital and Clinic probably
improved relations among the doctors working next door to one another. The end
of the war brought Army and Navy physicians—particularly Navy—flooding back
into practice, and the Hospital and Clinic doctors could each go back to doing what
they were best equipped to do, which at the Hospital was mostly acute care for local
residents, and at the Clinic was the assessment of chronic illness in visitors, many from a
long distance away, and conducting supporting research. In any case, the Clinic had no
surgeons and referred any patients needing operations out one door and in the other.

Relations had been warm enough at the beginning.
The archives of the Scripps Memorial Hospital Women's
Auxiliary [1] are a treasury of newspaper clippings, brochures,
and little snapshot histories of the early days on the
Prospect Street campus. The Auxiliary was founded in 1929,
with pioneering realtor Mrs. Anson P. Mills (a close friend
of Ellen Scripps) as president, and for the original purpose
of providing "a free bed in the hospital"[2] for a needy soul.
Annual dues were a dollar, but since the cost of a Hospital
bed was *more than nine dollars a day*, members had to raise
funds in other ways. Mrs. James W. Sherrill, whose husband
was director of the Clinic, was a founding member of the
Hospital Auxiliary then, and she was still a member in
1953—years after the divorce between the Hospital and the
Clinic—along with Mrs. Edmund Keeney whose husband
would shortly follow as director of the Clinic. Wives from
both sides of the aisle produced costumed Charity Balls at
a new (1924) and "elegant, luxurious hotel harmoniously
situated on the edge of the sea"[3] called Casa de Mañana—
donated by the visionary owner (and Auxiliary member),
Isabel Morrison Hopkins.

Mrs. Anson P. Mills was the
first president of the Scripps
Memorial Hospital Women's
Auxiliary. The group was
created in 1929 to provide free
beds for patients in need.
courtesy of San Diego History Center

The Scripps Memorial Hospital Women's Auxliary in 1934. Volunteer committees of the auxiliary folded bandages, transported patients, and raised funds for the Hospital.

courtesy of the archives of the Scripps Memorial Hospital Women's Auxiliary

The elaborate galas began in 1930 with the Washington's Birthday Ball in colonial dress (net profit to the Hospital $1,552.31), where Mrs. Hopkins' mother posed as George Washington, La Jolla's younger set danced the minuet, and a Miss Aida Underwood did an "old-fashioned eccentric dance" (a type of vaudeville routine with loose-limbed and contortionist-like moves). The events were sell-outs and continued on yearly in good-sport fashion, with such themes as the Irish Ball; Costumes of Many Nations Ball (twice) and the Hollywood Ball, with cigarette girls dressed in "modernist calico and cellophane"[4] to look like cigarette packs.

The outbreak of World War II brought total blackouts to the coast of California and the end of gaieties with the February 1942 Phantom Ball, which existed only in the imagination. The tickets were sold at the cost of "the dress you won't have to buy, the beauty parlor you won't have to visit, and the cost of all the aspirin for your headache the next day which you won't have now."[5] More than a decade elapsed before the prewar Charity Balls were revived with the first Candlelight Ball, staged December 1953, at La Jolla Country Club—a venue that was practically venerable at twenty-five years old. After 1953, the holiday Candlelight Balls so vital to philanthropy

In 1942, the Scripps Memorial Hospital Women's Auxiliary held a "phantom ball" for the benefit of the hospital. Declaring that wartime was not the time to have a ball, the women mailed invitations that suggested guests contribute the money they would have spent on the dance to the hospital. Among the original founders of the auxiliary are, left to right, standing, Mrs. E.H. Decker; Mrs. Morrison Hopkins; seated, Mrs. Rowland Hayden; Mrs. J. Lewis Morse; Mrs. J.C. Harper; and Mrs. H.W. Childs.

courtesy of the archives of the Scripps Memorial Hospital Women's Auxiliary

at Scripps Memorial would proceed uninterrupted through the decades in elegant rooms all over town. *The San Diego Union* described one such gala in 1969:

> The historic halls of Scripps Miramar Ranch resounded with the gaiety of a big party once again [as] Oriental rugs were taken up for dancing before a roaring fire and the portrait of E. W. Scripps.[6]

Annual Garden Bazaars in the summer also brought in funds and were held most often at the home of Florence "Floy" Scripps Kellogg (1870-1958). "Floy" was a niece of Miss Ellen through her brother, William Armiger, and began wintering in La Jolla in 1895, even before her Aunt Ellen built her own house. Floy was a socially vibrant beauty who was apparently happy to continue hosting parties through her eighties. She and her late husband, Frederick Kellogg, owned La Jolla Beach and Tennis Club, and their spacious house and grounds, called Chelsea, stood immediately south of Scripps Memorial, so that patients who opened their windows could hear the goings-on next door.

But the daily work of the Women's Auxiliary was less glamorous and much steadier than balls and garden bazaars. In the 1920s and 1930s, they sewed and mended hospital linens, visited patient rooms, created a lending library and a motor corps for transporting patients in their private cars. In wartime, due to the extreme shortage of help, Auxiliary members rolled up their sleeves at the Hospital to cook, serve food, and clean.

This advertisement for the 1952 Annual Garden Bazaar is held by auxiliary members, left to right, Mrs. Keith Jeffrey and Mrs. Richard Tullis.
courtesy of the archives of the Scripps Memorial Hospital Women's Auxiliary

In 1927, on Ellen Browning Scripps' ninety-first birthday, San Diego named a La Jolla Park after her, Ellen Browning Scripps Park in 1951.

courtesy of Scripps Health

In the seven years remaining to her after her medical institutions were up and running, Ellen Scripps donated funds for a college (Scripps College, Claremont, 1926), tower and chimes for St. James By-the Sea Episcopal Church (1929), an athletic field at La Jolla High School (1930), the Children's Pool (1931), a cottage-retreat for women students at San Diego State College (1931), and the list would no doubt have gone on forever if she'd lived that long. People kept trying, against all her protestations, to honor her publicly. When the name of the park above La Jolla Cove was officially changed to Ellen Scripps Park on her ninety-first birthday, Miss Scripps had this one comment for the *La Jolla Journal:*

> The only regret I have is that I do not bear a more euphonious name for such a distinction. The one little ironical vowel buried in its six barbaric Nordic consonants makes a combination unfitted for the name of a thing of joy and beauty.[7]

Ellen Browning Scripps made the cover of *Time* magazine in 1926.

courtesy of Scripps Health

But the signal event of the decade following the gifts of Scripps Hospital and Clinic to the people of La Jolla was the loss of their magnificent friend. In January 1932, Miss Ellen fell in her home "against a gas jet, striking her head."[8] After that she grew steadily weaker and more bird-like. Her attorney, Jacob Harper, continued to visit every day, as he had since 1916, until he was himself stricken with a serious illness in July 1932 and was admitted to Scripps Hospital for "a major surgical operation," so that he was not with Miss Ellen on August 3, 1932, when she died at home. She was ninety-five and had retained her intense interest in all things about her, as well as her wicked sense of humor, nearly to the end.

Scripps Memorial Hospital and Scripps Metabolic Clinic founder Ellen Browning Scripps died in her home in 1932. Miss Ellen left a rich legacy, having donated funds to scores of institutions in San Diego, including The Bishop's School, the La Jolla Children's Pool, and San Diego State, as well as founding two medical institutions that bear the family name. *courtesy of Scripps Health*

Just as Ellen Scripps requested of Mr. Harper, her ashes were placed in a box without fanfare— "no funeral, no gathering of the family, no flowers on the porch"— and later consigned to the sea below her home from the deck of the *Scripps*, a boat of the Scripps Institution of Oceanography.[9]

A biographer of the Scripps family adds this touching postscript:

> For the rest of his life, Jacob Harper cherished a letter received from a fellow attorney, Newton Baker: "Ever since the death of Miss Scripps I have found myself thinking of you with admiration and professional pride…I find myself happy to have known a lawyer to whom so beautifully a trust was given and who so beautifully and completely fulfilled it…[10]

To return to the postwar era at Scripps Hospital: Dr. William Doyle (1915–2000), La Jolla's first pediatrician, wrote this account of his first general staff meeting as its newest member. Recently discharged from the Navy, he had driven to the village from New York a few days before and was still awaiting the arrival by air of his surgeon-wife Dr. Anita Figueredo, and their three young children:[11]

Dr. William Doyle, c. 1964, was chief of staff at Scripps Memorial Hospital in 1964.

courtesy of Scripps Health

In October 1947, about a dozen physicians were gathered in the living room of the Nurses' Home of the Scripps Memorial Hospital in La Jolla, California. With feet on chairs and pipes in hand, these doctors were earnestly and informally discussing their patients and immediate medical problems of the hospital. This tiny group represented practically the entire active staff of the hospital, and of the adjoining sister institution, the Scripps Metabolic Clinic, as well.[12]

In October 1964, exactly 17 years later, I presided over my last general staff meeting of Scripps Memorial Hospital as outgoing Chief of Staff. The speaker of the evening was Jonas Salk. It now takes a sizeable auditorium in a brand new Scripps Memorial to accommodate a general staff meeting. The Hospital looms starkly from a sage-dotted mesa just out of town while a horde of earthmovers reshapes the landscape; [and] our old Nurses' Home on Prospect has been marvelously transformed into the Cardiopulmonary Institute of the renamed Scripps Clinic and Research Foundation. The story of this change is largely the story of America's great westward migration.[13]

DOYLE-FIGUEREDO HOUSE

Scripps Memorial Hospital and Scripps Metabolic Clinic, 1955.   *courtesy of Scripps Health*

Scenes such as this were common at Army base Camp Callan during World War II. The war brought a plethora of physicians and nurses to San Diego.

courtesy of San Diego History Center

The war did bring about a huge migration to San Diego of physicians and nurses—and cooks, welders, and pipefitters—many of whom had discovered paradise (or what they thought would be paradise after the war) while stationed at one of the Army or Marine Corps camps or Naval bases in town. There were at least a dozen of these. Early in the war San Diego was chosen as the new headquarters of the Pacific Fleet after the headquarters left Honolulu in the wake of Pearl Harbor. On Torrey Pines Mesa, the Army had Camp Callan and the Marine Corps Camp Matthews (both of which would combine later on to make the University of California, San Diego), but the huge pieces of military real estate were Camp Joseph H. Pendleton[14] Marine Base north of Oceanside (126,000 acres); the Naval Air Station off Coronado; the Naval Training Center in Point Loma (now Liberty Station); and the Naval Hospital at Balboa Park, which had 10,500 beds in 241 buildings covering that many acres[15] and was the largest hospital in the world.

It was the Navy that brought modern cardiology to San Diego in the person of medical officer (eventually Rear Admiral) Dr. David H. Carmichael, who would later lead Scripps to the forefront of cardiac care, along with Dr. William J. Kuzman at Sharp. In a talk with Dr. Kuzman before the San Diego Medical Society in 2006, Dr. Carmichael spoke of the early heroism of Dr. Francis M. Smith at Scripps Clinic, who managed to practice cardiology with nothing but a stethoscope, and similarly of Dr. Anton Yuskis at Mercy Hospital. But extraordinary inventions and interventions in cardiology—which had been at the tipping point of research before the war—erupted afterward in an unstoppable cascade, and Dr. Carmichael was brought from Naval Station Great Lakes to San Diego in 1953 specifically to set up a fellowship program at Balboa Hospital that would make it the best of the best.

In a way, modern cardiology began in 1929 with one of the more amazing medical experiments in history when a twenty-five year old German physician named Dr. Werner Forssman (1904-1979) performed the first human cardiac catheterization—on himself:

> Dr. Forssman hypothesized that a catheter could be inserted directly into the heart, for such applications as directly delivering drugs, injecting radiopaque dyes or measuring blood pressure. The fear at the time was that such an intrusion into the heart would be fatal. In order to prove his point, he decided to try the experiment on himself.
>
> He ignored his department chief and when a nurse tried to stop him, he tied her to an operating table. Then, he anesthetized his own lower arm and inserted a cannula into his antecubital vein threading it 65 cm all the way to his heart. After that, he walked up three flights of stairs with one end of the catheter in his arm and the other in his right atrium, for an X-ray.
>
> Facing disciplinary action for self-experimentation, he was forced to quit cardiology and take up urology.[16]

After a lot of other indignities, including being a German prisoner of war in WWII and then a lumberjack, Dr. Forssman was finally vindicated when Drs. Andre Cournand and Dickinson Richards read his paper and introduced cardiac catheterization at Bellevue Hospital in 1948, for which all three physicians won the Nobel Prize in Medicine in 1956.

Dr. David H. Carmichael led Scripps Memorial Hospital to the forefront of cardiac care. Dr. Carmichael served as chief of staff from 1970 to 1971.

courtesy of Scripps Health

And the astonishing advances kept coming, including the invention of the heart-lung machine by John Gibbon of Philadelphia in 1953—the year Dr. Carmichael arrived at Balboa Hospital. The machine was brought with much fanfare to San Diego. But Dr. Gibbon's original prototype kept balking in the operating room, so Dr. Carmichael and several others met with Convair engineers (who had switched from making B-24 bombers to supersonic jet Interceptors),[17] and together they developed a successful pump-oxygenator for San Diego.

Moving forward a few years and back to the Clinic:

In 1960, revered cardiologist Dr. Francis Smith was unwell and hoping to retire. Dr. Edmund Keeney looked to the University of Kansas to recruit Dr. E. Grey Dimond, who was professor and chairman of the Department of Medicine, as well as president that year of the American College of Cardiology. Dr. Dimond accepted the invitation to establish a cardiovascular section at Scripps Clinic and brought with him to La Jolla his wife, Audrey,[18] and a young associate named Dr. John Carson.[19] The young man with Kansas family values was originally dubious about Southern California as a place to raise children until he came down to look things over in April—when the snow was still high in Kansas—and "got my bald head burned over lunch on the Beach Club patio."[20] That did it. Dr. Carson called his wife, Elizabeth, and bought the house in which they would raise their large family, before flying home to pack.

Dr. Carson might well have remained at the Clinic forever, except for a contretemps over his annual summer job and family vacation, which was a month every July as physician at Lake Mohonk Mountain House in New Paltz, New York. Dr. Carson had established this routine (which would endure for more than 50 years) in 1958, even before arriving at the University of Kansas, and his chief was well aware of it.

But in the summer of 1961, Dr. Dimond somehow forgot to tell Dr. Keeney about the arrangement when one of his cardiologists went missing for 30 days, and Dr. Carson was called on the carpet when he returned. The rebuke stung, as well as the perceived lack of support—and meanwhile, Dr. Carmichael had moved to private practice from the Navy and chosen Scripps Memorial as the nearest good hospital to his home in Pacific Beach; for five years, from 1958-63, anyone needing an EKG at Scripps would get it from Dr. Carmichael's machine, which he kept in the back of his car. He and Dr. Carson "would see each other at midnight in the Hospital because both of us worked so hard."[21] (To clarify: all patient beds were then at Scripps Memorial and shared by Clinic and Hospital doctors alike.)

Dr. Carson also "wanted to put down roots in La Jolla and not see people from Los Angeles, where most of our Clinic patients came from at that time."[22]

Before long, Drs. Carmichael and Carson decided to work together and in 1962 set up practice on La Jolla Boulevard where their landlord was E.F.F. Copp, the diabetologist and erstwhile second-in-command at Scripps Clinic (who reportedly quit in a huff when passed over for the top job, after the death of James Sherrill).

The new partnership was hugely busy from the start. Dr. Carson recalls:

> "As the first boarded cardiologist in San Diego, David Carmichael was sought after as THE cardiologist, and from early morning to late night he was in every hospital in San Diego and Imperial Counties… and was having children and race horses named after him."[23]

Within a year there was a need for new associates: Dr. Ernest Pund from Georgia, who was briefly head of cardiology at Balboa, where Dr. Carmichael "ran into him and recognized his worth;" endocrinologist Dr. David Beary and cardiologist Dr. Jim Jordan" from that same cradle in the Navy:" and then Dr. John Trombold, All-American baseball player from Kansas who trained at the University of Utah with the "father of hematology," Dr. Max Wintrobe.[24] Drs. Beary and Trombold were the first noncardiologists of a thirty-three-member group that became Specialty Medical Associates and established a gold standard for medicine at the new Scripps Memorial Hospital on Torrey Pines Mesa after 1964.[25] But that first year, the budget was so stretched at Scripps Hospital that the administration could not equip a state-of the-art cardiovascular section. This was accomplished with a $75,000 donation from William Harmon Black of the Black and Gordon Oil Company of Wichita, Kansas—the first of many such crucial gifts from members of the extended Black family through the years.

And there were other memorable SMH physicians in the Prospect Street era, of course, many of them chiefs of staff, including fine generalists Everette Rogers and the "great raconteur" JT Lipe; and the unforgettable J W Johnson,[26] who would become both Chief of Staff at Scripps La Jolla (1968) and President of the San Diego Medical Society (1975), but died too young of an old renal tumor metastatic to the brain, and was memorialized with an annual lecture series at the new Scripps Hospital by the greatest names in American surgery.[27]

Surgeon Dr. Alan Berkenfield[28] says that on Prospect Street "everybody knew everybody" and met for Grand Rounds at lunch time in the glassed-in solarium on the roof, for a crab and shrimp salad buffet which was the best meal in town. There were four "not too sophisticated" operating rooms on Prospect, one reserved for urology with a screen built-in for pyelograms, but no intensive care unit: surgeons stayed up with unstable patients as long as it took, alongside regular nurses on the floor. As for operative notes, there were "two people, June and Shirley, in Medical Records and no machines except for a typewriter; you walked in and started talking,

Dr. Alan Berkenfield and staff at Scripps Memorial Hospital volunteered with the Flying Samaritans in Mexcio during the 1960s.
courtesy of the Flying Samaritans "How it All Began" video

and Shirley typed as fast as you could talk." The whole administration in the early '60s was two people, Fred Trader and his assistant, Mrs. Wilson.

> "It was a lot simpler then. You wanted something done, you could go to Fred. Like when we were with the Flying Samaritans[29] in El Rosario, Mexico and saw a little girl named Rosita with third-degree burns over 40 percent of her body. We couldn't leave her there, so Monday morning I went back up to Scripps with the head nurse, Fran Wicker, and into see Fred and said "Can we bring her up and take care of her? Because she's going to die if we don't." And he said, "Yes," but he looked at Fran and said, "I want to tell you something: you're in for a lot of work." There was no burn center, of course, and he said, "If the nurses have to put in a lot of extra time in taking care of this child, they have to do it on their own time." And Fran said, "Okay," because that's the way she was.
>
> So, by 11:00 in the morning we had a plane flying down to Baja and picked Rosita up, and in the meantime we cleared things with immigration so she just zipped right through Lindbergh Field. She had a temperature of 105, and, fortuitously, we had gotten our first cooling blanket a week before, so we could keep her temperature down, and we just cared for her and she survived."[30]

The emergency room was in the basement with three gurneys and a single nurse; all the general surgeons and a few GPs took ER call at home or in their offices "24/7 for two weeks at a time" with no established ambulance service and no EMS personnel. A big upgrade was the purchase by the police of station wagons with their back ends converted for accident victims; but the police still had no training beyond first aid and no way to alert the ER of what was on the way.

Both Hospital and Clinic had been remodeled over and over since 1924 and were bursting at the seams. In December 1950, a new wing of the Hospital opened on Prospect Street, bringing the total number of beds to 105, along with more and larger operating rooms and an extensive remodeling of the original buildings.[31] But the mortar was scarcely dry when it became obvious that this was a stop-gap solution.

> During the early 1950s, all departments doubled and tripled their operations…departments were literally scattered from "cellar to garret" extracting a heavy penalty from efficiency… there were patients on stretchers in halls and in beds in the library and reception room. [32]

With 5,000 new residents pouring into San Diego every month, hospital overcrowding was a countywide phenomenon: "from August to November 1956 there were many weeks when there were no beds available at Scripps Memorial, at Mercy or at Sharp."[33] Two years earlier, in 1954, Scripps Hospital Administrator Gerald Crary had initiated plans for yet another addition, to front on South Coast Blvd and raise bed capacity to 190. But the addition was never built.

In 1950 at Scripps Memorial, Dr. Anita Figueredo was on staff at as the first and only woman surgeon; she was also an eagle-eyed friend of the poor. When the hospital was remodeled and enlarged that year:

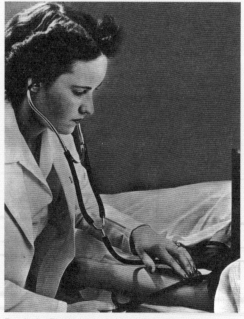

Dr. Anita Figuerado was the first female surgeon at Scripps Memorial Hospital and in San Diego County.
courtesy of Scripps Health

she managed to acquire the dismantled pieces, doors and window frames, hardware and old equipment and had it hauled away to Tijuana, Mexico where an entirely "new" Hospital of the Sacred Heart was erected from the discards. And then forever after at Scripps, a network of sympathetic nurses organized by Dr. Figueredo gathered up disposables, scrub brushes and gloves and suturing silk on crescent-shaped needles, and carloads of barely outdated infant formulas and drugs. [These things were] sorted and boxed for the *Casa de los Pobres,* a place in Tijuana where Franciscan nuns fed and nursed the poor of *"cartón-landia",* a riverbed colony of homeless people in cardboard boxes, who were washed out in flash floods year after year.[34]

But when the decision was made to move the beloved village hospital out to a wilderness of sage and chaparral that many La Jollans had never even seen—as there was no Interstate 5, no shopping,[35] and no reason to make the trek, except perhaps to shoot rabbits— a firestorm of debate erupted among neighbors and friends.

A pamphlet, called *La Jolla's Hospital Dilemma: How Did It Come About?*,[36] produced by "a non-profit corporation formed by La Jolla citizens for the sole purpose of preserving a community hospital in La Jolla," explained what happened this way:

> At about the time when the University of California announced its desire to locate a major new campus in the Torrey Pines area, and city property was being allocated for this and other purposes, a request was made to save a site for future hospital development in this area when the need arose. The proposition was put on the ballot, approved overwhelmingly by the voters, and a 40-acre site set aside on Miramar Road for this purpose. It was apparent to all that when a projected 25-50,000 new inhabitants had moved into the university area in the next ten years, they would then be able to share in the construction costs on a site already provided. This plan seemed eminently reasonable.

But the surprise was that in 1959—before UCSD was built—the Scripps Memorial Hospital Board of Directors voted to abandon Prospect Street altogether and relocate Scripps Memorial to that 40-acre site on Miramar Road, which a lot of villagers had expected someone else would build on, and leave Miss Scripps' little seaside hospital alone.

The doctors of the active medical staff were horrified and:

> In November 1959 passed, by an overwhelming majority (54-6) a resolution to the board of directors opposing any plan for hospital development for La Jolla which would entail loss of the present hospital.[37]

But the Scripps Hospital Board of Directors—then, as now—were a thoughtful, sophisticated, and extremely hard-working group of volunteers, and at that time were nearly all La Jollans themselves and/or relatives (Nackey Scripps Meanley and William Scripps Kellogg) of Ellen Browning Scripps.[38] Mrs. Burl Mackenzie, for instance, had been donating time and treasure to the Hospital since arriving in La Jolla from Wichita in 1945 and was now head of the new Building Committee, which involved driving up to Los Angeles every Monday at 5 a.m. to meet with architects.[39] The directors had grappled with the limitations of the village site for years and believed what history has borne out: that medicine was changing so rapidly and San Diego growing so fast, a move was inevitable and in the best interests of the majority.

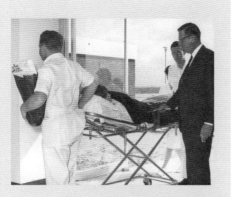

Executive Director Louis Peelyon, front right, greets the first patient to be admitted to the new Scripps Memorial Hospital. The Hospital moved to forty acres on the Torrey Pines mesa in 1964.
courtesy of Scripps Health

Still, when plans for the move proceeded inexorably, more than 3,500 La Jollans signed petitions to the state attorney general in his capacity of protector of charitable trusts, with the principal complaint that Ellen Browning Scripps had created a hospital for the village of La Jolla in perpetuity and that Miramar Road was not La Jolla. But by the time Stanley Mosk, attorney general of the State of California, filed suit against Scripps Memorial Hospital in Superior Court in February 1964, the new red-brick tower on the mesa was all but complete. Two months later, on April 22, 1964, Judge Eli Levenson decided in favor of the Board of Directors. In his findings, the judge stated that:

> The area of the City of San Diego known as La Jolla is not, and never has been a political entity and does not have any official boundary.[40]

"The court is satisfied," he said, "that Ellen Browning Scripps, by using the words 'in La Jolla', had in mind a general hospital facility in the general area of La Jolla to service people of all communities without identity."

When the daily papers carried the news, Louis Peelyon, hospital executive director, said "If there is no appeal, the new hospital will be ready to accept its first patients in the first week of May."[41] And the president of Save Our Hospital, Izetta Jewel Miller (a gracious and much-admired actress of the East Coast stage), told the press:

> The directors and members of the La Jolla Community Hospital Foundation will accept without rancor or reservation Judge Levenson's decision. We also will continue to be interested in the new Scripps Hospital and the future development of hospital care for this community.[42]

The new Scripps Memorial at 3770 Miramar Road did admit its first patient in May 1964, with much assistance from the doctors, including Chief of Staff William Doyle, who put newborns in bassinettes in the back of his wife's "Woody" station wagon for the transfer. Dr. Doyle was a sailor, as well as a card-carrying member of the Save Our Hospital Committee, and at the end of his term of chief of staff in November 1964, he received this note from Mr. Peelyon:[43]

> Dear Bill,
> Thanks for all your assistance and guidance as Chief in 1964.
> It was a rough year; thanks for helping "hold a'steady as she goes."
> Our patients received good care.
> Respectfully, Lou

Over the years, the Clinic grew to become a world-class biomedical research institute integrating basic and clinical research with patient care. Noted physicians and scientists from academic institutions throughout the United States came to conduct research in the La Jolla institution. *courtesy of Scripps Health*

CHAPTER SIX

Scripps Clinic and Research Foundation

1955-1977

WHEN DR. EDMUND KEENEY was summarily appointed director of Scripps Clinic after the death of Dr. Sherrill—six years after joining the research staff in 1949[1]—there was a brief undercurrent of revolt. In wider circles, Dr. Keeney was much-admired; William F. Black, who would later serve many years on the Clinic Board, said of the director:

> Ed Keeney was the consummate gentleman, articulate, well spoken, had an aura sort of to the manor born. He had a wonderful bedside manner. He was an excellent administrator and probably the best fundraiser I've ever encountered - and I've been involved with a lot of fundraising endeavors over the years. But he was the best. He really, I think, put Scripps Clinic on the map.[2]

Dr. Edmund Ludlow Keeney succeeded Dr. Sherrill as director of Scripps Metabolic Clinic in 1955.
courtesy of Scripps Health

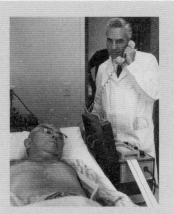

Dr. E. Grey Dimond established the Institute for CardioPulmonary Diseases and practiced at Scripps Clinic from 1960 to 1968. While at the Clinic, Dr. Dimond developed innovative, continuing education programs for physicians to update their cardiovascular disease diagnosis and therapy skills.
courtesy of Mandeville Special Collections Library, UC San Diego

But some of the more senior staff felt seriously upstaged, and Dr. Keeney acted with typical decisiveness in taking control. Years later, one of the early Clinic physicians, endocrinologist Dr. Tom Lambert, told the younger Dr. Sherrill what happened:

> "Well, the first day after your father's funeral we had a meeting and Ed Keeney came in and said, 'I am your new Director and you have two choices: either join me, and accept me as your leader, or leave. But do not get in my way.'"[3]

Most people stayed and went back to work, and Dr. Keeney set about revitalizing the Clinic. He had in mind a world-class biomedical research facility in the image of the Rockefeller Institute in New York and signaled his intent by changing the name to Scripps Clinic and Research Foundation (SCRF) nine months after taking over, on October 26, 1955.[4]

Dr. Keeney also began recruiting physicians from academic institutions around the country. Through the end of the 1950s he concentrated on clinical appointments: Drs. Solon Palmer and Lee Monroe in gastroenterology; Dr. Willard VanderLaan from Boston to build the division of endocrinology with Thomas Lambert; Dr. Herman Froeb from University of Southern California in pulmonology and Dr. Fred Ziegler from Johns Hopkins in psychiatry. After them in 1960 came cardiologist Dr. E. Grey Dimond, along with his Brazilian fellow, Dr. Alberto Benchimol, who organized the catheterization lab. Dr. Dimond spent eight years in his Clinic office, which was adorned with antique stethoscopes, and in that time established the Institute for CardioPulmonary Diseases in the old nurses' annex of Scripps Hospital, as well as a series of highly regarded seminars in Sherwood Hall, on the adjacent block along Prospect Street (the site of Miss Ellen's old home), before taking leave of La Jolla in 1968 to build a new School of Medicine at the University of Missouri, Kansas City. He was replaced by Dr. Richard Kahler from Yale.

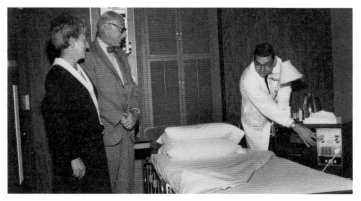

Dr. Richard L. Kahler demonstrated a patient control and communication console at the new intensive care unit at Scripps Clinic and Research Foundation to donor Edgar J. Marston Jr. and his wife. Dr. Kahler replaced Dr. Dimond at the Institute for CardioPulmonary Diseases.
courtesy of Mandeville Special Collections Library, UC San Diego

But the appointments that changed the institution were those which broadened the scope of the Clinic to include scientists doing full-time basic research. The first of these, in 1959, was Dr. A. Baird Hastings (1895-1987), head of the Department of Biological Chemistry at Harvard, who—at the age of sixty-three—was wishing to retire from administration and return to the laboratory "to again enjoy personal experimental work." Dr. Hastings began research by himself at SCRF and was awarded his NIH grant for seven years, "rather than the cautious three years he had requested, thus extending support through his seventieth birthday;" and Dr. Hastings later wrote of the "excitement and pleasure he derived from almost two decades in the second, La Jolla, phase of his career."[5]

Noted biochemist Dr. A. Baird Hastings came to Scripps Clinic in 1959 to conduct basic research. The next year, Dr. Baird was awarded a seven-year grant from The National Institutes of Health, although he had only requested a grant for three years.

One of the first of Dr. Keeney's new recruits, Dr. Charles Cochrane, says that the director of Scripps Clinic understood a problem facing scientists at universities in the 1960s which was:

> that if you wanted to do research, you had to do that in association with a teaching schedule, with clinical activities, with committees the school set up for you, and therefore research became almost a passive entity in your life. If you were really going to do research with expansion of knowledge at the molecular level, you had to do it full time.[6]

In 1961, pioneering immunologist Dr. Frank Dixon and four associates, Drs. Charles Cochrane, William Weigle, Joseph Feldman, and Jacinto Vazquez, were immersed in basic research in immunology at the University of Pittsburgh.

Dr. Dixon was a fascinating personality, born in St. Paul, Minnesota, and educated in Minnesota through his medical degree, then at Harvard Medical School's Department of Pathology, and at Washington University, St. Louis, until he arrived as chair of the Department of Pathology at the University of Pittsburgh in 1950, when he was thirty years old.[7] According to Charles Cochrane:

> The University of Pittsburgh was then a third rate institution, but the Andrew Mellon family had been putting money into it and they brought in Frank Dixon and Jonas Salk and some people from Harvard, and were getting the various departments moving. And that was one of the best decisions of my life, to go down and join this group of young people doing immunology. And it was all straight research even though it was in the department of pathology.[8]

Pioneering immunologist Dr. Frank Dixon, center, and four of his colleagues arrived from the University of Pittsburgh in 1961 to establish a Department of Experimental Pathology. Left to right, Drs. Charles Cochrane, Joseph Feldman, Frank Dixon, Jacinto Vazquez, and William Weigle came to Scripps to focus on basic research without administrative duties or teaching responsibilities. *courtesy of The Scripps Research Institute*

But then everything changed at Pittsburgh when "they got a new President from Smith-Corona Typewriter and he came in and started running the University like a typewriter business." All sorts of bureaucratic restraints caused the researchers to consider leaving. They were evaluating multiple offers from universities from around the country, when:

> One person stood up in front of us and this was Edmund Ludlow Keeney, from the Scripps Clinic. He was a big, tall, handsome man with a wonderful way about him – a remarkable person – and he realized exactly what we needed. And what he wanted was people doing research right next to the clinicians…to build science and clinical activities together. So he brought us out here to look at the place.

After meeting with Dr. Keeney on his home ground on Prospect Street, Dr. Dixon's team was convinced that he meant what he said, "that we would bring our own salaries and grants and do everything ourselves"—unmolested by other demands from the institution—"and that he'd build a new building for us with Admiral Wilder Baker[9] as the Chairman of his Board." So the five Pittsburgh scientists packed up and moved their large operation, along with ten postdoctoral fellows and twenty staff for technical support, to a village no one in the East had ever heard of, and to the amazement of their colleagues in Eastern universities who predicted they'd be back within the year.

But the team sank roots and flourished. In 1964, with the transfer of Scripps Hospital to Torrey Pines Mesa, *San Diego Union* and *Tribune* Publisher James Copley provided one million dollars for the purchase of the vacated hospital—along with a no-compete agreement that the Clinic would not bring in surgeons or run a general hospital for at least five years.[10] The old hospital was renamed the Copley Center; and the promised new building was completed in 1965 as the Timken-Sturgis Research

Laboratories, fronting on South Coast Boulevard and donated by patient Valerie Timken Sturgis Whitney,[11] whose father W.R. was owner of the family firm making roller bearings in Canton, Ohio, and founding donor of the Timken Museum of Art in Balboa Park.[12] Dr. Keeney ever after referred to the Timken-Sturgis as "the building a urinalysis built" because the donor had been admitted to the Clinic unable to use her legs, was found to have a correctable illness, diabetes, and walked out under her own steam.

Dr. Frank Dixon (1920–2008) became founding director of the Department of Experimental Pathology in 1961 and ultimately director of the Research Institute of Scripps Clinic until his retirement in 1986, after a quarter century of leadership. He and his associates got no salaries (as opposed to people recruited to a university). Their incomes were dependent on the grant support they raised; and Dr. Dixon espoused a concept called "scientific Darwinism," which said "you didn't have to tell people if their research was good or bad because if they couldn't get funding from a national organization they wouldn't be around Scripps." As Dr. Cochrane said:

Dr. Frank Dixon established a thriving research program at Scripps Clinic and Research Foundation. When he retired in 1986, the Clinic was the largest independent, nonprofit biomedical research center in the country. Its funding from the National Institutes of Health was $39 million per year, surpassing the Mayo Clinic.

courtesy of The Scripps Research Institute

> Frank realized that the strength of the department would be created by individuals thinking their thoughts in research and developing their own areas. I could pick what I wanted to work on and then it was my job to work in that area.

> We established the institute with our own grant support. Not everybody did this. Not everybody did well. And so it was really the four of us, Frank Dixon, Bill Weigle, Joe Feldman and myself, who stayed on in the department and built the new structure.

Dr. Dixon was a complex and sometimes difficult man who attracted many talented people, but sometimes drove them away; he worked obsessively hard and had trouble understanding why his researchers might not want to be in the lab twenty-four hours a day, seven days a week— unless it was to play bruising squash on the rooftop court of the lab. He was also a natural recruiter, "very bright and wonderfully articulate."

> He had a vast circle of friends in Europe and in this country and he would charm people so well with his words and his brilliance that people would naturally think that this would be a great place to work.

Accomplished scientists in immunology from the U.S. and abroad chose to leave their universities and join the group in La Jolla, including Dr. Ralph Reisfeld from the National Institutes of Health, Dr. Hans Müller-Eberhard from the Rockefeller Institute, "who was a real champion," a member of the National Academy of Sciences, and would later be awarded the first endowed chair at the Clinic,[13] and Dr. Dick Dutton from the Hammersmith in England.

> And then immunology had grown to a point that with all of the talks that we were giving at national meetings, everybody got to know that this was Scripps on the West Coast and it was strong in immunology. And we began to get postdoctoral fellows applying from Asia, this country and Europe.

One of Dr. Dixon's postdoctoral fellows, Dr. Michael Oldstone, came to the Clinic in 1966 from Johns Hopkins and—in an address to the La Jolla Historical Society along with Dr. Cochrane[14]—painted this nostalgic picture of La Jolla when he arrived:

> There was no Highway 5. That meant the beaches were empty when you went to the beach. The Unicorn and the Cove[15] were the two movie theaters, and there were only two places to eat at 9 o'clock at night after the movie – the La Valencia or Alfonso's Mexican…and on Fridays we would go over to the C&W Delicatessen on Girard and have abalone sandwiches.

Dr. Oldstone also made this observation in the address about relations in the early days between the clinicians and basic scientists:

> When we were small and lived on Coast Boulevard, we used to meet and have free lunches. And there is something about a free lunch that attracts everybody, no matter how bad the lunch is [and so] we knew all the clinicians and it was very easy to form relationships and collaborations. Also, at that time, the clinicians used to attend our Wednesday afternoon seminars [since] they were not pressured to see patients every 15 minutes. They had a lot more free time and we had a lot more interrelationships.

And Dr. Cochrane commented about the scientific cross-fertilization among La Jolla's three new

This Ansel Adams photo of Dr. Charles Cochrane as a medical student at the University of Rochester appeared on the cover of the university's magazine in 1952. Dr. Cochrane was twenty-two at the time. Dr. Cochrane was recruited to conduct basic research at Scripps Clinic and Research Foundation.

© 2012 The Ansel Adams Publishing Rights Trust

institutions: the UCSD School of Medicine, the Salk Institute, and Scripps Clinic and Research Foundation. The group met in the library conference room which was "about 12 x 18 feet":

> David Bonner [first Chair of Biology at UCSD] was putting together the medical school up on the hill; Jonas Salk, whom we had known at Pittsburgh, came to work upstairs in our lab while he was building on Torrey Pines Mesa; and [the early UCSD people and Salk people] and our group of five met in one room. And we should have had pictures taken because that group of fifteen scientists then expanded into what is today the third largest complex of medical science and biotechnology in the country after San Francisco and Boston.
>
> You can imagine the germination of ideas that came from all this mixed talent during those meetings.

Dr. Cochrane went on to describe his first encounter with a medical student who would shape Scripps Research in years to come:

> I remember the day down in Timken Auditorium on Prospect Street when we had a meeting of the clinical and research staffs. In a premeeting, there were a number of postdocs and other people present; and one of the new people who was thinking of coming was apparently an officer in the National Guard. He was sitting on the stairs next to the chairs in the auditorium. And when it was time to dismiss everybody except the staff, Ed Keeney looked around, and he saw this fellow in the National Guard uniform and said, "Excuse me. But we're having a staff meeting here, and you'll have to leave the room."
>
> And that was Richard Lerner. I'll never forget it.

The back of Scripps Clinic looked out on South Coast Boulevard. By the 1970s, it was apparent the Clinic would have to move from its Coast Boulevard location, even though space had been added with the Copley Center and the new building housing the Timken-Sturgis Research Laboratories, left.

courtesy of Scripps Health

Under the leadership of Dr. Edmund Keeney, far left, Scripps Clinic and Research Foundation expanded throughout the 1960s and 1970s, boosting its reputation biomedical research.
courtesy of Mandeville Special Collections Library, UC San Diego

Dr. Keeney said in a 1986 lecture[16] that from the time of his appointment in 1955 he had worked to build three strong medical research departments: Experimental Pathology [Immunopathology], Biochemistry, and Microbiology, and he accomplished this very quickly. After his hugely successful strategy for experimental pathology, he turned to Dr. Frank Huennekens from the University of Washington for biochemistry (1962)—giving Dr. Hastings his leisure for research—and to Dr. John Spizizen from Minnesota for microbiology (1964). And then all the new space created by the vacated Hospital allowed the promotion of expanded clinical departments in radiology, hematology, allergy-immunology-rheumatology, and dermatology, as well as the solidly established cardiology and endocrinology with its historical emphasis on diabetes— soon to be recognized as an immunologic disease.

Then all that new space was filled. By 1970 it became apparent that the Scripps Clinic and Research Foundation would have to move—despite 70,000 square feet of five-year-old laboratories and the reluctance of Dr. Keeney, who loved the old site and his own allergy office where he still saw patients every day. Chairman James Copley and the board of trustees understood that the Clinic had to move in order to grow, just as Scripps Memorial did a few years before. But Mr. Copley was Dr. Keeney's best friend and golfing partner and could not convince him of what needed to be done. So he hired James Lewis Bowers, Ph.D., with whom he had worked on the Nixon-Agnew Presidential campaign of 1968, to fly out from New York as consultant. Mr. Bowers (who would later become executive director of Scripps Memorial Hospitals Foundation) interviewed a list of seventy-five stakeholders, city officials, heads of corporations, and community leaders, as well as Scripps Clinic doctors, nurses, and board members. The clearest message came from San Diego Mayor Frank Curran, as James Bowers describes:

Mayor Curran said to me when I interviewed him, "Young man, let me tell you one thing right now. If you people think you're going to do anything, add one brick to that place in La Jolla, no. Not until you build a garage for five hundred cars. Because," he said, "our office gets calls from La Jolla people every day complaining about parking, because your Scripps people take over all the spaces by the beach early in the morning and never leave."[17]

When the consultant's report confirmed the need for a move, the vote was thirty-two to one in favor, with a foot-dragging Dr. Keeney against. (The other significant opponent, who didn't have a vote, was Dr. Dixon who said, when the Clinic finally decided to build, "then go ahead and build a hospital and surgery and whatever else, but let me stay down here and just run the research"—and, indeed, the immunologists did stay down by the beach several years after everyone else had left.[18] For his part, Dr. Keeney changed gears and persuaded the New York consultant to stay in La Jolla as his assistant and manage the move. James Bowers, who was reveling in the January La Jolla sunshine, asked someone in Manhattan to pack up and ship his belongings, and went on to a long career of service to the entire Scripps medical family.)

By this time, it was apparent that La Jolla's center of medicine and science had shifted, with Scripps Memorial Hospital, UCSD School of Medicine and the Salk Institute, to the Torrey Pines mesa. It so happened that the Clinic's desire to relocate to the mesa dovetailed exactly with the desire of a landowner there, Dow Chemical, to move quickly and quietly away. This was the time of relentless demonstrations against Dow by college students opposed to the company's manufacture of napalm and Agent Orange for the Viet Nam War; and a Clinic Board member at the time, Don Ballman, was a retired Dow executive who perceived what would happen if the company followed through on plans to move their operation to a site next door to the young and liberal UCSD. So Ballman convinced the company to give to Scripps Clinic and Research Foundation its thirteen prime acres (valued at $888,000) overlooking Torrey Pines Golf Course and the sea.[19]

William F. Black was persuaded to take the reins of the Scripps Clinic and Research Foundation Board of Trustees from retiring Chairman Edgar Marston in 1972. Left to right seated, William Black, chairman; and Edmund Keeney, MD, president. Also elected in 1972 were, left to right standing, James Ridgeway, Frank Kockritz, and William Elser. Mr. Black served as chair until 1978.
courtesy of Mandeville Special Collections Library, UC San Diego

James Copley, publisher of the San Diego Union and Tribune, proved a good friend to Scripps Clinic, providing funds for expansion in 1964 and chairing the capital campaign for a new complex on the Torrey Pines mesa..

courtesy of Scripps Health

The gift of land enabled Dr. Keeney to contact his friends again for money, including the faithful James Copley, who chaired the campaign, which raised $11.6 million—enough for a new building in the 1970s—but did not live to see it.[20] Chairman of the Clinic Board from 1972-1978, the crucial six years of campaign and construction, was William F. Black, who recalled wryly that:

> When Jim Copley recruited me, he said, "Now, Bill, this won't take any time at all. It's mostly ceremonial."
>
> It was by far the biggest fundraising ever undertaken in San Diego up until that time. I think it was noted then that the main reason it was successful was that so much of the support of the Clinic in those days was from out of town. Our fundraising efforts weren't limited just to 92037. We had enormous support from not only around the country but from foreign countries as well, especially Mexico. Mexico was always a good market for Scripps Clinic back in those days.[21]

Dr. Keeney chose the famed Edward Durrell Stone, architect of the Museum of Modern Art (MOMA) in New York and the John F. Kennedy Center in Washington, D.C. Mr. Stone's design for the new SCRF—including what is now Scripps Green Hospital and Stein Clinical Research—was completed in 1974 and was his final project before retiring that same year.[22]

In 1974, ground-breaking ceremonies for the new institution were led by Dr. Edmund Keeney, center, who wielded a five-foot aluminum scalpel. Left, William Black, chair of the board of trustees, and, right, Mayor Pete Wilson, used conventional shovels.

courtesy of Scripps Health

Groundbreaking for the new institution occurred in April 1974 in an atmosphere of great anticipation, but, within a month, the state of California was demanding huge institutional change.[23] The *California Medical Practice Act* of 1974 declared a specific prohibition against the corporate practice of medicine, citing the "principal evils" as "the conflict of standards between the professional obligations of doctors and the profit motive of the corporation employer."[24] The Scripps Clinic and Research Foundation was to reorganize into three corporations to conform to state codes:

1. SCRF, which included an embedded division for research called the Research Institute of Scripps Clinic (RISC);
2. A separate Hospital; and
3. The first Scripps Clinic Medical Group.

With this, and after nearly thirty years in control of it all, Dr. Keeney decided it was time to step down as director, though he retained the title of president for three more years. Dr. Dixon became CEO of both SCRF and RISC, Horace Warden president and CEO of the Hospital, along with neurologist Dr. Don Dalessio as first chief of the Hospital Medical Staff, and radiologist Dr. John Smith president and CEO of Scripps Clinic Medical Group. The umbrella title overall was the Scripps Clinic Medical Institutions (SCMI).[25]

In December 1975, the three boards of the Scripps Medical Institutions together recognized the many gifts of their most devoted donor couple by renaming the Hospital of Scripps Clinic "The Cecil H. and Ida M. Green Hospital of Scripps Clinic." Mr. Green was an MIT-trained engineer and founder of Texas Instruments, which entered the semiconductor business in 1952 and produced the first pocket-sized transistor radio in 1954. In 1970—before the move to the Mesa—the Greens established the Cecil and Ida Green Investigatorship at Scripps Clinic and Research Foundation, and subsequently the couple made gifts to help construct a hospital on the new campus.[26] The formal banquet in celebration was the highlight of an otherwise very challenging time.

Left to right, Dr. Cecil H. Green and his wife, Ida M. Green, with Dr. Hans J. Müller-Eberhard, the first appointee to the Green Investigatorship in Medical Research. The Hospital of Scripps Clinic was renamed The Cecil H. and Ida M. Green Hospital in honor of the Greens, who were both patients in 1958.

courtesy of Scripps Health

Formal dedication of the new Scripps Clinic facility on the Torrey Pines mesa occurred in November 1977, after Dr. Charles C. Edwards had arrived to take on the role of president of the Scripps Clinic and Research Foundation.

courtesy of Scripps Health

In the fall of 1976, "about half" of the research staff began moving north from the Timken-Sturgis building—to be followed by the rest in 1980, when a free-standing Immunology Laboratory was built on open land to the south. This was Dr. Dixon's building, and he requested a special interior, with all laboratories against the perimeter walls and the center as a two-story atrium with upholstered benches, tables, and armchairs, and good art—including Alexander Calder on the wall and mobiles overhead—for relaxed encounters with colleagues at work on different projects.[27]

A third research center, Molecular Biology, was funded by Johnson & Johnson in 1983; and it is worth noting here that one of the more stately pieces of monumental art on the campuses stands between Molecular Biology and Immunology: Andy Goldsworthy's *Oak Cairn 2004* in memory of William O. Weigle. The cairn is sixteen feet high, of curvilinear lengths of bleached grey English oak, and is hidden behind a wall of trees in a stepped-down, sandy gravel square near the green grass and sea.

Oak Cairn 2004 by Andy Goldworthy

The addition of all this space to the Research Institute was essential in view of continued recruitment of professional staff in each department from this country and abroad. In addition, postdoctoral scientists from all over the world were knocking at the doors: in the first fifteen years, the number of professional staff grew from the Founding Five to seventy-four and "postdocs" from seven to more than a hundred—all a harbinger of exponential growth in the decades to follow. [28]

In February 1977, the clinicians from Prospect Street and their patients made the transfer to Scripps Green. Formal dedication of the new facility at Torrey Pines occurred during a long week in November 1977, a few months after the arrival on the scene of a new President of Scripps Clinic and Research Foundation:[29] Dr. Charles C. Edwards, Mayo Clinic-trained surgeon and veteran of high-level government commissions and private boardrooms, who had a transforming vision for the path ahead.[30]

Dr. William Doyle painted *View from the Bridge* of the new Scripps Memorial Hospital. The oil won first prize in oil realism category from the San Diego Art Institute in 1967.   *courtesy of San Diego History Center*

CHAPTER SEVEN
Scripps Memorial Hospital
1964-1991

WHAT PHYSICIANS AND
HOSPITAL EXECUTIVES of a certain age
now think of as the golden age of medicine
in San Diego—which is to say the time when
they felt most in control of their own fates—
roughly covered the last decade of Scripps
Memorial Hospital on Prospect Street and the
first two on Miramar and Genesee. Rules of
medical practice were simple: anyone who
came to your office seeking care was your
patient ever after, and you (or your partner on
your day off) saw that patient day or night in
the office, at home, or in the emergency room;
wrote admitting orders if necessary; made
daily hospital rounds at least once; organized
specialty care by colleagues; and went back
to the office for the day. You were paid more
or less what you asked and developed your
practice based on your reputation, rather than
your patient's insurance plan. Patients generally
had *a* doctor and knew who the person was.

Aerial of La Jolla, c. 1965. The original entrance of Scripps Memorial Hospital on the Torrey Pines mesa faced Miramar Road, at the time the main road to the hospital. Construction of Highway 5 changed the configuration of roads.

courtesy of San Diego History Center

Louis Peelyon was the first executive director at Scripps Memorial Hospital. Mr. Peelyon was hired in 1961 to help oversee expansion of the Hospital.

courtesy of Scripps Health

Similarly, hospital beds could scarcely be made up fast enough for the growing population—so that competition with other institutions was not so charged an issue—technology was developing at a furious rate, and the mandate of the hospital executive was straightforward: to expand—to build or acquire big centers of healing with the most up-to-date equipment to be found. The first person with the title "Executive Director" at Scripps Memorial, Louis Peelyon, was hired in 1961 as an expert in hospital construction, with skills acquired under the Hill-Burton Act, a postwar federal program designed to create "4.5 beds per 1000 people."[1]

Mr. Peelyon had been the construction supervisor at Grossmont Hospital in La Mesa [2](1955) and loved technology; the new Scripps Memorial with 240 beds had gifts from the Space Age, including microwave ovens, meaning that "meals could be prepared a day in advance, kept refrigerated until needed and then delivered to the floors."

There was a system of pneumatic tubes—"three quarters of a mile" of tubes whisking cylinders four inches wide and a foot long through the eight floors of the building with "messages, prescriptions, paper work, drugs and X-ray film" to any part of the hospital in seconds. There was a "completely controlled environment" of double-paned windows sealed with neoprene and "never a need to open the window."[3] Several members of the board and nearly everybody at Save Our Hospital regretted those windows. Burl Mackenzie, board member of the Building Committee, said:

> The one thing I remember very clearly about the building plans, because I was always sorry when it didn't last, was that we saved regular windows for the more expensive corner rooms, so you didn't have to have air conditioning – so you could open your windows and feel the fresh air.[4]

But the noisy flight path overhead from Miramar Naval Air Station dictated otherwise. Patients in a special intensive care unit on the third floor had wires taped to various body parts and attached to machines with control panels and alarms so that nurses could record every aspect of the patient's condition.

But construction couldn't stop. By 1969, a Renaissance man named William E. Nelson built the first medical office building west of the hospital at 9844 Genesee. Bill Nelson was an attorney with a Ph.D. in economics from the University of Wisconsin (for which he had a "free ride" after winning a contest in mathematics)

Scripps Memorial Hospital moved to Miramar Road in 1964. The new hospital had 240 beds to serve the growing population of San Diego, as well as the most sophisticated technology of the time.

courtesy of Scripps Health

and now writes erudite newsletters about economics and the human condition with Latin and Shakespearean epigrams. He got into building, he explained, because "as a lawyer in L.A., I met people who wanted to develop things." He met Louis Peelyon after completing his first office building in La Jolla. Mr. Nelson subsequently undertook a number of projects for both Drs. Edmund Keeney and Charles Edwards at Scripps Clinic, and has a key role later on in this story.[5]

Plans for a second building phase at the hospital were also under way with groundbreaking in 1971 for an entirely new second tower, remodeling and expansion of the first, and four new operating rooms called the Kelsey Surgical Pavilion, in honor of Preston Kelsey, former president of the board. The remodeled first tower was named for a colorful La Jolla lady named Frances Nunnally Goodrich Winzer (1891-1981). She was a patient of Dr. John Carson, who told this story:

> I first saw her about 1965 when she lived on Electric Avenue [modest neighborhood] with her soon-to-be husband. And I thought she was poor and didn't send her a bill. And then she moved to a house on Waverly, and when I made a house call and went through the corridors, here were pictures of Mark Twain. And I said, "Did you know Mark Twain?" She said, "Yes. I was one of his Angel-fish." And Angel-fish were young ladies between the age of twelve and sixteen who promised to write Mark Twain every few months and in return were "appointed to his Aquarium" and sent a little angelfish pin.
>
> And Frances Nunnally Winzer was the daughter of James H. Nunnally who bought the Coca Cola Company [with his wife's cousin] from Asa Candler. Mrs. Winzer's first cousin was Robert Woodruff who gave a hundred million to Emory University. So I started sending her bills after that.
>
> And one Sunday in March 1972, I came up to make rounds and Joe Thompson had fixed her hip. And the nurses said, "Mrs. Winzer is just beside herself. She needed a special commode chair and none was available." So I went in, and she said, "Dr. Carson, what would it cost to get a commode chair?" And I said, "About a million dollars." She said, "I'll give it to you." And the lawyer was there the next day and she gave us our first million."[6]

Leaders at Scripps Memorial Hospital watch the second building phase, which added a second tower, remodeled and expanded the first tower, and added four new operating rooms. With the addition of the second tower, the Hospital had a total of 344 beds. *courtesy of San Diego History Center*

The second tower, which brought the total number of beds to 344, was dedicated on May 6, 1973, and named for James Copley (1916-1973)—the man who had been honorary chairman of the building fund at Scripps Memorial, on top of his huge contributions to Scripps Clinic, and despite being gravely ill.

But there were winds of change, and powerful forces at work rethinking how medicine would be delivered and paid for in this country. January 1973 saw the implementation of the infamous Professional Standards Review Organization (PSRO) legislation, which so inflamed many physicians that a near-riot erupted at the meeting of the American Medical Association (AMA) in Anaheim that year.

PSRO for the first time imposed utilization controls on the services provided through Medicare and Medicaid[7] and was viewed as a slippery slope toward socialized medicine. The officers and high-level staff of the AMA were actually trying to cooperate with the Nixon administration so as to have a say in how the PSRO program was developed, but their voices were shouted down. The January 1974 newsletter of the *American Association of Physicians and Surgeons (AAPS)* said this:

NIXON WANTS DOCTORS PERMANENTLY CONTROLLED

Three times in three weeks President Nixon told the nation's physicians that in effect they deserve no better than to be permanently burdened with oppressive government controls over their fees and the way they practice medicine.

In February 1974, Mr. Nixon sent to Congress his scheme to nationalize medicine ("an idea whose time has come in America," he called it.) The scheme would allow states to set physicians' fees, drugs prices and hospital charges and would extend those vicious PSRO controls beyond the elderly and indigent to encompass everyone - all practicing physicians and all their patients.

And there was no help from the left side of the political aisle:

NEW BILL ATTACKS MEDICAL FREEDOM

Sen. Edward M. (Ted) Kennedy and his ideological fellow travelers are determined to destroy private medical practice one way or another. He has introduced legislation (S. 2994) designed to wipe out medical freedom in the guise of health planning. [This bill] is as vicious in concept as the dangerous and deadly PSRO law. It would create health planning agencies in each state...under direction of state health commissions which, in turn, would be regulated and controlled by the Secretary of HEW.[8]

At Scripps Memorial Hospital, the board of trustees decided they needed outside help to plan for what lay ahead and hired Tribrook Healthcare Consultants. Tribrook, in turn, persuaded the board they needed to reorganize into a more "corporate-type" structure with a president/CEO—someone from one of the newer hospital administration degree programs that had sprung up at a few universities in the country—and a nationwide search produced about forty candidates. The ultimate choice, Ames Early, was at that time president of Mercy Hospital Miami, Florida, and was already known to Tribrook, since he had hired them at his own institution.

Scripps Memorial Hospital continued to expand in the 1970s to meet the needs of the growing San Diego community·   *courtesy of Scripps Health*

Ames S. Early became president of Scripps Memorial Hospital in 1976. Mr. Early helped the Hospital weather the changes under way in the delivery of health care, including how physicians were paid for medical services.

courtesy of Scripps Health

Ames S. Early was born on his grandparents' farm in Butler County, Iowa, and grew up in Rinard, a town of 120 people, where his father sold lumber. From a high school graduation class of twelve students, he went on to the big city lights of Des Moines and Drake University where he did premed, followed by a year in medical school at the University of Iowa. Mr. Early's interest in medicine arose from nearly losing his leg as a twelve-year-old to a staph infection in a knee banged up by hockey, and being saved by an attentive orthopedic surgeon. But in medical school he was "overwhelmed by biochemistry" and:

> I decided to try to find something else – but bear in mind, where I grew up, you were a farmer, a businessman, a teacher or a preacher. I had to take some tests at the university counseling facilities to find out what else there was; and I learned there was something called "hospital administration." There was a small program at the University of Iowa which had been in existence only a few years – one of eighteen programs in the country at the time – and I was accepted into the program of one year on campus and another in residency at the University of Minnesota Hospital in Minneapolis, 1960-61.[9]

Those were heady days at Minnesota where C. Walton Lillehei was pioneering open-heart surgery; Ames realized he had found his calling and stayed on staff at Minnesota for seven years before taking his first chief administrator post at Newton, Iowa, "home of the Maytag Company."

Before long, he and his wife, Beryl (whom he met in third grade in Rinard, Iowa), missed the larger world, and they moved on in 1968 to Mercy Hospital, Miami—"one of the most beautiful hospital locations you could ever imagine, right on Biscayne Bay looking across to Key Biscayne"—where Mr. Early was "the first person in management who was not a religious" and was able to help the Sisters[10] create a board and expand the hospital from 300 to nearly 500 beds. Seven years later in 1975 when the name "Ames Early" was presented to the Scripps Memorial Board, trustees Dick Hibbard and Harry Collins, along with medical Chief of Staff Dr. Carson, made the trip to Miami for due diligence and felt that they had found their man.

Ames Early took over as president of Scripps Memorial Hospital on February 2, 1976, and was received in a "helpful and gracious, cordial and friendly" manner by Louis Peelyon, who retired to a little house in Julian.[11] He also was courteously received by the medical staff, although he felt he had to earn the respect of a strong and independent group of "outsize personalities who at that time were their own boss." Dr. Ernie Pund was a member of the board and always helpful as "a voice of reason." Prior to his arrival at Scripps, Mr. Early read over board minutes and said "I found my eye always returning to statements made by Dr. Pund." When they discussed differences with the medical staff, Mr. Early's position was:

> You know there are bound to be differences. How we manage to deal with them is what's important.
>
> I always felt that the strengths of the institution were the doctors and the nurses that most closely supported them, and that my job was to do the best I could to keep that strong.
>
> And somehow you've got to blend all of this energy and ambition into something that works for the greater good as well as for the individual. That's not always a clear-cut path.

Scripps Memorial did have strong doctors and nurses in those years, and one of those strengths was in the operating rooms—which served both the Hospital and Clinic until after the latter moved up to Torrey Pines Road in 1977. Patients were coming to the Clinic from all over the world. As Dr. Charles Edwards would later say, recalling his early days as director of the Clinic:

> Every morning, patients would receive a fresh rose. Every evening, they would be offered cocktails. The patients the clinic attracted consisted of a few Hollywood stars – including Greta Garbo, Elizabeth Taylor and John Wayne – and an elite group of wealthy executives from Southern California and around the world.[12]

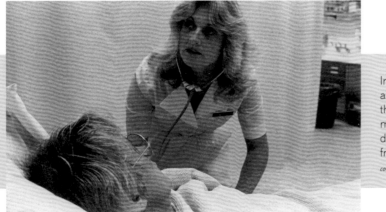

In the 1970s, nurses and health care staff in the emergency room made sure the patient did not feel alone and frightened.

courtesy of Scripps Health

Dr. A. Brent Eastman arrived at Scripps Memorial Hospital in 1972. Dr. Eastman was one of the founders of the Trauma Center at the Hospital in 1981 and instrumental in helping develop the San Diego County Trauma System in 1984.

courtesy of Scripps Health

But they got their surgery—general, vascular and thoracic—at Scripps Memorial from the group called North Coast Surgeons, whose original partners were Dr. Dick Jones and Dr. Donley McReynolds from the University of Rochester in New York. Drs. Jones and McReynolds joined forces in 1970 and incorporated as North Coast Surgeons in 1971; they were joined a year later by Dr. David Baker from the University of Southern California and Los Angeles County Hospital. Similarly in that era, a trio of young physicians from New York and Virginia—Paul Brenner, who set up the department of obstetrics and gynecology at San Diego County Hospital; Russell Holcomb, an early obstetrical specialist at Encinitas; and Alan Blank, the first laparascopist in San Diego—assembled themselves into North County OB-GYN, headquartered at Scripps Memorial.[13]

The fourth member of North Coast Surgeons was Dr. A. Brent Eastman, who arrived at Scripps Hospital in 1972 from the University of California at San Francisco and the San Francisco General Hospital, which was then one of only two *de facto* trauma centers in America. He joined North Coast Surgeons in 1974.[14] Dr. Eastman said of that era:

> My remembrance of Scripps Hospital at that time was that first and foremost it had an excellent medical staff, excellent in terms of virtually every specialty represented by physicians and surgeons, who, it appeared to me, could have had an academic career any place of their choosing but chose to be at Scripps. Many of the medical staff at that time had joint appointments at the new medical school, the University of California San Diego, where they pursued their interest in teaching.

> Scripps Memorial also had a strong historical relationship with the Scripps Clinic and Research Foundation, which continued to be one of the leading not-for-profit medical research institutes in the United States – "leading" based on NIH grants, the ability to attract top talent, and high awards in the field.[15]

And Dr. McReynolds[16] said:

> Until Green Hospital was built we did all of the surgery for the Clinic. It was ironic that people came from all over the world to have their physicals. Then when they needed surgery we'd transfer them to the Hospital, after which we'd send them back to the Clinic to convalesce. They would think they'd had surgery at the world-famous Scripps Clinic.

Drs. Eastman and McReynolds, as well as Dr. Alan Berkenfield and anesthesiologist, Dr. Bob Andrews, all said independently, "We had great nurses." One legendary team[17] ran the operating room in the mid-to-late 1960s and 1970s. Head nurse Edna "Bunny" Carroll was tiny and trim and had been to dancing school in Los Angeles with Shirley Temple; Bunny was "very calm and cool – a joy to work with," according to fellow nurse, Marla Hess. Canadian Marla Hess arrived in June 1964, one month after the move to the mesa, and was head nurse from 1969-1979, when Bunny became supervisor. Marla said:

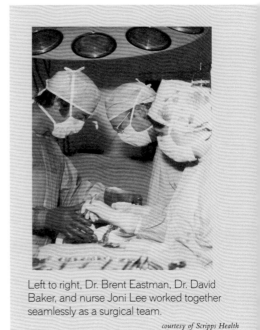

Left to right, Dr. Brent Eastman, Dr. David Baker, and nurse Joni Lee worked together seamlessly as a surgical team.

courtesy of Scripps Health

We weren't very busy at first out on Miramar Road. It took us about a year to get busy, and in the early days you had to be careful opening cupboards when you came in the morning, in case someone on nights left the door open to get some air and a rattlesnake crawled in.

In the early days, everybody did everything [that is, scrubbed on all types of cases] until specialization crept in with the heart team and orthopedics. There was marvelous camaraderie among the nurses.

Louise Favor from Montana worked thirty-eight years at Scripps, from 1966-2004. Her original claim to fame was that she graduated from nursing school on the night of the Great Yellowstone Earthquake of August 17, 1959,[18] and started out as operating room supervisor at Bozeman Deaconess Hospital on her first day as a nurse the following Monday, treating victims of the earthquake. But Louise also loved internal medicine and chose the medical floor when she came to Scripps Hospital, 7 West with cardiologists Drs. Carmichael, Carson, and Jordan, before making her way back to surgery later on.

And Joni Lee from Springfield, Illinois, was at Scripps Hospital for one year, 1973, before traveling the world with her family. When she knocked on the door again three years later, Bunny's only question was, "When can you start?," and Joni rejoined Bunny, Marla and Louise and has been in the operating room there ever since.

It was the new vision of Dr. Charles Edwards for the Clinic in the fall of 1977 that inadvertently added bricks to what came to be called "The Berlin Wall" between the Scripps Institutions east and west of Highway 5. As Dr. Eastman explained:

> When Dr. Edwards came to take over the helm at Scripps Clinic, he decided to create a Department of Surgery for the Clinic and, because of the very positive and very strong collegial relationship that had been established, we were invited to create that department.
>
> Dr. Edwards' other initial recruitments to head surgical subspecialties were also from Scripps Memorial, including Drs. Tom Waltz in Neurosurgery and Clifford Colwell in Orthopedics.
>
> But we at North Coast Surgeons debated the option and in the end decided not to make the move, principally, I think, because of David Baker's intense commitment to the private practice of surgery. And so we remained at Scripps Memorial.[19]

Dr. Clifford Colwell,[20] who accepted Dr. Edwards' invitation, had arrived at Scripps Memorial in 1970 from the Air Force, after a fellowship in trauma at Los Angeles County Hospital. He joined the inimitable Dr. Tom Laughlin in practice. Dr. Laughlin, who had been an orthopedic resident with Dr. Colwell's older brother, John, was— John told Cliff—"the best technical surgeon I've ever seen." Another strong draw was that Scripps Hospital physician, Dr. Bruce Kimball, was running the department of orthopedics at UCSD as a part-time position, and Dr. Colwell wanted to teach and do clinical research. So he came to La Jolla, and the most admired physicians on staff were completely welcoming and "instrumental in developing my practice."

> They already had good orthopedists, such as Joe Thompson and Bruce Kimball, in addition to Tom Laughlin. And so they didn't have to send patients to me. But they did, and they got me integrated, helped in my growing, developing, got me interested in the working of the hospital committees and so forth. And it was a great experience.

Dr. Colwell had been at Scripps Memorial seven years, when he was invited to establish the department of orthopedics at Scripps Clinic. And he realized that the strong feeling among the Hospital physicians was:

> 'We're not going to do resident training, we're not going to do research. We are going to take good care of people.' Which they did. I don't think you had a better community hospital. But they were not interested in teaching residents.[21] And I had always been interested in that.

So Dr. Colwell went across the freeway to the Clinic, assuming that he could do it all, and established a highly-esteemed center for research and treatment of musculoskeletal disease.[22] But his huge referral base at Scripps Memorial dried up overnight. There was private practice, and then there was the Clinic.

Scripps Memorial Hospital had always taken good care of people in its own community and, after the move to the mesa, the Hospital became a true tertiary care center for San Diego and Imperial Counties, for nearly every medical condition. Innovations became the rule. One which brought a deluge of positive publicity from around the country was the establishment in the newborn nursery of "the nation's first and only professional grandmother," Lanie Carter, who nurtured thousands of new parents through the first months of their babies' lives (1977-1997). [23] [24] Another was a local revolution in the care of the seriously injured patient.

Emergency care had been steadily evolving since the days of using police station wagons as ambulances and transporting dying patients unannounced to hospital basement rooms with no physician in house. Landmarks in this evolution were the federal Emergency Medical Systems Act of 1973, which provided for an organized approach to emergency medical systems nationwide.[25] A second was the recognition of emergency medicine as a specialty in 1979.[26]

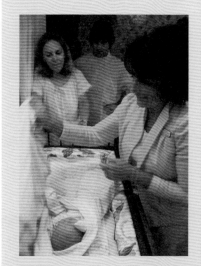

Lanie Carter was established at Scripps Memorial Hospital La Jolla as a family care consultant in 1977. As the country's first "professional grandmother," Mrs. Carter saw every new baby born at Scripps La Jolla and acted as a consultant to every new parent. She was available by phone twenty-four hours a day, seven days a week.

courtesy of Scripps Health

Scripps Hospital had a state-of-the-art emergency department (ED) with a specialist-director, Dr. Robert Eggold, receiving patients from well-equipped ambulances and trained paramedics. But the death rate for victims of trauma was still unacceptably high at Scripps Hospital, as it was everywhere else in the county (and in most of the country). The fundamental problem was the same as it had been twenty years before, which was that if a patient is bleeding to death he needs a surgeon *now* – and an ED physician, however well-trained, is not a surgeon. Dr. Eastman said:

> I had come to San Diego direct from the San Francisco General Hospital (SFGH), which was at that time the single great trauma receiving hospital of the city and county of San Francisco. Ambulance drivers picked up their victims all over town and sped directly to the famous "Mission Emergency" at SFGH – with no thought of stopping at the many community hospitals along the way without a committed staff standing by to save a life. We young surgeons at "The Mission" in that era were baptized by immersion in trauma, and we left our training with an abiding passion for the care of injured patients.
>
> So that when I arrived in San Diego in 1972, I became aware of the fragmentation of trauma care in our County. Here, injured patients were taken to the nearest hospital, regardless of the nature of the

calamity or the resources available to treat them. It was the luck of the draw — if you were in danger of bleeding to death from a ruptured liver or spleen, the ED you entered might or might not be able to locate the surgeon on call, have staff trained to resuscitate, or even have a lab tech at work after midnight. Injured patients arrived at hospitals alive, only to die anyway of what the newspapers still called "internal injuries" — meaning that no surgeon had even determined the cause of death. I was one of a handful of young surgeons fresh from training where things were done differently — San Francisco, Viet Nam - and we slowly found one another and began plotting to build a new system.[27]

San Diego at that time had three surgeons who had graduated from serious trauma training programs: Dr. William Long at UCSD, from Maryland Shock-Trauma; Dr. Richard Virgilio at Mercy, prior head of the Trauma Unit at Navy who "trained" with the Marines in Viet Nam; and Dr. Eastman at Scripps. They knew first-hand that optimal care of the injured patient required a finely-tuned system, and Dr. Virgilio voiced the apprehension of all three when he stated publicly in 1977:

> If you are seriously injured on a major highway in San Diego, you have less chance of surviving than a Marine seriously injured in Viet Nam.[28]

Dr. Virgilio[29] had been a surgeon in Da Nang ten years before, and he knew what he was talking about. After his year at war, when he was sent to Balboa Hospital in 1971 to set up a trauma unit, he was theoretically responsible for any sailor who got injured anywhere in San Diego County and ended up in a civilian hospital. And Dr. Virgilio said:

> Before long I realized that people were getting less than optimal care after major trauma all over San Diego County, not just in South Bay or East County. It became clear because I was seeing preventable deaths. We could get to any outlying hospital with our trauma van and then get the patient back to Balboa before they could even get a hold of a general surgeon to come in and see the patient.

So by the time Dr. Virgilio left the Navy at the end of 1978 and was looking for a civilian job, he wanted to do something unorthodox, which was not to have a private office, but to concentrate on trauma and surgical intensive care "in-house." In the era before hospitalists, this was a decidedly suspect idea. Fortunately, the administrator at Mercy Hospital at the time was a "hard-charging Italian nun" named Sister Joanne De Vincente.[30] And although the pulmonary physicians covering the intensive care units were opposed and the other surgeons as well,

> Sister Joanne basically just said, 'Virgilio's coming in here.' Maybe because I was Italian.

> So Sister had my back but I was pretty unpopular at Mercy for a long time. I mean I'd walk down the hall by myself, and a couple of the other docs would say, "Here comes Virgilio with all his friends." [31]

But Dr. Virgilio and Dr. Eastman, along with Dr. Steven Shackford from the Navy (who soon replaced Dr. Long at UCSD[32]) and a young UCSD surgical resident named Dr. David Hoyt,[33] kept working to build trauma centers at their own hospitals with a longer-range plan for a system county-wide. Ultimately, surgeons, trauma nurses, and ED physicians began meeting monthly in a self-imposed Medical Audit Committee—an unprecedented sharing among competitor hospitals about what they were doing right and what they were doing wrong.[34]

At Scripps Hospital, the opening of the Trauma Center in 1981 required the commitment of not only the dozen or so trauma surgeons[35] who agreed to stand by no more than twenty minutes away, but also of virtually the whole hospital staff of nurses, anesthesiologists, radiologists and laboratory personnel—not to mention the commitment of administrator Martin Buser, under Ames Early, and the Board of Trustees, who had to hope that "trauma" would not consume every other resource in the Hospital.

Although the fledgling trauma system clearly saved lives, a bruising political battle followed, as hospitals that saw their emergency rooms being bypassed fought to retain the status quo and enlisted their county supervisors in the fight.

> The political hurdles were formidable. We were aided in our quest by publication of the sentinel autopsy study by Trunkey and West[36] comparing the preventable death rate in San Francisco, which had a trauma system, and Orange County, which did not. As expected, the study showed a 20-fold increase in preventable deaths (i.e., deaths of persons who could have been saved with prompt care) in our northern neighbor, Orange County.

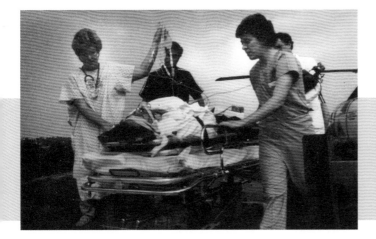

Scripps signed an agreement to share the helicopter services of Life Flight with all San Diego hospitals in 1983. Left, a trauma victim who fell from the Torrey Pines cliffs was rushed to Scripps Memorial Hospital La Jolla via Life Flight helicopter.
courtesy of Scripps Health

When the major political debate over trauma care erupted in San Diego, a similar investigation, the Amherst Study[37], was conducted here – and again, the results were the same. Injured patients in San Diego were 20 times more likely to die unnecessarily than in cities with an organized trauma system. An interesting and compelling bit of data from the Amherst Study was that *it was not a matter of good and bad hospitals*: the preventable deaths were spread among all thirty hospitals in the County with EDs. Rather *it was the lack of a system* to ensure that patients were transported directly to designated trauma centers with the resources immediately available to care for any injury.[38]

Finally a community consensus emerged regarding six trauma centers (five adult and one children's), all verified by the American College of Surgeons and designated by the lead agency of San Diego County Emergency Medical Services under Chief Gail Cooper. Recommendations were formally adopted by a politically courageous County Board of Supervisors in November 1983, and on August 1, 1984, the San Diego County Trauma System was born.[39] Over the next year the preventable death rate dropped from 21 percent to 1 percent and has remained at that level ever since.

On the occasion of its twentieth anniversary celebration in 2004, keynote speaker Vice-Admiral Richard H. Carmona, MD, Surgeon General of the United States (and a trauma surgeon from UCSF) told the crowd at the San Diego Marriott

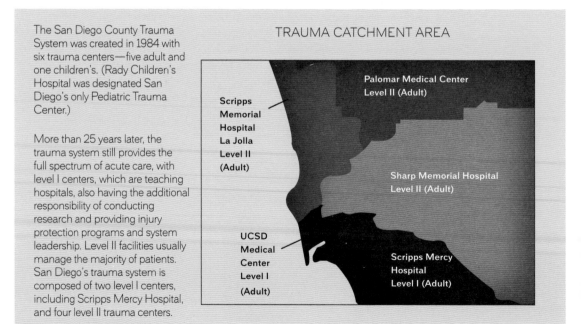

The San Diego County Trauma System was created in 1984 with six trauma centers—five adult and one children's. (Rady Children's Hospital was designated San Diego's only Pediatric Trauma Center.)

More than 25 years later, the trauma system still provides the full spectrum of acute care, with level I centers, which are teaching hospitals, also having the additional responsibility of conducting research and providing injury protection programs and system leadership. Level II facilities usually manage the majority of patients. San Diego's trauma system is composed of two level I centers, including Scripps Mercy Hospital, and four level II trauma centers.

TRAUMA CATCHMENT AREA

Palomar Medical Center
Level II (Adult)

Scripps Memorial Hospital La Jolla
Level II (Adult)

Sharp Memorial Hospital
Level II (Adult)

UCSD Medical Center
Level I (Adult)

Scripps Mercy Hospital
Level I (Adult)

Hotel, "The San Diego Trauma System is the envy of the nation."[40]

And there was much else going on at the campus of Scripps Memorial, including the building of several institutions funded by the Whittier family of Los Angeles, who in 1979 sold Belridge Oil to Shell Oil for the then-record price of $3.65 billion.[41] The first was the Whittier Institute for Diabetes and Endocrinology under the direction of Dr. Willard VanderLaan, and the way this came about is a case study in the vagaries of philanthropy.

Dr. VanderLaan, who was then at Scripps Clinic (as he had been since 1956), had two connections to philanthropist N. Paul Whittier—one conventional (he was the physician for Mr. Whittier's first wife)—and the other a shared automobile. They were the first and second owners of a 1959 black Mercedes with a red interior that Mr. Whittier recognized in the parking lot on his first visit to Scripps Clinic in 1969, and which caused him to seek out Dr. VanderLaan in the first

Dr. Willard VanderLaan with his wife, Eileen. Dr. VanderLaan was the first director of the Scripps Whittier Institute for Diabetes and Endocrinology, which opened in 1982.
courtesy of Scripps Health

place. When Mr. Whittier formed his Confidence Foundation to distribute some of his vast wealth, he offered the new president of Scripps Clinic, Dr. Charles Edwards,

The Whittiers watch four children with diabetes place a time capsule below the dedicatory plaque at the dedication of the Whittier Institute for Diabetes in 1982.
courtesy of Scripps Health

James Bowers, PhD, spent thirty-five years working with Scripps. In the 1970s, he oversaw the move of the Scripps Clinic and Research Foundation to the Torrey Pines mesa. In the 1980s, Mr. Bowers, as executive director of Scripps Memorial Hospital Foundation, led the largest capital improvement campaign undertaken by a community hospital at the time.

courtesy of Scripps Health

$5 million to form an institute for endocrinology, with the proviso that Dr. VanderLaan be director for at least ten years. Dr. Edwards turned him down. [42]

Meanwhile, Paul Whittier had formed a side connection to Scripps Memorial Hospital. That particular Scripps alliance was through Joseph Jessop, leading back to Miss Ellen's free-wheeling brother, Fred. Joseph Jessop Sr. was related to the Scripps family by marriage: he was the youngest child in the family who lived on a 40-acre plot next door to Miramar, and his much-older sister married Fred before little Joe was born. [43] The grownup Joe Jessop and N. Paul Whittier were yachtsmen who met in San Diego Bay and went sailing with James Bowers, director of the SMH Foundation.

Soon Ames Early was accepting the gift that Dr. Edwards declined. Dr. VanderLaan left the Clinic across the freeway, and the first red brick triangle of the Whittier Institute for Diabetes and Endocrinology opened its doors on the campus of Scripps Memorial in 1982. [44] At the threshold, four young patients with diabetes left their handprints and buried a time capsule containing a glass syringe, insulin and a food exchange list. [45]

The following year (1983), Helen Whittier Woodward donated $4 million to establish the Mericos Eye Institute, in memory of their father Mericos Whittier (who was not only an oil man, but also the developer of Beverly Hills.) [46] And finally, in 1991, the original philanthropist, Paul, died at Scripps Memorial after a long illness. [47] Always intellectually curious, Mr. Whittier loved to discuss the new trauma system with his surgeon, Dr. Eastman, and to watch through his hospital window as the Life Flight helicopters touched down; his ultimate bequest to Scripps was a $1 million endowment of the N. Paul Whittier Chair in Trauma—the first endowed Chair of Trauma in the United States—with Dr. Eastman as recipient in August 1991.

And meanwhile, in his first decade as president of Scripps Memorial, Mr. Early agreed to buy and bring into the Scripps family two other hospitals, from opposite ends of the county: San Dieguito Hospital, Encinitas (1978) and Bay Hospital Medical Center, Chula Vista (1986).

The Growing Family

SCRIPPS ENCINITAS AND SCRIPPS CHULA VISTA

In 1961, while plans for the new Scripps Memorial on the mesa were going forward, two other community hospitals arose north and south of La Jolla in the building boom sweeping the county. Both were constructed piecemeal at a time of minimal outside regulation and took a few years to develop as effective acute care hospitals under physician owners—after which they served their communities well for some years, until the changing face of medical economics caused their leaders to look around for more support.

Main Street in downtown Encinitas (historic U.S. Highway 101) in 1929. The Southern California railroad established the downtown in 1881, starting with a water tower by the tracks to power the steam engines. The most prolific decade of construction in downtown Encinitas was in the 1920s, but the stock market crash in October 1929 brought an end to the prosperity. La Paloma (The Dove) Theater opened in 1928 and was one of the first theaters to show talking pictures.

courtesy of San Diego History Center

CHAPTER EIGHT
The Growing Family
SCRIPPS ENCINITAS

ENCINITAS MEDICAL DENTAL BUILDING (1961)
ENCINITAS CONVALESCENT HOSPITAL (1964)
ENCINITAS HOSPITAL (1966)
SAN DIEGUITO HOSPITAL (1975)
SCRIPPS MEMORIAL HOSPITAL ENCINITAS (1978)

THE NORTH COUNTY DISTRICT OF SAN DIEGUITO is mostly the area of two old Mexican ranchos back-to-back. Rancho Los Encinitos (meaning "little oaks" for the ubiquitous scrub oaks in the chaparral and later misspelled as Las Encinitas) encompassed present day Leucadia, Encinitas, Cardiff-by-the-Sea, and Olivenhain. Rancho San Dieguito (or "St. James the Lesser") was renamed in 1906 by the Land Improvement Company of the Santa Fe Railway and is now Rancho Santa Fe.[1]

Along with the communities of Solana Beach and Del Mar, the whole of San Dieguito was without a local doctor[2] until the arrival in 1926 of Dr. C. Victor Lindsay (1898-1971). In a 2010 interview,[3] his son, Dr. Charles V. Lindsay, Jr., said that his father and his mother Mary, a registered nurse, were both trained at the College of Medical Evangelists at Loma Linda and were traveling the coast south of Santa Barbara "looking for a place to serve" and camping as they went. In the village of Encinitas, they stopped in at Westbrook Hardware, were invited to camp in the storeroom, and opened their medical practice in gratitude for the hospitality.

Paul Ecke Sr., and his wife, Magdalena. Mr. Ecke moved his poinsettia business from Los Angeles to forty acres of land in Encinitas in 1923, helping to make Encinitas the flower capital of the world.

courtesy of San Diego History Center

The Lindsays arrived in Encinitas nearly simultaneously with the Paul Eckes and their brilliant Mexican poinsettias (1923)—the winter-blooming flower of the Aztecs, discovered by the first U.S. Ambassador to Mexico, Joel Poinsett (1779-1851), who was a physician himself and later founded the Smithsonian Museum.[4] Before poinsettias, the primary crop was lima beans—also a staple of the Aztecs, but originally cultured in what is now coastal Peru and shipped by the Spanish in crates stamped with the name of the Peruvian capital.[5] Lima beans could be "dry-farmed," since water was scarce and well-water brackish.

The settlers of the old Encinitas community with the ironic name Olivenhain, meaning olive grove, learned this the hard way, as described in the Arts and Community website of Encinitas:

> Olivenhain was established as a German colony in 1884. Many of the pioneers were enticed by newspaper ads promising they could make fortunes from olive groves. When they arrived, however, they found the land too dry to support olive trees, or anything else needing much water. The hardy immigrants who stayed…farmed lima beans which, conveniently, needed little water as their broad leaves hold the morning dew. [6]

One of those hardy immigrants was Alwin Wiegand, older brother of Herman, a key figure in the story of Encinitas Hospital; Alwin Wiegand farmed lima beans in the whole of Green Valley, which is now the long stretch of El Camino Real from Encinitas Blvd. to La Costa and gave the family name to Wiegand Plaza.[7]

A general store in Olivenhain at the turn of the century. Olivenhain was founded by German immigrants in 1884, including the Wiegand family. Herman Wiegand would become a staunch supporter of the hospital in Encinitas.

courtesy of San Diego History Center

Dr. Victor Lindsay's practice was crucial for fifteen years, until interrupted by the Second World War, when he was drafted for administrative duty; after the war, he was chronically ill with asthma. By 1958, he was semiretired with an office in his Leucadia home.[8] Local physician, Dr. C. Fred Brass (from the first graduating class at San Dieguito High School, where his mother taught English and math), had taken over Dr. Lindsay's practice for a time, but Dr. Brass moved south to Solana Beach— where he was a hugely popular physician with a specialty he described as "the skin and its contents"[9]—and an excellent opening appeared in Encinitas for a pair of family physicians from Kansas.

Drs. Charles Clark (1929-2011) and Dwight Cook were great friends at Kansas University Medical School, after which they departed for service in the Air Force and Navy respectively. In the spring of 1958, flight surgeon Dr. Cook, on the carrier *USS Hancock*, received this letter from Edwards Air Force Base, California:

12 May 58

Dear Dwight,

Dot and I are leaving the Air Force June 1st. This deal came along about a month ago…and since everything is all set I'll see what you think of it.

Encinitas is a small seacoast town just 30 miles north of San Diego…A doctor Hazan there is primarily a research man…and will be leaving July 1st.…

I am paying him $7,000 total for his practice, inventory and equipment, which includes a 100 amp GE X-Ray, a Burdick ultrasonic unit, a new Sanborn ECG and a completely equipped laboratory. There is a new waiting room, two fully equipped treatment rooms and a pediatric room, also a lovely set of office furniture for the doctor…

The office is not large but it is adequate and I consider it only a temporary place to hang my shingle, as I want to build as soon as possible. There are no projected increases of new doctors and the area is growing like mad. The new walk-ins are averaging $10.00 per week…

I would like for you to come to Encinitas with me… I know we can't miss here, as hospitals are reasonably close and privileges will be available and gosh knows the people are in the area and need care… The fishing is good, some of the best deep sea fishing on the coast… and Lake Hodges (bass, bluegill and crappie) is 12 miles away. The climate is always warm…

Here's hoping you will decide to come in on this deal. I'm keeping my fingers crossed.

Sincerely,
Charlie

Drs. Clark and Cook did join forces and, "in order to share the nurse and three exam rooms, one of them saw patients in the office (at 745 Second Street), while the other did rounds" at Scripps La Jolla on Prospect Street eighteen miles away; they reversed the process in the afternoons. Dr. Cook said in an interview, while turning pages of a remarkable memory book:

> We had a little office on Second Street in Encinitas, just an old house. And that's where we were for a year. But we got tired of driving to La Jolla every day, all the way down to Prospect Street along the coast route 101. We were delivering babies there, going twice a day and making rounds and it was just pretty obvious we needed a facility in our area. So we bought some land on Santa Fe where we thought the freeway was going through.[10]

Dr. Clark had said from the start that he intended to build. So in 1960, the partners bought property on Santa Fe Drive and Devonshire Road from flower grower Robert Hall, whose late father had owned the entire forty-acre rectangle that would be split on the diagonal by Interstate 5.[11]

The doctors bought most of what would become the western half. Within months, they had built medical and dental offices with a clinical laboratory on site and secured a third physician and two dentists as tenants.[12]

The Encinitas Medical-Dental Building opened for business in February 1961 and was the first structure to appear at 360 Santa Fe Drive. Pictures from the grand opening in March show a single-level structure with a U-shaped roof and stylish stone pillars in front.

Exterior of St. Mark's Lutheran Church

courtesy of John Eisenhart

Historic Buildings

The Encinitas Medical-Dental Building was not alone on Santa Fe Drive for long. The second structure was St. Mark's Lutheran Church, built a few months after the Medical-Dental Building on the corner of their shared site. The church with its "shell-like shape and vibrant stained glass" was razed after forty-five years, along with a ball field in 2006 to make way for a much-needed hospital expansion.[13] The Medical-Dental Building, called "the clinic," is still standing and in use as Medical Records, with the big new hospital wrapped around it.[14]

The Encinitas Clinic gave the doctors better quarters, even though they were still commuting to La Jolla. Dr. Cook said:

> We didn't yet have a hospital, but we did have a special area in the Clinic with a pretty active emergency room. We even did tonsillectomies there and quite a bit of orthopedics. A couple of guys from Tri-City came down and did anesthesia. And we had our own lab and X-ray. So we were basically able to handle twenty-four hour care. We didn't man it twenty-four hours. We would just go in when we needed to.

After two years at the Clinic, in 1963, the two physicians from Kansas were joined by a third, tall Dr. Ronald Summers, who had been a freshman when they were seniors at Kansas University Medical School and was referred to them by fellow-Kansan, Dr. John Trombold at Scripps. By the time Dr. Summers arrived, the original partners had already decided that their Clinic was not enough and that the commute south to La Jolla for hospitalized patients (or nearly as far north to Tri-City Hospital in Oceanside) was still too hard on all concerned. As Dr. Cook said:

> We needed a hospital. We decided that the thing we could afford to do would be to build a sort of convalescent hospital where we could admit patients needing longterm care. That's the next thing we did, in 1964.

This would be a first-stage hospital— not full-service at first, but a convalescent hospital, a facility which would be "the answer to the question of interim care for patients recovering from illness or surgery, yet unable to remain at home."[15] There was available space on land adjacent to the Encinitas Clinic (east of the church, which hugged the southwest corner), but insufficient money to build. For construction funds the doctors turned to a favorite patient and friend.

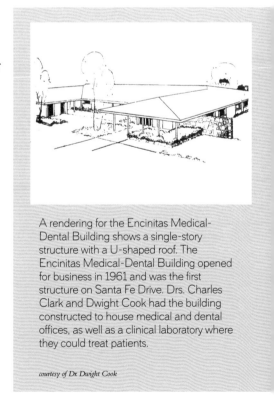

A rendering for the Encinitas Medical-Dental Building shows a single-story structure with a U-shaped roof. The Encinitas Medical-Dental Building opened for business in 1961 and was the first structure on Santa Fe Drive. Drs. Charles Clark and Dwight Cook had the building constructed to house medical and dental offices, as well as a clinical laboratory where they could treat patients.

courtesy of Dr. Dwight Cook

Left to right, Dr. Charles Clark, Herman "Pop" Wiegand, Dr. Ronald Summers, and Dr. Dwight Cook. Mr. Wiegand, a patient of Dr. Clark, guaranteed a loan to build a convalescent hospital in Encinitas where the doctors could admit patients needing longterm care.   *courtesy of Dr. Dwight Cook*

Herman "Pop" Wiegand [1890-1993], was a cattle rancher and "patriarch of one of the original homestead families in Olivenhain"[16] and was a patient of Dr. Clark. Mr. Wiegand was seventy-three when the doctors approached him about their hospital project, and he agreed, on a handshake, to co-sign a loan with his own Bank of America stock as collateral. His grandson, J. Byron Wood—born at Scripps Memorial on Prospect Street in 1947, and later one of the first general surgeons at Scripps Encinitas— relates the following story:

> My grandfather lived to be 103, and when he was around 70, he was still an active cattleman. One day in maybe January or February, it had rained a lot and there were sinkholes. And, in a place that would usually be dry, he walked his horse into a hole full of water. The horse couldn't get out of the hole and was drowning –so my little 155 pound grandfather grabbed the reins and sort of pulled this horse up out of the water. And he got real wet, cold, and kind of strained from the exertion. A couple days later he started having chest pains. So he went to see Dr. Clark, and they had this fancy machine that could actually trace the electrical activity of your heart.
>
> So on the basis of the tracing and his family history—Pop's own father had died of a heart attack at 72[17]—Dr. Clark told him that he was having a bad heart attack. He put him on heparin and told Pop "he should get his affairs in order because there was no telling how long he was going to have left." So that's when Pop started cutting back on the cattle operation, selling off his property and investing the money in stocks—which is why he had stocks to put up as collateral for the new hospital.
>
> He lived another thirty years, never had any trouble with his heart, and was always grateful to Dr. Clark for saving his life with that heparin.[18]

Drs. Charles Clark and Dwight Cook are ready to signal the beginning of construction on the first hospital in Encinitas. Left to right, architect Don Hartfelter, Dr. Cook, Dr. Clark, and contractor E.A. Reis, at the groundbreaking ceremony in October 1963.

courtesy of Dr. Dwight Cook

With the building loan now guaranteed, the project went forward with a design by architect Don Hartfelder[19] for a one-story hospital adjacent to the existing medical office. Pictures of the groundbreaking in October 1963 show Drs. Clark and Cook together holding the handle of the shovel, and within six months they had their first hospital.

And Dr. Summers said:

> We did a couple of other things with that money. We bought five houses along Devonshire Drive, thinking we could sell them later at a profit and do great things at the hospital. (They never did appreciate much before we sold them off). But then we also decided to grow flowers on three or four of our vacant acres, as a holding operation to cover taxes and carrying costs.
>
> The property we bought from Robert Hall was bare. But Charlie Clark had another grateful patient named Tom Minami who grew flowers. So Tom helped us propagate carnations. We did it for a year-and-a-half, and then decided to hire a real pro. We got this guy from Colorado State who told us we should expand to South America. He took 100,000 of the propagated "sets" we had down to Bolivia and was never heard from again.
>
> Later we heard that Bolivia was growing and shipping carnations to the U.S., so we figured we had done something for international trade.[20]

Encinitas Hospital became the San Dieguito Hospital when it expanded to 94 beds and became a full service hospital in 1975. The new hospital fulfilled the dream of founders Drs. Charles Clark and Dwight Cook.

courtesy of Dr. Dwight Cook

The doors opened in April 1964 to the 60-bed Encinitas Convalescent Hospital, another one-story structure with an interior courtyard, similar in style to the Encinitas Clinic next door—as it happens, just about the time a Superior Court judge was ruling that Scripps Memorial could finally move up from Prospect Street to the Torrey Pines mesa. The new Encinitas hospital had complete X-ray, laboratory and physical therapy services, and a professional administrator, Harry Mercer. By the time of the grand opening three months later—with a thousand guests enjoying 2,000 cookies and several gallons of iced tea—the press was reporting that "of the twenty-five patients admitted so far, ten have regained their health to a point where they could return to their homes."[21]

At the outset many rooms were intended for elderly patients requiring long-term care, but the convalescent hospital did obtain a general medical license and rooms were gradually converted to acute care. Dr. Cook said:

> The original license for the Convalescent Hospital was "long-term care" and after a while we got what was called a "medical specialty license" (which no longer exists)—and we converted some of our long term care beds to acute beds, and then we could take care of medical illnesses—but not surgical. And somewhere in there we added psychiatric beds as part of the mix.
>
> Then we stopped doing obstetrics—began referring pregnant women to Dr. Gary Vandenberg in La Jolla—and that helped cut down the travel even more. By 1966, Dr. Cook said, "we upgraded the facility to a specialized hospital for internal medicine" and renamed it Encinitas Hospital.

But the doctors continued to plan for a full-service hospital with surgery.

> The big thing we wanted to bring in was surgery and that's where the big expense was. Meanwhile we bought more land to the north.

In 1967 they bought an adjoining parcel of land to the north to accommodate future development. Now the acreage included what had been John Lorang's chicken ranch, plus some of his brother Harry's fields of squash, beans and chilies.[22]

And finally, after eight more years, the founding doctors joined forces with an investor named William Powers from Los Angeles[23] and settled on Health Care Development (HCD) of Newport Beach as partners and managers for a $4 million expansion of Encinitas Hospital to 94 beds with full medical-surgical capability, an intensive care unit and one of "the first full-fledged Emergency Departments found anywhere in San Diego,"[24] under the direction of Dr. Thomas J. Ruben. The newly named San Dieguito Hospital opened in October 1975, and Chief of Staff Dr. Cook told reporters that the opening of the hospital addition is "what we've always dreamed about."[25]

Drs. Cook, Clark and Summers recreated their practice as the Encinitas Medical Group and started convincing physicians to migrate to North County, "like Peter Pool, Antone Salel… Paul Woody, the first orthopedist,"[26] and surgeon David Baker, who had previously handled all general surgery for the Encinitas doctors in La Jolla.

But the same changes in payment for health care that were so challenging everywhere else were daunting in Encinitas. The founders had built the hospital they envisioned for their community, but were faced with hard economic realities. In 1977, they approached Scripps Memorial about a possible sale. Dr. Cook said:

That's about the time we were 'absorbed' by Specialty Medical Group—they needed a referral base in North County, and we were using them as specialists anyway. I mean it was a natural—so we became a part of Specialty Medical Group, and those doctors I'm sure had a lot to do with selling us to Scripps.

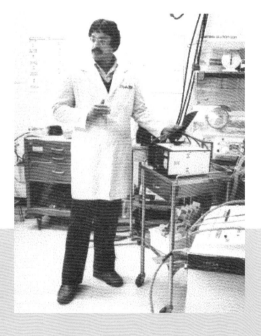

In 1983, Dr. Thomas Ruben was chief of staff at Scripps Memorial Hospital Encinitas and director of emergency services. Right, Dr. Ruben explains some of the equipment in the hospital's emergency department.

courtesy of Scripps Health

As Ames Early recalled:

> The founders of San Dieguito Hospital were struggling with the complexities and the financial aspects of Medicare. So they brought in business partners to try to take a different approach…but they concluded they wanted to sell the hospital, and it was going on the block.
>
> We at Scripps were concerned about national for-profit corporations (such as Hospital Corporation of America [HCA] and American Medical Inc [AMI], which already had Mission Bay Hospital and Valley Medical Center, El Cajon). This is when we were still thinking about trying to spend no more than was necessary on capital improvements and equipment—not to shortchange ourselves, but to say, 'What sense does it make for every hospital to duplicate every piece of expensive equipment? But if one of these corporations comes in to North County with lots of money, the first thing that's going to happen is we're going to have a medical arms race.
>
> And we said, "Maybe we ought to do something to head that off."

According to Insight, the 1977 annual report of Scripps Memorial:

> It was natural for Scripps to take more than a passing glance at the opportunity. Both hospitals have served the same population for the past several years. Over three-quarters of the members of San Dieguito Hospital's medical staff also are members of Scripps Memorial's medical staff. They have been able to admit their patients to either hospital as convenience and individual preference required.

Mr. Early also said:

> We were fortunate that we had a board with business-minded people who were used to market risk, who were development minded, Dick Hibbard, Harry Collins and Dick Poole – a strong, positive, steady force who said, "We had better see if we can do this." So we set about to do it.

Scripps purchased San Dieguito Hospital in January 1978.

courtesy of Scripps Health

Left to right, Dr. Dwight Cook, co-founder of San Dieguito Hospital; Scripps Trustees Richard Hibbard and H.M. Poole; and Ames Early, president of Scripps, signed the transfer of ownership of San Dieguito Hospital to Scripps in 1978.

courtesy of Dr. Dwight Cook

In August 1977 Scripps Memorial announced its decision to purchase San Dieguito Hospital, with transfer of ownership complete on January 30, 1978. Scripps Trustee Harry Collins was quoted in the *San Diego Union* as saying,

> "We felt obligated from the beginning to pursue this purchase. We always have considered north San Diego County a primary part of our health service area [and] have an obligation to expand our services to other parts of the county if asked."[27]

The purchase price of the new Scripps Memorial Hospital – Encinitas was $5.15 million. Administrator Paul O'Neill, who had assumed his post at San Dieguito in 1976, continued on. Ames Early became chief executive of the two hospitals, and Senior Vice-President Lauren Blagg the new administrator at La Jolla.[28] And Dr. Cook said:

> When Scripps bought us, we actually accomplished what we had wanted from the beginning. We wanted to be involved with Scripps. That was always our aim.

One of the first new physicians to arrive at Scripps Memorial Encinitas was surgeon J. Byron Wood, Pop Wiegand's grandson, who joined the practice of Dr. Sam Winner[29] in 1978. Following shortly after was ED physician Ron MacCormick (Chief of Staff at Encinitas three decades later in 2010), who was fresh from medical school at the University of Texas, Houston, and a flexible rotating internship at Mercy Medical Center, San Diego. Dr. MacCormick said:

> At Mercy I met a heart surgeon, Leland Housman,[30] who knew Tom Ruben had the contract for the Emergency Department up here, and put me in touch with him. So back in 1979 when I finished my training, Tom hired me and I've been here ever since.[31]

In those days there was still no formal residency for emergency physicians—1979 was the year Emergency Medicine was recognized as a specialty—but Dr. MacCormick knew early what he wanted to do and went after it: "All my years in undergraduate school I was always working in an emergency department with many different physicians; and then in medical school, all my elective rotations were in EDs at USC, Valley Medical Center and others."

Dr. MacCormick, like so many others in this story, became interested in medicine after needing a doctor's help himself. He was in junior college when he had a snow skiing accident, "had to go to physical therapy; got interested and switched my business major to physical therapy, then kept going on into medicine."

Asked what Scripps Encinitas was like in 1979, Dr. MacCormick said:

> It was much smaller. This whole front half where all the patient care area is, the second floor and the main lobby were all added later. We only had five beds in the emergency department and one of them was used as the GI suite, where Dr. Michael Kimball would come down and do his endoscopies and colonoscopies and we would use the other rooms to run the ED. They had a baseball field right next door—an open field with just weeds—and we'd go out there and watch the kids play when we weren't busy.
>
> It was a very close-knit family of people that worked here. We knew what was going on with everybody's family and kids—there was a real community feel.

The San Diego Trauma System was still five years away and Dr. MacCormick said:

> In the first years that I worked here, I was doing burr holes [for bleeding in the brain] and opening chests and doing everything that you would expect in a trauma center. I came out of a really good training program and concentrated on emergencies – but when you don't get that many cases, let alone the personnel working with you—they don't know how to do the procedures and support you. So the trauma system was absolutely a good move.

In 1987, Scripps Memorial Hospital, Encinitas, had a groundbreaking for the East Wing Addition. In Herman "Pop" Wiegand's honor, the groundbreaking was held with a white horse and plow. Dr. Charles Clark held the reins.

courtesy of Scripps Health

In 1985, after seven years in the Scripps family, the hospital was approved by the State of California for expansion and renovation and a serious fundraising campaign for the East Wing Addition began.

> Twenty-two years after he guaranteed the loan to build Encinitas Convalescent Hospital, Pop Wiegand was named Honorary Co-Chair of the Capital Campaign along with Paul Ecke, Sr. In Pop's honor, groundbreaking in May 1987 was conducted ceremoniously with a white horse and plow, with Dr. Charlie Clark holding the reins.[32]

The support of the Leichtag Family Foundation is helping build a two-story, 60,000-square-foot critical care building with a state-of-the-art emergency department on the campus of Scripps Memorial Hospital Encinitas. The $10 million donation was made in honor of Lee and Toni Leichtag, who made their first donation to Scripps Encinitas in 1979. Toni was a founding member of Circle of Life 100, a women's service organization that supports Scripps Encinitas, and also served on the hospital's community advisory board for more than two decades.

courtesy of Scripps Health

A few things had to be moved for the $17 million dollar expansion, including Kentucky Fried Chicken on Santa Fe Drive—about which the *Los Angeles Times* reported "The Colonel Gets the Bird, Landmark Bucket and All"[33]—but by 1990 Scripps Hospital Encinitas had an "airy 99,000 square foot addition in Southwestern style," including a two-story atrium entrance, a meditation room adjacent to a new landscaped courtyard, and 146 new beds including "the wing's proudest feature, its 30 bed Rehabilitation Center."[34] Dr. Michael Lobatz[35] and his partner Dr. Thomas Chippendale[36] were building the strong Neurology Department at Encinitas which would set the stage for the systemwide "rehab center" of the next century—the only certified comprehensive rehabilitation facility in northern San Diego County for stroke and brain injuries, with a remarkable brain injury day treatment program giving full lives back to wounded warriors and to civilians from throughout the Scripps Health system.[37]

Dr. James LaBelle arrived in Encinitas in 1987 as an Emergency Department physician just as Charlie Clark was following along behind the plow in groundbreaking for the expansion. Originally from the state and University of Washington, Jim LaBelle had completed a residency in internal medicine at UCSD where he was a member of the junior faculty. Dr. Scott Eisman (now in charge of

The 90,000 square-foot addition opened in 1990 with a two-story atrium, a meditation room, and 146 new beds.
courtesy of Scripps Health

the Encinitas Intensive Care Unit and chief of staff-elect) was also junior faculty at UCSD, and the two physicians began moonlighting in the Encinitas ED, fifteen nights a month each. Dr. LaBelle would eventually direct the Emergency Department (and after that ascend to the complex duties of corporate vice president of Quality, Medical Management and Physician Co-management). He said of his first years at Scripps:

> When Ames Early was in charge, Scripps Encinitas was a healthy hospital. The community was growing. The services were great here. Credentialing was tight and the doctors were really quality. In the early days it was hard to get in – it was a small hospital with not a big market share. So the early docs really set the bar high.
>
> And even though we've grown a lot, we still have a very family oriented culture here and can make decisions real easily. I think our reputation in the system is that this is a good place to do pilots because we're flexible and people don't get mad if things don't work out. We just try something else.[38]

But sometime in the 90s, things began to change. There were multiple reshufflings of leadership at "corporate" and a breakdown in communication. Dr. La Belle said:

> We had a wonderful administrator, Gerald Bracht, who was loved by the medical staff, who was very focused on developing this campus. And somewhere around 1997 or '98 they took Gerald kicking and fighting to corporate…and people here realized that Scripps was changing direction and there was just a lot of fear. Nobody knew what was going on. Nobody could really even read a hospital balance sheet to know how the hospital was doing.
>
> I realized that none of the physicians up here knew anything about business and how the whole business of medicine worked. So I decided to go to UC Irvine in 1998, to a healthcare MBA program for physicians—like remedial business school for docs—and got an MBA.
>
> Jan Zachry was a nurse with me in the ED at the time, and we were both really frustrated with a lot of things that were going on. And somebody said to us, "Well, if you think you can do any better, why don't you do it?" So Jan and I both decided to go to business school at the same time. I went up to Irvine, and she went to the University of Phoenix for an MBA focused on nursing, which was offered on site at Scripps La Jolla.

Ultimately, both would play key roles in what transpired at Scripps Encinitas in the tumultuous decades to come.

Above, in 1957, Chula Vista was on its way to becoming the second largest city in San Diego County. The citrus groves and produce fields that once characterized Chula Vista disappeared after World War II, when many of the factory workers at Roher Aircraft Corporation and thousands of servicemen stayed in the area.

courtesy of San Diego History Center

CHAPTER NINE
The Growing Family
SCRIPPS CHULA VISTA

SOUTH BAY MEMORIAL HOSPITAL (1961-64)
BAY GENERAL HOSPITAL (1964-84)
BAY HOSPITAL MEDICAL CENTER (1984-1986)
SCRIPPS MEMORIAL HOSPITAL CHULA VISTA (1986-2004)
SCRIPPS MERCY HOSPITAL, CHULA VISTA (2004)

IN 1961, THE HOSPITAL that would become the fourth campus of Scripps was built but shuttered tight on H Street in Chula Vista, abandoned by its builders, and it stayed that way for three years until January 1964, when it opened its door to the community as South Bay Memorial. Meanwhile, ten miles south of the hospital of the Sisters of Mercy and twice that far from Scripps Hospital and Clinic in La Jolla, a group of young physicians trained after World War II was looking for a medical home and considering building its own.

The border town of Chula Vista, at the outbreak of World War II, was farmland deep in celery and lemons.[1] In 1940, the 5,000 residents were served by a handful of family physicians and the small private Chula Vista Community Hospital (CVCH), which began as a nursing home in an old two-story house on F Street.[2]

But, in 1941, Rohr Aircraft Corporation arrived with more jobs than there were citizens in town, and suddenly farms and orchards gave way to houses. Growth was explosive. The population tripled to 16,000 by 1950;[3] and, as in the rest of the county, the servicemen who discovered San Diego during the war very frequently decided they had found the Promised Land.

One of these returning servicemen was Dr. Anthony Pierangelo,[4] who had multiple careers in San Diego: first (1944) as a twenty-one-year-old Navy antisubmarine warfare officer; then, after medical school at Tufts, as a resident in obstetrics and gynecology at Mercy Hospital (1952), when Mercy had the largest obstetrical service in the nation with 500 deliveries a month; next as general physician with Dr. Tom Lococo in National City (1953-57); and finally, after a second residency in anesthesia, returning to Chula Vista from 1958 onward in general practice, with added services in anesthesia.

The young Dr. Pierangelo soon found himself among other colleagues with postwar training who wanted to improve the quality of medicine in Chula Vista "to match the rest of the county." In that endeavor, he was joined by pathologist Dr. Lewis Palmer from the University of California San Francisco Medical School, who had state-of-the-art training in pathology at Valley Forge Army Hospital, in Japan at the central laboratory for the Far East Command, and at Huntington Memorial Hospital in Pasadena, before coming to Chula Vista in 1953 to join pathologist Dr. Stanley Lloyd at CVCH. Acting simultaneously as the chief of pathology at San Diego County Hospital (1954-1961), Dr. Palmer met leading physicians in the greater medical community, including Dr. Lee Monroe of Scripps Clinic, during Dr. Monroe's volunteer term as chief of staff at County Hospital. This particular friendship led to Dr. Palmer's role as consultant in pathology at Scripps Clinic.

As the 1950s and 1960s wore on, Drs. Pierangelo and Palmer were among a group of like-minded physicians, "disappointed with the broken promises" at the increasingly "dilapidated" Community Hospital (which in years to come would have its own dramatic story of growth and resurrection as Sharp Chula Vista).[5]

The doctors, who couldn't wait for that theoretical up-to-date facility, decided to purchase a 54-bed hospital at 435 H Street with a short, but wildly checkered, history: built in 1961 by investors in multiple small hospitals, who promptly went bankrupt before ever opening the doors; mournfully vacant for three years; finally opened to patients in 1964 as South Bay Memorial Hospital by a new set of Los Angeles investors, who were evicted by the sheriff within months for nonpayment of rent; taken over by the mortgage holder, Home Federal Savings and Loan, and renamed Bay General Hospital; only to be forced onto the auction block when Home Federal was advised they could not—as a savings and loan— legally run a hospital and began looking around for buyers!

Dr. George Cave had actually been a member of the medical staff of the 1961 hospital that never was. From Vancouver and the University of British Columbia, he arrived in Chula Vista in 1958 and joined the locally prominent McCausland-Robinson Clinic in general practice. In 1961 he returned to Vancouver for a residency in general surgery (and would return to Chula Vista as a surgeon in 1967), but before he left he attended the first and only staff meeting of the ghost hospital:

> I can recall that the parking lot and the driveway had not been completed, it was a rainy winter night and we had to exit the hospital over planks to get out of there. It was a swamp.

And Dr. Palmer blew the whistle on the bankrupt owners who had built a number of small hospitals in town as quick producers of cash. Dr. Palmer said:

> In 1961 I was invited to be pathologist at the new Lake Murray Hospital at 70th Street and I-8 [out near San Diego State]. The hospital received good medical support, but the creditors did not get paid. The Administrator was embarrassed and ashamed. The operating corporation had no investor's capital – the working capital came from a loan on accounts receivable and an examination of the books showed that some money had been siphoned off. After six months at Lake Murray I put that hospital in involuntary bankruptcy. What I didn't know until later was that the same corporation had started on a new hospital in Chula Vista.[6]

At the start of all the new activity in 1963, the *Chula Vista Star-News* had run a front-page story with a picture of Chula Vista's "white elephant" hospital under a huge canary palm and the headline "Million Dollar Hospital to Open Nov. 15." The text said:

> The new 27,000 square foot hospital will be known as South Bay Memorial. It will have 54 beds, including 10 maternity, two surgical suites and a modern obstetrical suite. No purchase price was officially announced, but it was reliably reported to be about $950,000, fully-equipped... Administrator Kurt Nork emphasized that there is an acute shortage of hospital beds in the area even with the addition of the 54 beds.[7]

And the accompanying editorial was titled "Badly Needed Facility:"

> The news that Chula Vista's never-opened hospital on H Street finally will go into operation in November certainly is good news for the community. The ultra-modern, beautifully equipped plant, which had remained idle and empty for three years, has been an unhappy example of what can happen when the ambitions of developers exceed their financial capacity...It is to the interest of the entire community that this new South Bay Memorial flourishes. It is badly needed in the area, as the State Dept of Public Health has pointed out. Even with its 54 beds, the South Bay will be 74 beds short of what it should have. It will be there for quick and convenient use of the ailing in time of need.

In fact, the hospital opened in January 1964. But by December 12, 1965, the *Star-News* headline was "Bay General Hospital on Auction Block" with text stating:

> The operating group was evicted by the sheriff last April [1965] for non-payment of rent and operation of the hospital was taken over by a new operating company owned by Home Federal. The name was changed to Bay General Hospital. EH Sorensen, administrator, stressed that the auction of the land and building at 435 H Street would in no way affect the operation of the hospital…

Onto this stage with ever-revolving scenery stepped the twenty or so physician-investors of "Chula Vista Group Properties," with Dr. Anthony Pierangelo as chairman of investors and Lewis Palmer as president of the hospital corporation that would lease the land and buildings and run the program.

In the summer of 2010, five of the senior physicians of that era met to discuss what took place.[8] Dr. Palmer said:

> What impressed me about Chula Vista was that the doctors were very concerned about having an improved hospital. They'd been promised a new hospital by the management at CVCH and were disappointed. Their primary purpose was to buy this hospital as the basis for a really modern medical center, along with an office building for physicians. We offered every physician in town the opportunity to participate.

Obstetrician-gynecologist, Dr. Leroy Miller, from Winnipeg, Manitoba, with medical training at Loma Linda and Wayne State Universities, had come to Chula Vista in 1963, originally to CVCH. Dr. Miller said:

> There was a group of practitioners in town who had been here a long time and considered it sort of a private preserve and that anybody coming into town came on their invitation….The "insiders" at the time were really in control of Chula Vista Community Hospital, a private institution. The doctors peripheral to that inside group felt they were not being dealt a fair hand in the practice of medicine there and, to their credit, went ahead and built the facility the community really needed.

And this, from family medicine physician, Dr. Charles Camarata, originally from Chicago with training at Oregon Health Sciences and the Naval Hospital at Balboa and MCRD, who arrived in Chula Vista in 1960:

> We wanted a first class facility and we attempted to collaborate with the existing community hospital [CVCH], to avoid duplication. I actually approached their Board and said, "Why don't we figure this out and work together, to do what's best for the community?" But they wanted no part of it.

In December 1965, the physicians made a conditional offer to purchase and entered escrow on Bay General Hospital with clearly-stated intent to enlarge and develop the institution.

They immediately drew up plans for the new facility and appeared before the City of Chula Vista Planning Commission. Permission was granted to proceed, but set off a political war between supporters of Bay General and supporters of CVCH that raged for years. Archives of the *Star-News* list nineteen headlines in the twenty-four months from February to February, 1967-69, with titles like "Fight between Bay General and Chula Vista Community Hospital continues;" "Hospital Nonsense;" "Hopes for agreement between feuding hospitals dims" and "Any further talks would be unproductive." Forward progress stalled, while appearances were made before multiple committees of the Comprehensive Health Planning Association. It was only when city council members were replaced, including the mayor, that the plan was finally approved.

In December 1966, the physicians had successfully purchased Bay General Hospital from Home Federal and were running the small hospital successfully; what the fight was about was the expansion plan. Finally, in January 1969, "the Chamber of Commerce held a hush-hush meeting to urge the Comprehensive Health Planning Association to endorse Bay General's expansion"[9] and on February 6, the plan was approved.

Politics aside, the physician group had been scrambling for financing for the new addition at a time when money was tight. Dr. Pierangelo explained how they got the money:

> The going rate was two to three "points" to the broker for a loan, but it was difficult to obtain long-term financing. After about a year of searching, we found a broker in Los Angeles who wanted *13 points* for his commission…and we agreed to it! But at that point, Dr. Tom Lococo (who was a big bear of a man, 6'3 or '4, and Sicilian) went with our attorney and this broker to Chicago to meet with directors of the Teamsters Union. According to Dr. Lococo, when the Chairman of the Teamsters Board looked at the application, he raised his eyes to look at the LA broker and said, "This says 'thirteen points'… but you really mean 'three points', don't you?" The guy said, "Right!" and we were in business.

At that time the Teamsters were being investigated by the Justice Department. It is my own opinion that they needed a showcase loan on their books because they were the only people we dealt with who were <u>gentlemen</u> and who made sure that no one took advantage of us. (I received calls from the FBI for years afterward seeking information on the Teamsters…and delighted in telling them this.)[10]

Groundbreaking for the $2.5 million expansion of Bay General Hospital took place on January 25, 1970, with California Assemblyman Wadie Deddeh ("pride of the Chaldean community"[11]) holding the pick and Dr. Anthony Pierangelo ("chairman of the board of the hospital corporation and master of ceremonies") the shovel. By the time the new hospital wing was formally opened on May 13, 1971, it had become a "$4 million dollar, 108-bed addition and [one of] the largest red-brick structure[s] in San Diego County."[12]

A special eight-page section of *The Star-News*[13] shows the architect's drawing of the original one-story, white-roofed hospital, dwarfed by the four-story addition to the north and the legend "what Bay General Hospital has done with $5 ½ million dollars to provide you with the most modern, up-to-date health care possible."

Also shown is Chief Administrator William Wagstaff in a memorable plaid jacket. Text reads, "Happy patients mean patients with the best chance of recovery! Of the 108 beds in the new wing, 60 are in private rooms!" Mr. Wagstaff was quoted earlier about forecasting hospital trends years in advance:

Most new hospital construction shows a strong trend toward single-bed rooms. We anticipated this back in 1967 when our plans were first-drawn, and we've been proven right. The big advantage of the single-bed room is that a patient will not be disturbed by other patients. He can talk freely with his physician, nurse or family about confidential matters without embarrassment.[14]

In 1970, a ten-foot shovel and a pick were used to break ground for the $2.5 million expansion of Bay General Hospital. Left to right, Assemblyman Wadie Daddeh, Chula Vista Mayor Will Hyde, Supervisor Henry Boney, Senator James Mills, Rep. Lionel Van Deerlin, and Dr. Anthony Pierangelo helped commemorate the occasion. The new hospital opened in May 1971. *courtesy of San Diego History Center*

A special section of *The Star-News,* May 16, 1971, focused on the opening of the new wing of Bay General Hospital.

On the back page of the special insert is a "Table of future expansion:" Phase I was the first hospital tower just completed with remodeling of the original hospital. Phase II (1973) would include a new medical office building, multilevel parking garage and second hospital tower; and Phase III (1975) a third tower. An issue of *Bay General Hospital News*, which is undated but claiming "New Medical-Service Center on Schedule" (so presumably 1972), shows the architect's rendering of the new five-story medical office building "with narrow bronze-tinted windows shaded by white metal fins:" and announces that groundbreaking ceremonies are imminent on Fourth Avenue adjoining the hospital.[15]

The doctors had their new hospital and medical office building and, in 1974, decided it was time to go nonprofit. Dr. Pierangelo said:

> Being a member of the Board and learning a lot about running a hospital, what I found was that we had a lot of negative publicity about being a "business" – even though we poured every cent back into the facility, people would say, "Well, you're keeping patients an extra day."

> So we brought in an advisory board of community leaders and taught them the ins and outs of running the facility. Then they became the new board of directors and that was how the transition occurred. When we turned the hospital over to the non-profit organization we left them a million dollars of working capital.

An architect's rendering of a planned five-story medical office building adjoining Bay General Hospital was featured in the hospital newsletter. The medical office building opened in 1973.
courtesy of Scripps Health

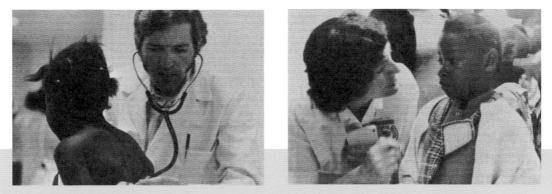

In the spirit of Ellen Browning Scripps, Bay General Hospital donated countless hours to the Chula Vista community. Above left, Dr. Melvin Ochs was one of three Bay General Hospital doctors who volunteered to give free physicals at the southeast Boys and Girls Club. Right, Mrs. Anthony Pierangelo, a member of the hospital auxiliary, also helped out at the event. *courtesy of Scripps Health*

Dr. Cave, who was in Canada in the early 1960s and, therefore, was not an owner, reflected:

> From the standpoint of a non-owner physician who practiced in this hospital from 1967 through 1974 when it went non-profit, I can speak for a lot of other people in my position and say that we were very happy with the arrangement, with the doctors as directors and an administrator administrating. It ran very efficiently.

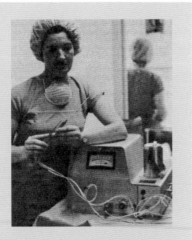

Bay General Hospital was in the vanguard of technology. In 1972, the hospital purchased the county's first middle ear cryo-probe to remove vascular tumors. Previously, patients had to go to Los Angeles for the surgery.
courtesy of Scripps Health

Within a year, Dr. Pierangelo said, the non-profit administration "had already gone through the million dollars we left them, so they floated $3 million in bonds." But all the founding physicians continued to work at Bay General, and it was a good place to work.

> Departments like pathology and radiology improved, kept up with the times, got new equipment. The operating room continued to thrive and was very efficiently run. We had several good nursing supervisors there, and on the wards, the same thing. We developed an intensive care unit. It was a very efficiently-run institution.[16]

Much of how well the hospital worked after the transition and in the early 1980s was due to the skill of administrator, Marty Comella, a retired Army colonel who had been in premed himself for a time, but dropped out with some illness and eventually went into the Army in medical administration. Mr. Comella came to Chula Vista originally as manager of the doctors' business partnership, and they were impressed enough to hire him as hospital administrator. And things went well until Marty Comella resigned in 1984, just as Bay General Hospital was changing its name to Bay Hospital Medical Center;[17] Mr. Comella's assistant Bob Larson, was reportedly "not his first choice" to succeed him, but the board did not search for another candidate, and Mr. Larson took charge.

Dr. Cave was chief of staff in 1986, when "the place came completely unglued." In January, the Chula Vista City Council was considering "a plan to turn the financially troubled, non-profit Bay Hospital Medical Center over to a private corporation, National Medical Enterprises of Los Angeles."[18] President Larson said the hospital's troubles stemmed from its inability to pay off $15 million in tax-exempt bonds and revenue notes, sponsored by the City of Chula Vista. Records from the city council meeting noted that "Bay Hospital Medical Center is in financial difficulty despite the fact that its 72.6% occupancy rate is second in San Diego only to Children's Hospital," and "Mayor Greg Cox expressed some concerns about the proposed agreement."

Dr. Cave said:

> I became aware during my first four months as Chief of Staff that this particular Board seemed to be taking a lot more direction from the hospital administrator than I thought a Board should. After three Board meetings, it became obvious that this hospital was in big trouble. The financial report we saw showed a million dollar profit, but it didn't make sense to me.
>
> In between meetings, I questioned some of my medical colleagues in the doctors' lounge, not referring to specifics, but asking them in generalities what they thought about the type of accounting I was seeing—and they didn't think it was correct.
>
> In May of 1986, Mr. Larson left on an African safari, and before he left he called me into his office and royally chewed me out for talking about the accounting with my colleagues. It turned out the doctors' lounge had been fitted with a microphone, but nobody knew it at the time.

While the director was away, nurse executive Ruth Blank was acting CEO and she discovered that Bay General Hospital was on the verge of financial collapse. She instigated the corrective action by calling in a bankruptcy attorney, "a very good, knowledgeable young man from Los Angeles" who began sorting out debts and creditors.

Ruth Blank, acting CEO of Bay Hospital Medical Center, approached Scripps about purchasing the failing hospital in 1986. Bay General Hospital changed its name to Bay Hospital Medical Center in 1985.
courtesy of Scripps Health

Meanwhile, Ms. Blank was "auditioning other groups, including Mercy Hospital, a group from Arizona, Chula Vista Community Hospital, and eventually Scripps Memorial, which turned out to be our white knight."[19] The founders said:

> Most of us didn't feel that keeping it in Chula Vista with two hospitals under one Board was a wise idea because this hospital was so indebted we didn't want to sink the other one. The other hospitals consulted really wanted to put Bay General into receivership, because coming out of bankruptcy would be a lot cheaper. This was going on from May to September. As each party came along and made their presentation, it became evident that this hospital could be made into a second rate facility, handling things like outpatient physiotherapy and no longer operating as an acute care hospital. None of us wanted that.
>
> And Scripps was the one that guaranteed maintaining the hospital in its present state and with its present mandate. Scripps, to their credit, was the only one that would agree to take on the debt and take over the hospital. Mr. Larson was relieved of his duties and left for Mexico.

Of these events, Ames Early said:

> The first approach to us from the acting CEO, Ruth Blank, was to Lauren Blagg, who was Senior Vice-President and Chief Financial Officer at Scripps. Lauren Blagg worked with a man named Bob Gregg, an independent Medicare Reimbursement Consultant who was part time for both Scripps Memorial and Bay General, and Bob had already told Lauren, "There's a problem developing down there."
>
> But the first thing Ruth Blank said directly to Scripps was, "We have payroll coming next week and we don't have the money to pay it? Can you help us?"
>
> We did work out some way of making sure that their payroll was covered, yet didn't obligate Scripps at first; and we asked for a ninety-day period to do due diligence. And at the conclusion of the ninety-day period we understood the difference in payer mix there, which was disadvantageous, but we also understood the importance of Bay General Hospital to that community. The community could not afford to be left without that hospital.
>
> And we thought we could bring some advantages of economy on the management side, and that it ought to be kept going. So our Board agreed that Chula Vista would be added to the Scripps group.
>
> And I found myself saying that the Scripps Hospitals came to serve everyone, patients who could go anywhere in the world, and patients who had nowhere else to go.[20]

Jeff Bills became the first administrator of the Scripps Memorial Hospital Chula Vista in 1986, when Scripps purchased Bay Hospital Medical Center.

courtesy of Scripps Health

Mr. Early's first administrator for the new Scripps Memorial Hospital Chula Vista in 1986 was Jeff Bills, who had started his administrative career at Scripps La Jolla, after an internship in Salt Lake City at Intermountain Healthcare. A year later, in 1987, Mr. Bills recruited an assistant, Tom Gammiere, from St. Benedict's Hospital in Ogden, Utah. (Jeff Bills was also from Ogden, and both men had played serious baseball in college, one as catcher and the other shortstop and second base.) Five years later, in 1992, when the Scripps Institutions of Medicine and Science were formed, Jeff Bills was recalled to La Jolla as chief executive, and Tom Gammiere took the reins at Chula Vista.[21]

Dr. Francisco Gracia was a leader at Scripps Memorial Hospital Chula Vista, serving as chief of surgery and chief of staff.

courtesy of Scripps Health

General surgeon, Dr. Francisco Gracia,[22] was chief of surgery at Chula Vista during much of this period (1984–85 and 1987) and chief of staff in 1991 and 1992, when he was photographed shaking the hand of the new administrator, Tom Gammiere.[23] Dr. Gracia's career was in many ways emblematic of the changing face of the medical staff at that time. Born in Sonora, Mexico, Dr. Gracia earned his medical degree at the National Autonomous University of Mexico and then came to this country for internship in Ohio and surgical residency in Arizona. He returned to Mexico in 1972 and set up practice in general and vascular surgery in Tijuana. After a few years and "for many reasons," he left Mexico for good, took the California licensing exam and opened a practice in Chula Vista in 1980—along with his brother, Edgardo, also a surgeon. Dr. Gracia recalled:

> Most of the surgeons when we arrived were non-Hispanic, of course, and not very receptive to us at first. But in a short while we established very well and, as a matter of fact, four years after I started my practice here I became Chief of Surgery.

> We were not the first Hispanics – there was another surgeon and a few internists, but minimum. It was later on in the '80s when more came along – mostly Mexicans and Peruvians, a couple Colombians, one or two Argentineans and Brazilians and a few from the Caribbean, Puerto Rico and the Dominican Republic.

> The makeup of the patient population was more or less the same as it is now. I would say 80% of them are Hispanic and 20% a mix. A physician that comes here not able to speak Spanish is kind of lost for a few months, but then they learn the basics, the medical Spanish, and they get along very well.

Ames Early, president of Scripps, held a press conference with the Chula Vista team to announce the sale of the Chula Vista hospital to Scripps.

courtesy of Scripps Health

Discussing what happened before and after the acquisition by Scripps, Dr. Gracia said,

> It was difficult when the administration was in shambles, and they didn't know what to do. In 1986, I was in the operating room and I asked for some simple thing like a cannula and they said, "We don't have it." And I asked for something else – "We don't have that either." Dr. George Cave, who was the senior surgeon here (and I relate to him very well) said, "Francisco, maybe this is the last surgery we do here, because right now we don't have money to pay the salaries."
>
> So that was before Scripps came along. We were told the financial situation was precarious and the hospital was about to close. So when we learned that Scripps was coming along we were happy because we knew that was the salvation of the hospital. We didn't think too much about Scripps. We just thought, well, good, the hospital will continue.

After a while came second thoughts. The bills were paid. But some of the doctors began to think, "the only thing we have received from Scripps is the name and a coat of paint for the hospital."

There was disenchantment, grumbling. Some people thought that "the local administration couldn't make any decisions because they were just reporting to La Jolla" or that maybe Chula Vista was just a "training ground for administrators," and the best ones would soon move up and away (as Jeff Bills moved back to La Jolla in 1992, and Tom Gammiere to Mercy in 1999.)

Part of the unrest may have been cultural, Dr. Gracia said:

> Here, the difference in the medical staff from the rest of Scripps is very simple. In the north, in La Jolla, Encinitas, all of them, they follow the rules. They follow protocols. That is the way it is, systematic. Here we follow protocols, but we rebel against anything that appears to be imposition without information.

An aerial view of Bay Hospital Medical Center in 1985 reveals nothing about the financial shambles of the hospital Scripps purchased in 1986.

courtesy of San Diego History Center

> Now, somebody who knows both cultures, he can navigate them. And I was in a position where I navigated both worlds.

Dr. Gracia was recognized as a leader at Scripps Chula Vista and became a member of the board of directors of the Scripps Foundation from 1995-98, after which he served two terms on the Scripps Health Board of Trustees from 1998-2003. As he served in those corporate positions, he said two things happened: the first was that

> I learned how difficult it is. I knew the budgeting and how they go about managing money, so I understood many things – my impression became different from some doctors who did not have that experience.

But Dr. Gracia was also in a position to invite the administrative leaders down to Chula Vista to see for themselves the problems and opportunities. In 1991, the year he was first chief of staff, Scripps Memorial Hospitals and Scripps Clinic "remarried" as the Scripps Institutions of Medicine and Science (SIMS), and both the president and vice president of SIMS, Charles Edwards and Ames Early, came down to Chula Vista every two weeks "for at least six or seven meetings."

Dr. Gracia felt the leaders learned many things, and the medical staff as well. As leadership at "corporate" changed—and it did change often in the '90s—those new leaders also came down to see for themselves.

And eventually, in 1999, there was "something really positive:"

> The something positive was the creation of the ICU and the Emergency Department, which at that time was the best in the city. La Jolla was pale in comparison because ours was the top of the line – *beautiful*.[24]

Left to right, Wilbur Moore, director of Facility Support Services for Scripps Memorial Hospital Chula Vista, and Tom Gammiere, vice president of Scripps Chula Vista, review plans for the hospital expansion and remodel.

courtesy of Scripps Health

The new twenty-four-hour emergency department, intensive care unit and lobby added 40,000 square feet and doubled the number of ED and ICU Beds.[25] The *Update Summer 1999* issue,[26] from Scripps Health Foundation, described the lovely change:

SCRIPPS CHULA VISTA RENEWED:
New ER, ICU and Lobby Pave Way for Expansion Plans
Construction of the $19 million expansion project, underway for the past 20 months, nears completion.

The renovation brings a whole new look and brand new feel to the 38-year-old hospital. "Many of the new features were designed to reduce stress in the hospital setting for patients and families, as well as staff," said Linda Mitchell, lead interior designer with Jain Malkin, La Jolla. "Open areas in both the interior lobby and exterior courtyards give patients' families enough space to wait comfortably for their loved ones."

The circular shape of the lobby serves two purposes, according to the project's architect, Ed Ruegg of James Leary, San Diego. "It has a healing effect because it embraces and welcomes you into the hospital, while the natural light from the cone-shaped skylight has a soothing, spiritual quality." The rotunda also acts as the focal point for all future expansion and connects the existing building to the new addition.

To fund the project, Scripps contributed $7.25 million from cash reserves. The remaining funds came from charitable sources, including $800,000 raised from Scripps employees, medical staff and community leaders.

Chief of staff when the new addition opened in 1999 was pathologist Dr. Carla Stayboldt, herself emblematic of the diversity of the medical staff, as a non-Hispanic woman.[27] A graduate of the University of California at Los Angeles and Oral Roberts University Medical School, Dr. Stayboldt came to the University of California at San Diego for her residency in pathology (1983-87), during which time she did an elective in dermatopathology at the downtown San Diego lab of Dr. Palmer.

Dr. Stayboldt joined the medical staff at Chula Vista in July 1987, about nine months after the take-over by Scripps, and soon after also joined Palmer Laboratory Medical Group, which had the pathology contract for Scripps Chula Vista; in doing so, she became medical director of clinical laboratories there.

Dr. Carla Stayboldt became the first female chief of staff at Scripps Memorial Hospital Chula Vista.
courtesy of Scripps Health

There were only a few women physicians at Chula Vista in 1987, including emergency department physician Dr. Mary Margaret Loehr, and radiologist Dr. Lucy Perkins. Dr. Stayboldt recalled:

> Every lunch time around 12:30 PM I'd go up to the physicians' dining room with this one long table where everybody would sit and chat. And pretty much 99% of the time I was the lone woman at the table. On rare occasions Mary Margaret and I would both be there, or Lucy and I would both be there. But usually I was it. And I didn't feel really any sexism. I felt like I was just kind of part of the gang.

Dr. Stayboldt had majored in Spanish for a while in college after six years of precollege Spanish and living with a family in Spain. About the lunch room conversation at Chula Vista, she said:

> If there were just Spanish speakers there, they'd be speaking in Spanish but as soon as an English speaker would show up they, out of respect, would switch to English because they didn't want that individual to feel like they were talking about them.

Always interested in leadership, Dr. Stayboldt joined the San Diego Medical Society, "jump-started" the young physicians section there, then moved on as chair of young physicians at the California Medical Society.

Dr. Ahmed Calvo with residents of the Scripps Family Practice Medical Residency Program. Accredited in 1998, the program accepted its first class in June 1999.

courtesy of Scripps Health

At her own hospital, she was involved in committee work regarding such things as the appropriateness of specific surgical cases. And then she was nominated to fill the post of medical staff secretary-treasurer, which was ordinarily a two-year position, but had been vacated early by an emergency department physician, "who was into holistic healthcare and wanted to go off and do a private holistic practice." [28]

Secretary-treasurer ordinarily led to chief-of-staff elect, and the following year, Dr. Stayboldt was nominated for that position as well, and in due course became the first woman chief of staff at Scripps Chula Vista—though not without a little flurry of angst among some of her tradition-minded colleagues.[29]

The late 1990s was a challenging time to be in medical staff leadership at Chula Vista— as well as everywhere else in the Scripps system. But just before the close of the decade, an infusion of young physicians arrived on campus in a sort of spiritual match to the fresh new architecture. The Scripps Family Medicine Residency Program admitted its first class of six residents in 1999 (and has filled 100 percent of its openings in the ensuing decade). A dream of the former Director of Medical Education at Scripps Chula Vista, Dr. Ahmed Calvo, and now directed by Dr. Marianne McKennett, the UCSD-affiliated program trains family physicians in primary care for underserved communities along the U.S. border with Mexico. Medical students are recruited for their commitment to community medicine, cultural competency and scholarship.

Nearly half the entering residents are Latino themselves, some—a profoundly satisfying cadre—are graduates of local high schools; and so far, when the residents finish their program, two-thirds have gone on serving. Young physicians who grew up in the area come back home to train—and stay.[30]

A renovation in 1999 added 40,000 square feet to Scripps Memorial Hospital Chula Vista. The $19 million expansion included a new emergency department and doubled the number of emergency department and intensive care unit beds.

courtesy of Scripps Health

CHAPTER TEN
Scripps Clinic Medical Institutions
1977-1991

SCRIPPS CLINIC RESEARCH FOUNDATION
GREEN HOSPITAL
SCRIPPS CLINIC MEDICAL GROUP

IN 1977, THE BOARD OF TRUSTEES of the Scripps Clinic Medical Institutions chose Dr. Charles Cornell Edwards as third President and CEO[1] in a half-century.[2]

Dr. Edwards came with impressively wide-ranging credentials. He was first of all a surgeon—not just a physician, but a surgeon—and trained at the Mayo Clinic, which he would believe for the rest of his life was "pound for pound, the best medical institution in the world."[3] He was a veteran of academic medicine at Mayo (residency and junior faculty, 1952-58), of private surgical practice in Des Moines, Iowa (1958-61), and of organized medicine with the American Medical Association ("point man" for the AMA with Congress over Medicare, 1962-66); of remarkable government service, including the Central Intelligence Agency (undercover agent briefly 1961, then "open" special agent "several years"); the Food and Drug Administration (Commissioner 1969-73) and the Department of Health, Education and Welfare (Assistant Secretary for Health, 1973-75); and even industry, before government service with a management consulting firm (Booz, Allen, Hamilton 1966-69); and after, with a medical device company (Becton Dickinson Senior Vice President 1975-77).[4]

Besides all that, Dr. Edwards was a very handsome man. His brief private practice at Mercy Hospital in Des Moines coincided with Ames Early's stint there as a laboratory assistant, working his way through Drake University as a twenty-one-year-old kid when Dr. Edwards was thirty-five. Mr. Early said:

Dr. Charles Cornell Edwards had an ambitious agenda for the development of Scripps Clinic when he became president and CEO in 1977.

courtesy of Mandeville Special Collections Library, UC San Diego

> I remember asking about him because we were in a cafeteria line, and he looked so sharp. He looked as if he were the surgeon out of central casting.[5]

The two men, who would eventually have much to do with one another at Scripps, didn't speak back then in 1958, but their paths did cross years later before they came to La Jolla. In 1973, when Dr. Edwards was Assistant Secretary for Health at HEW, he gave a lecture at a summer course at Harvard University in health policy administration, attended by Ames Early, who was then executive director at Mercy Hospital, Miami. And Ames said:

> They had a nice little reception out on the lawn afterwards. And so I made it a point after the speech to say hello to Charlie Edwards. That was the first time I met him. And then the next time, of course, was when he appeared in La Jolla.

When Dr. Edwards did appear in La Jolla in 1977 (the year after Ames Early), his vision for Scripps Clinic did not match what he found. In his later autobiography, *Tough Choices: My Extraordinary Journey at the Heart of American Politics and Medicine,* Dr. Edwards wrote:

> What I saw when I flew out to visit Scripps Clinic and Research Foundation intrigued me.
>
> It wasn't much, really. The clinic was small, with only 45 or 50 doctors – all diagnosticians, no surgeons. The research component was also small, but had an outstanding scientific staff. Money was tight.
>
> But I saw the potential for more – much more.[6]

He went on to say:

> The reality of the Clinic bore little resemblance to my ambitious vision for it. The hospital catered to the few who could afford it.
>
> My vision was to build this small clinical operation into a large multi-specialty clinic and, with the prestige of the research institute, transform it into one of the top medical providers in the country.
>
> I began to increase the institution's resources and enlarge its patient base. The first step was to recruit surgeons.[7]

Dr. Edwards promptly recruited surgeons, some from afar and some locally (as recounted in chapter seven). The number of doctors at the Clinic "increased significantly, eventually growing from about 75 to more than 500."[8] But the success in recruitment led to lack of space, and, without an expansion, the Clinic could not recruit medical specialists necessary to increase outpatient volume. The "critical turning point" for the Clinic came with a multimillion dollar gift from George and Thelma

Anderson to fund the 164,000-square-foot Anderson Outpatient Pavilion, which opened in 1983.[9] With the Outpatient Pavilion open and waiting, Dr. Edwards said:

> The challenge then became to attract patients. That's when we conceived of satellite clinics [which] would refer surgery and other specialized care back to the La Jolla campus. Our satellites would be established in locations close enough to be managed from the founding institution, but far enough to attract their own doctors and new patients.[10]

With more than three decades of giving, philanthropists Darlene and Donald Shiley have a legacy of generously supporting Scripps Clinic. Darlene's first gift was to endow the Donald P. Shiley Lectureship, a surprise gift to Donald. *courtesy of Scripps Health*

The first satellite opened in Borrego Springs, the second in Rancho Bernardo, and ultimately, there were "almost a dozen satellite clinics around the region…providing a steady stream of patients for surgeons and other specialists on the main campus."[11]

But Scripps Clinic Medical Institutions needed capital, and in the 1980s, Dr. Edwards wrote, health care on the national scene was moving rapidly from the nonprofit model to a for-profit system. Dr. Edwards decided to investigate a joint venture, and eventually signed a landmark agreement with the best proprietary group to be found, which was Hospital Corporation of America (HCA), founded and managed by the Frist family of Tennessee.[12] He wrote:

> Our landmark agreement with HCA enabled Scripps Clinic to grow to another level of size and importance. In the deal, HCA agreed to supply the capital for needed improvements – including construction of a new hospital wing, additional surgical suites, a parking garage and the Shiley Sports Center. In exchange, we agreed that HCA would manage the hospital operation. To our good fortune, Richard Bracken – one of the most competent administrators that I have had the privilege to work with — was our hospital administrator.[13]

The relationship with HCA was one of the best and most important decisions I made as head of Scripps Clinic and Research Foundation.

The second satellite clinic of Scripps Clinic Medical Institutions opened in Rancho Bernardo. Ultimately, almost a dozen clinics were established throughout the region to refer patients for specialized care and surgery to the La Jolla campus.
courtesy of Mandeville Special Collections Library, UC San Diego

The medical specialty that was perhaps changing most dramatically at that time was cardiology, from what was dubbed "stethoscope cardiology" to interventional, meaning a change from clinical diagnosis—with or without referral for open-heart surgery—to the use of devices threaded through veins into the heart or coronary arteries to repair whatever was wrong.

"In the 1950s", Dr. David Carmichael said, *"coronary artery disease was captain of the men of death."*[14] The sitting United States President Dwight Eisenhower suffered a left anterior myocardial infarction in 1955, and between that event and August 1968 had "seven heart attacks and fourteen cardiac arrests." The treatment was bed rest.

In 1967, Scripps philanthropist William Harmon Black had a heart attack on the golf course of the La Jolla Beach and Tennis Club and died without treatment of any kind; La Jolla was still without an organized response to medical emergencies outside the hospital. In response, his widow Ruth Black donated the very first La Jolla Emergency Heart Ambulance to Scripps Clinic.[15]

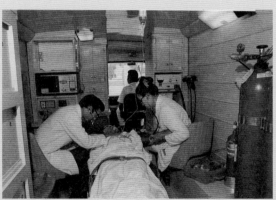

After Scripps philanthropist William Harmon Black died without treatment for a heart attack, Scripps Clinic received its first La Jolla Emergency Heart Ambulance from his widow, Ruth Black. The mission was to bring free emergency care to heart attack victims within ten to twenty minutes of the time the call came into the Clinic. The custom-built vehicle was equipped to care for patients at the site and on route to the hospital.

courtesy of Mandeville Special Collections Library, UC San Diego

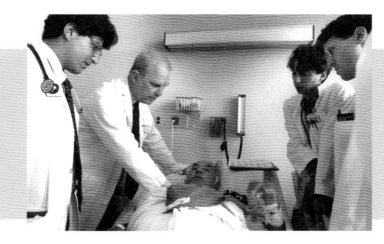

Dr. Allen "Skip" Johnson
discusses a patient's case
with fellows at Scripps Green
Hospital. Dr. Johnson was
one of the first cardiologists
to come to Scripps Clinic
who specialized in cardiac
catheterization.

courtesy of Scripps Health

Meanwhile, at the Clinic, Dr. Richard Kahler, an excellent clinical cardiologist, had come from Yale to replace Dr. Grey Dimond as director of the department and served from 1968-81. But, over those years, the field of cardiology tilted sharply toward intervention, and in 1979, Dr. Allen "Skip" Johnson arrived at Scripps Clinic at the head of a long line of innovators, which would include Drs. Guy Curtis, Paul Teirstein, Richard Schatz, and Mimi Guarneri. Dr. Johnson[16] was raised in Evansville, Indiana, where his grandfather was mayor, and first thought about being a doctor as a seven year old in the 1948 Labor Day polio pandemic, when he was hospitalized for six weeks on a huge ward of afflicted children. He said: "You were in awe of the nurses, in awe of the physicians. So that got me really tuned in to medicine."

Trained at Johns Hopkins in the 1960s, Dr. Johnson encountered the pioneering treatment of congenital heart disease by surgeon, Dr. Alfred Blalock, and pediatric cardiologist, Dr. Helen Taussig, and then made his way to San Diego in the wake of the great Eugene Braunwald who founded the Department of Medicine at UCSD.

Dr. Johnson arrived at UCSD in 1970 and remained there nearly a decade as chief of cardiology at the Veterans Administration Hospital, before being recruited to Scripps Clinic in 1979 by Dr. Edwards. Dr. Johnson said:

> They had done some cardiac catheterization with Grey Dimond at the old Scripps Clinic facility on Prospect Street, but in those days cardiac catheterization was done more on patients with congenital and valvular heart disease. Coronary artery disease was still off the map.

> And then the Clinic more or less abandoned cardiac catheterizations and when they moved up here had no cath lab per se. But cardiology was literally exploding in the era of 1965-80. So when I arrived I was obligated either to do our cardiac catheterizations elsewhere or build out our own lab. We did both.

Cardiac catheterization was a new diagnostic tool for cardiac care in the 1970s. Right, a physician holds an example of a catheter that will be used in the state-of-the-art catheterization lab that opened at Scripps Clinic in 1984. The lab was the precursor to the groundbreaking Heart, Lung and Vascular Center that opened in 1989. Scripps became renowned for its cardiology program, receiving numerous national awards and accolades, including recognition by *U.S. News & World Report* as being among the best in the nation for cardiology and heart care.

courtesy of Mandeville Special Collections Library, UC San Diego

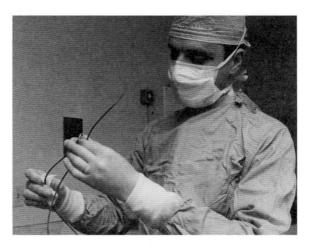

Dr. Guy Curtis[17] was born in still-segregated St. Louis, Missouri, at the all-black Freedman Hospital, owned and operated by his grandfather. Dr. Curtis said:

> Every generation of my family had a physician in it, and so I was expected to become a physician also. My early days were spent sitting around the living room listening to these guys who were general practitioners talk about their cases and I found that pretty fascinating.

But, before medical school, Dr. Curtis first earned a Ph.D. in pharmacology at the University of Michigan:

> And the way that happened was, I was working in a cardiology research lab where we were looking at arrhythmias and pacing. Back then cardiac catheterization was just getting going, and so I put some of the early dyes in animals, and found that this was much more interesting than anything I'd ever run into, so decided to do the pharmacology. We did electrophysiology which means the study of abnormal rhythms of the heart, trying to understand their mechanisms and then how to stop them – and this was before anybody else was doing it. And after that I decided I needed the MD.
>
> Fortunately the NIH was supporting that kind of thing, thanks to Eugene Braunwald and his group. There was this idea that you could produce PhD / MDs who could work on the interface between the basic science lab and the clinical world. And so that's how I got my support to get through.

Dr. Curtis arrived at UCSD in 1975 as a cardiac fellow under Dr. Johnson—who was considered an exceptional invasive cardiologist—and, although the program was generally excellent,

> one of the things they didn't have was electrophysiology. And I had done all of this stuff in dogs. So when I was done with my fellowship I was able to get a job as Director of Electrophysiology. I was the only one at UCSD.

The two young invasive cardiologists recognized that they had very similar interests; both won top awards in teaching[18] and were committed to providing the best clinical care. So, in 1984, when Dr. Johnson was looking to start a fellowship program at Scripps Clinic and to add electrophysiology, it was a natural to invite Dr. Curtis to join him.

The first up-to-date cardiac catheterization lab at the Clinic opened that year, and soon Drs. Johnson and Curtis were planning a remarkable new facility for the diagnosis and treatment of cardiovascular and pulmonary disease, a center where the entire infrastructure—offices, laboratories, operating rooms (including the first hybrid operating room-cath lab in the country), plus intensive care units—was gathered in a brilliantly compact space one could reach from any direction in thirty seconds. And, for that, they had the full support of the new administrator for Green Hospital, hired by Dr. Edwards: Richard Bracken. According to Dr. Johnson:

> He was inspired. We said, 'We have this vision.' And he said, 'Tell me more about it.' He analyzed it very quickly and said, 'That sounds like a winner. I'm going to support it.' And it went from vision to completion in lightning speed.
>
> In 1989, the groundbreaking Heart, Lung and Vascular Center of Scripps Clinic opened its doors.

The president of the Scripps Clinic Medical Group at this time (1981-91) was pathologist Dr. Robert Nakamura, who started his career at Scripps in 1967 as a researcher in William Weigle's lab. Dr. Robert Sarnoff, current medical group president, said of his predecessor:

> Bob was quality through and through. He oversaw the expansion and the development of most of the divisions here in the 1980s which was a real period of growth for our Clinic. The Anderson Outpatient Division was built in that time. The Green Hospital Heart Lung Vascular Surgery Center was built during that time, all under Bob's reign, so to speak. So, Bob was a real powerhouse, a very bright guy with a great sense of humor.
>
> He was Japanese and had been interned with his family in a camp in Arizona during World War II. And against all odds, he got into medical school. He was a tiger. I mean Bob was not somebody that you would take lightly, nor was Charlie Edwards. So I think that the interactions between the two of them were at times tumultuous.
>
> Dr. Edwards was a very interesting man. And Bob was wily and a character and it was sort of fun watching the two of them interact. But Bob was a real proponent of the Scripps Clinic Medical Group, a real defender, and a balance for Charlie.[19]

Dr. Richard Schatz[20] was an intern at Letterman Army Hospital in San Francisco in 1977 when he took the technology he learned in a research project at Duke University and became one of the first persons trained to do the *echocardiogram*, a test using sound waves to create a moving image of the heart. He said,

> Because of my research, I was one of only about three people in the world who knew how to actually do these things and interpret them. The very first commercial machines were coming out and no one knew how to use them. I actually talked my Chief of Medicine at Letterman into buying our first two-dimensional echo machine, and as an intern I read all the echos and founded the department, and did the same thing at UCSF.
>
> It was really exciting and that's where I felt the future was, until I discovered intervention.

In 1980, Dr. Schatz moved on as a fellow in cardiology to Brook Army Medical Center in San Antonio. Unusually, for a fellow, he was allowed to attend the very first Andreas Gruentzig Interventional Course in America in 1981. Dr. Andreas Gruentzig (1939-1985) was a German physician who did the first successful balloon angioplasty of a coronary artery in Zurich in 1977;[21] his course was thrilling. Dr. Schatz came back and told his chief, "Hey. We need to get into this intervention stuff."

> And that was pretty much the end of my echo career because I got excited about intervention and really liked being in the cath lab. So as a fellow in 1981 I started doing all the angioplasties for the group. And that's how it all started. Pretty soon I had the most experience of anyone in the city, so I went around town teaching people in the private sector.
>
> The battle then began with surgery versus angioplasty.

Coronary intervention at that point meant *angioplasty:* dilating narrowed arteries with balloons inserted via catheter and breaking up the plaque. This was an alternative to the CABG—pronounced "cabbage," or coronary artery bypass graft, which creates new routes around narrowed and blocked arteries with pieces of vein from the leg or with chest wall (internal mammary) arteries, allowing sufficient blood flow to the heart muscle. CABG requires open heart surgery; angioplasty does not.

The battle was a real one, because it wasn't clear that just stretching the arteries open was superior to bypass surgery; it was more convenient for the patients certainly, but frequently the ballooned arteries collapsed again. "So-called *acute closure* was very common: 10% of the patients would crash" (meaning the vessel closes, they have a heart attack and go to the operating room) "and then the *recurrence rate* was 30-40%" (meaning the vessel would close off later on).[22]

Dr. Schatz was still in the Army in San Antonio when he met the Argentine inventor-physician Dr. Julio Palmaz in 1985 at the Southwest Research Institute. The two teamed up to develop the first successful coronary artery stent—essentially modifying for coronary arteries 3-4 mm wide the prototype stent invented by Dr. Palmaz for larger vessels.[23]

The Palmaz-Schatz stent is a tiny, expandable stainless steel tube which holds coronary arteries open after angioplasty.[24] Closed it looks like a slotted silver tube, articulated to go around tight bends; opened, it resembles diamond-patterned mesh. Inserted into an artery clogged with plaque after a balloon has pushed the plaque to the side, the stent compresses the plaque further and holds the artery open.

By the time the Palmaz-Schatz stent was in clinical trials in 1988, the tremendously energetic Dr. Paul Teirstein arrived at Scripps Clinic after multiple cardiac fellowships at Stanford, Mid-America Heart Institute in Kansas City, Missouri, and the NIH, to initiate a program in coronary intervention. He was recruited by Dr. Johnson for his new Heart, Lung and Vascular Center. Dr. Johnson said of Dr. Teirstein that "he was young, ambitious and had vision, and could handle the emotional stress of angioplasty at that time. He also saw that the future was the stent."

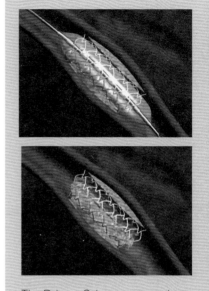

The Palmaz-Schatz stent was the first successful coronary artery stent—a tiny, expandable stainless steel tube that holds coronary arteries open after angioplasty.
courtesy of Scripps Health

Dr. Paul Teirstein was recruited to Scripps Clinic by Dr. Allan Johnson for the Heart, Lung and Vascular Center. Left to right, Dr. Teirstein discusses the new advances in cardiac care with Dr. Richard Schatz.
courtesy of Scripps Health

Center front, Mother Teresa received lifesaving cardiac care in 1991 at Scripps Clinic from, left to right, Drs. Paul Teirstein, Larry Kline, and Patricia Aubanel. Mother Teresa was able to receive the Palmaz-Schatz stent because Scripps Clinic was the only clinical trial center on the West coast with access to the device.

courtesy of Scripps Health

Innovative heart treatment for Mother Teresa

When Dr. Schatz left the Army after fourteen years, he took the post of director of the Arizona Heart Institute in Phoenix; and in 1990, when he had had enough of the heat in Arizona, he came to San Diego to interview at Sharp, which had up-to-date cardiologists, but old labs. He then toured the gleaming new labs at Scripps Clinic at the invitation of Dr. Teirstein and signed a contract. The stent was then for experimental use and by strict protocol only and specifically not for emergencies. But the day after Christmas 1991, Mother Teresa of Calcutta appeared at the door of Scripps Clinic with a failing heart.

The Clinic's first fellow in Interventional Cardiology had been the young Mexican physician, Dr. Patricia Aubanel, who now had a cardiac clinic in Tijuana and was attending Mother Teresa at the house there of her Missionaries of Charity. Mother Teresa had been in Tijuana for two weeks, on the last stop of a worldwide visitation to her communities, and became increasingly ill. She resisted treatment and the inevitable publicity. But Dr. Aubanel prevailed and reportedly tucked Mother Teresa into an ambulance bound for Scripps Clinic, alongside a Tijuana dignitary who was having a heart attack himself—so that reporters were distracted by the VIP they knew and did not discover the little nun on the adjacent gurney until later on.

Dr. Teirstein was on-call while Dr. Schatz celebrated the holidays with his family. Dr. Teirstein describes what happened:[25]

> Mother Teresa came in with coronary ischemia and congestive heart failure and pneumonia. She had low blood pressure and could hardly breathe. I did a cardiac catheterization with Patricia Aubanel and found three-vessel coronary disease. Two lesions responded well to balloon angioplasty, which was the standard of the time. (Mother

Teresa was much too sick for bypass surgery.) Her left anterior descending artery opened with the balloon angioplasty but the result was suboptimal, with an unstable "dissected" appearance. Therefore I used a Palmaz–Schatz stent to stabilize the blockage.

At that time, the stent was only available as part of a research trial. Thankfully, Scripps was the one center on the west coast with access to the stent. The procedure was very successful and I could tell the international news team, which by then had gathered in our large auditorium:

'All of us, including Mother Teresa, are breathing easier today.'

Another vital member of Mother Teresa's medical team was pulmonologist and critical care specialist Dr. Larry Kline, who was treating her pneumonia in lungs already ravaged by old tuberculosis–but he first had to persuade his patient to stay and accept care. Dr. Kline, who is Jewish, later told a convocation in Philadelphia that when he first met Mother Teresa she was trying to leave the hospital against medical advice; and he told her that if she left without treatment, it "'would interfere with her ability to do God's will," and that God was taking care of her by having her brought to the hospital for the medicine, which was also a gift from God. "Oh," Mother Teresa sighed, "don't bring Him into this." But she turned around and went back to bed.[26]

The fellowship in interventional cardiology, which eventually led to the preservation a little longer of Mother Teresa in this world, was part of a program in Graduate Medical Education at Scripps Clinic founded by Dr. Stanley Freedman and taken over by oncologist Dr. Michael Kosty when his predecessor stepped down. The fellowships (for physicians who had completed residencies elsewhere) came first in 1980; these were followed in 1987 by the residencies themselves, three-year rotations in internal medicine now under the direction of Dr. Joel Diamant.

Both programs have been hugely successful in terms of national ranking of applicants and in providing a steady stream of highly competent young physicians back into the Scripps Health system and the larger community. As of this writing, there are more than 30 sub-specialty fellows enrolled every year in 16 fellowship categories, 36 regular medical residents and 28 to 30 Navy residents rotating in, along with third-and fourth- year medical student "sub-interns"—all keeping clinicians and faculty, including the late and much beloved Dr. Philip Higginbottom (1947-2010),[27] at the top of their game.

A fellow in interventional cardiology after Dr. Aubanel was Dr. Erminia "Mimi" Guarneri,[28] who would ultimately found the Scripps Center for Integrative Medicine. Dr. Gaurneri had been raised in Brooklyn in a large, extended Italian family by an uncle who was a family physician with an office at home. She said:

Dr. Erminia "Mimi" Guarneri founded the Scripps Center for Integrative Medicine in 1999. *courtesy of Scripps Health*

My concept of medicine was one in which everyone is connected, family is connected, people are connected. It was very personal, not technological at all. I had a natural connection to people and healing and wanted to serve in that way.

After three years in cardiology at New York University— Bellevue Hospital, Dr. Guarneri was accepted in 1994 to the interventional fellowship of Drs. Teirstein and Schatz at Scripps Clinic— and during her first year at Scripps found herself in the gratifying situation of training her mentors from Bellevue, who flew out to La Jolla to learn to use the Palmaz-Schatz stent. Dr. Guarneri ultimately placed thousands of stents and had the opportunity when she finished her fellowship to go many other places. But she chose to stay at Scripps Clinic:

because the Clinic was pioneering. It was the first in everything. If there was a new stent we got it. If there was a new drug to trial, a new device, we were the first to get it. It was exciting to be at the front end of everything that was happening in cardiac care from an intervention side.

But at the same time, Dr. Guarneri began to realize that this mechanical fix was not really a permanent cure for cardiovascular disease—that it was addressing a small section of the vessel as opposed to the entire human being, and "we were really doing nothing for prevention of heart disease and chronic disease management.

And just as I was looking at that, I was asked by Paul Teirstein to participate as a principal investigator with Dr. Dean Ornish in a research study to look at whether or not we can reverse heart disease through diet and exercise, yoga and meditation.

I felt that this was not at all my paradigm. I wasn't competent in it. And to his credit, Paul said to me, "This is important work. I don't have the time to do it, so I'm asking you to do this study."

So Mimi Guarneri made her way to the Claremont Hotel in Berkeley, California, for a week-long retreat with hundreds of heart patients learning lifestyle change, and what she discovered would change her work profoundly in the decade to come and lead to the founding of the renowned Scripps Center for Integrative Medicine in 1999.

As to the basic science arm of the institution, when Dr. Edwards took over as CEO of Scripps Clinic Medical Institutions in 1977, acting CEO Frank Dixon gave up those particular reins, but continued on as director of what was still called the Scripps Clinic Research Foundation after the re-organization of SCRF. By all accounts, relations between these two brilliant and ambitious men were strained from the beginning.

For one thing, Dr. Edwards—still envisioning the Mayo Clinic model—pressed Dr. Dixon to build scientific ties between the research and clinical sides of the Scripps organization, but Dr. Dixon was first and last a scientist and had no interest in the clinical side, nor in teaching, which he had made clear from the beginning.

Dr. Edwards wrote:

> [But finally Dr.] Dixon agreed to recruit a key scientific investigator with more clinically related interests. In 1978, Ernest Beutler joined the team. He began to build a thriving program in molecular and experimental medicine – which later spilled back over into the clinical side helping to establish centers of excellence in fields such as bone marrow transplantation. Today the Scripps marrow transplant center [now under James Mason] is one of the most outstanding in the nation.[29]

But Dr. Clifford Colwell, who moved to Scripps Clinic from Scripps Memorial at Dr. Edwards' invitation, had this to say:

> Working with Dr. Edwards all these years, I think he was greatly disappointed by his inability to get the research and the clinical more integrated. He could not do that with the personalities he had to face. And I shared the disappointment. One of the reasons I left Scripps Memorial for the Clinic was to interrelate, to combine a clinical practice with world-class research. But we were never able to pull that off to the degree we hoped.[30]

In 1986, Dr. Dixon stepped down as director of the Research Foundation, and Dr. Edwards chaired the search committee that chose his replacement: Dr. Richard Alan Lerner.

Dr. Lerner was already at Scripps as chair of the department of Molecular Biology and was a towering personality who—as Dr. Edwards said:

> not only possessed a brilliant scientific mind, but also the unusual ability to digest information about almost any scientific topic. He understood science and the direction science was going. He thought big—and he had an uncanny ability to identify scientific talent.[31]

Dr. Charles Cochrane elaborated:

> Richard has two main attributes as I see it. One is that he is able to determine where research in various areas is going and so, therefore, to look beyond borders and do research to make the quickest steps into the future.

Dr. Richard Alan Lerner replaced Dr. Frank Dixon as director of the Research Institute of Scripps Clinic in 1986. *courtesy of Scripps Health*

And the other is recruiting people in those areas, K. C. Nicolaou, Ian Wilson, Peter Wright and others, and Gerry Edelman (1972 Nobel Prize in Physiology or Medicine for the structure of antibodies), bringing him in. So that he's able to penetrate into the darkness of the future with not only ideas but with people. And that's made The Research Institute boom.[32]

Dr. Lerner grew up in Chicago, the son of an oral surgeon, and was interested in science from the beginning. As a teenager he did chemistry at the University of Chicago on his summer breaks from high school. He attended Northwestern because it was close by and after three years left for Stanford University School of Medicine, which had just at that time (1959) moved from its old downtown San Francisco home to Palo Alto—the result of which was that the medical school had almost no community patients and was trying out a five-year program that allowed their students to do externships in other hospitals around the country halftime. Dr. Lerner explained:

> Basically at Stanford in those days, you learned about lupus and Hodgkin's disease. That's what they had. I mean, I probably saw five hundred cases of Hodgkin's disease and God knows how many kids with lupus, but nothing else.

So Stanford medical student Richard Lerner spent half his time back home in Chicago as a lifeguard on Chicago beaches during the day (perhaps not exactly what Stanford had in mind) and an extern at Cook County Hospital at night. About the latter, Dr. Lerner said:

> I don't think anyone in my class ever saw a fracture, ever saw a myocardial infarction. But I had seen it all in Cook County anyway, in spades.

> I was actually sort of an aide to the interns. And what that really meant in those days — and wouldn't happen today - is you did procedures, because they needed an extra pair of hands. So as an extern I learned how to do all kinds of things, spinal taps and draining cardiac tamponade. You would go on rounds and you'd see everything.

About medicine, Dr. Lerner said:

> I actually thought that I would go to medical school to be a practicing physician. But I soon realized that I wasn't very interested in that.

I admired the guys I went on rounds with at Cook County. But my problem with clinical medicine was that if you knew the answer, sort of everybody else knew it too. And if you didn't, nobody knew it. To me that wasn't very interesting.

I wanted to know things that other people didn't know.

As a medical student, Dr. Lerner also used his half-time "coupons" to go other places, including to Georgetown to work with nephrologist Dr. George Schreiner, which path would then lead directly on to Scripps Clinic. Georgetown Hospital was the opposite of Cook County in that externs were not allowed to touch the patients:

and I basically didn't have anything to do. So I decided to go to the library and learn everything there was to learn about kidney disease by reading, indiscriminately, every article in the *Journal of Clinical Investigations* about kidney disease. But I only read the physiology, you know, the salt and water stuff. So when we would go on rounds, George Schreiner would ask questions and I was the only one who knew the answers because the poor guys who were up all night taking care of these terribly sick patients didn't have the privilege of going and sitting in a library all day. And I didn't have to take care of these people because I couldn't, because I didn't have a degree. And so I knew everything there was to know and they knew nothing because they were there to take care of the patients.

But then one day it turned out that there was a patient with immunologically based nephritis. And this guy asked me if I knew anything about Frank Dixon's work. And I didn't. So I went and read it. And that's when I decided to come out here.

So Dr. Lerner came to Scripps Clinic in 1964, right before medical school graduation, to interview for a job with one of the world's leading immunopathologists, and he wore his National Guard uniform because the Viet Nam war was heating up and soldiers could fly for half-price. In 1965, he became Dr. Dixon's fellow, and within a short time Drs. Dixon and Lerner were the first to transfer an autoimmune disease from man to a primate—which settled an argument between the West Coast and the East Coast nephrology crowd. Dr. Lerner said:

That was published in the *Journal of Experimental Medicine* in 1966[33] and was the most important thing I did with Frank.

By the time Dr. Lerner took over twenty years later as director of SCRF, he was chairman of molecular biology and ready to return to his first love, chemistry (which was never a research department under Dr. Dixon). As soon as Dr. Lerner took over, the push for a Department of Chemistry began and was funded by ingenious and multimillion dollar agreements with industry, agreeing to "first right of refusal" for promising compounds. Suddenly the Research Institute had money of its own, was no longer dependent on patient care at the Clinic, and would never be dependent again.

Dr. Lerner's simple goal for the Research Institute was to be the best in the world. And to do that he used "the only competitive advantage we had"—without the massive endowments of Harvard and MIT—which was "the ability to create critical mass because we were not governed by an academic center." He only hired the top scientists in their field, and if there were four or five "best," he tried to hire them all.

A direct consequence of the emergence of the Department of Chemistry was the arrival at the Research Foundation for the first time of graduate students. The Founding Five immunopathologists from Pittsburgh had always had "post-docs," but Dr. Lerner said:

> You can't have a chemistry program without students. The work of the chemistry world is done mostly by graduate students.
>
> The final outcome of a piece of chemistry is wonderful. But it's a lot of factory kind of stuff in between. That's the *quid pro quo* in chemistry, you know: you want the labor and you teach.

Fortunately for prospective students, one of Dr. Lerner's first recruits after taking over the Research Foundation in 1986 was Dr. Norton B. "Bernie" Gilula (1944-2000), who came to found and chair the Department of Cell Biology. Dr. Gilula's vision was a graduate program recognizing that "most of the important problems in biology and chemistry today require an interdisciplinary approach to their solutions." And in 1989 SCRF established a unique graduate program—later called the Kellogg School of Science and Technology—to help integrate the disciplines of biology and chemistry, with Dr. Gilula as founding dean.[34] Dr. Cochrane observed:

> The graduate school started and that was a marvelous thing. And within not too long a time it became, according to the *U. S. News and World Report*, one of the best places for graduate students in protein chemistry and biochemistry and so forth in the country, along with MIT and Harvard and Yale and Stanford and UC Berkeley. The *Manchester Guardian* in one of its reviews called it the best place for protein chemistry in the world. And they were fifty miles from Cambridge.[35]

In that same year, 1989, SCRF acquired another 21 acres of land east across Torrey Pines Road to cope with its expanding size.[36]

Scripps Green Hospital opened in 1977 on the Torrey Pines mesa as part of the new Scripps Clinic complex, which also included the research institution   *courtesy of Scripps Health*

But Dr. Edwards was also coping with continuous change in the world of health care and the once-seamless relationship with HCA began to fray. Dr. Edwards wrote:

> While we worked successfully with HCA until 1991, the field of for-profit hospitals was becoming big business. HCA re-emerged as a public company in 1992 and was acquired by Columbia Hospital Corporation in 1994. The firm's focus shifted from providing quality care to boosting its stock price.[37]

So Scripps Clinic began to look around for another partner, and in 1991 rediscovered the one it had divorced forty-three years before when they were both young and restless on Prospect Street.

St. Joseph's and Mercy Hospital/Medical Center
Sister Administrators 1890-1983[1]

Mother Mary Michael Cummings	1890–1922
Sister Mary Angela Cooney	1922–1923
Sister Mary Liguori McNamara	1923–1929
Sister Mary Angela Cooney	1929–1932
Sister Mary Thomas Shanley	1932–1938
Sister Mary Beatrice Malone	1938–1944
Sister Mary Leonard Fahey	1944–1956
Sister Mary Eucharia Malone	1956–1965
Sister Mary Placida Conant	1965–1977 Executive Director 1972–1977★
Sister Mary Jo Anderson	1968–1972 Assistant Administrator
Sister Mary Joanne De Vincenti	1977–1983 Executive Director 1977–1983★
Sister Mary Jo Anderson	1979–1983 Assistant Administrator/VP

★During terms of the executive directors, Mr. Ed Hertfelder was appointed administrator.

In the 1920s, the Mercy Hospital campus overlooked Mission Valley. An aerial view of the hospital in 1927 reveals the north wing, which was added in 1926. *courtesy of Scripps Health*

CHAPTER ELEVEN

Mercy Hospital

1924-1985

THE LONGEST-SERVING CHIEF EXECUTIVE in Scripps Health history was Mother Mary Michael Cummings, who led the entire St. Joseph's community—hospital, convalescent home, convent, and nurses—for thirty-two years until the day she died. The founder was nearly an entire executive team unto herself, as we know it today, with the exception of chief medical officer and general counsel. She was certainly chief financial officer, strategic planner, chief of development and human resources, not to mention local superior and mistress of novices, and had incidentally built another hospital in Oxnard (St. John's) in 1912.

After Mother Mary Michael's death in 1922, with the change of the corporate title from St. Joseph's to Mercy Hospital in May 1924 and the opening of the new fireproof hospital in November of that year, a rolling documentary would show the Sisters of Mercy in slow procession through the roaring twenties, the Great Depression, the serious work of the Second World War, and the postwar relief and boom. For ninety-three years, the chief executives are nuns.

Ultimately, the final change to lay leadership in 1983 occurs because of profound changes in the religious community itself, beginning with the reforming Second Vatican Council of 1962-65 which, as one historian put it, "blew the hinges off" the convent doors.[2] There is a diversion in the stream of bright young Catholic women away from the cloister toward all the opening doors of the wider world.

Until 1968, the Sisters of Mercy wear the familiar black habit falling in folds from the throat to the feet, with the white, starched half-moon bib called the *guimpe*, long black veil, leather cincture, and rosary with ebony cross—except in direct patient care, when they wear pristine, soft, and easily washable white. Then, in 1968, the familiar begins to shift. Sister Mary Placida Conant appears in an A-line navy blue dress several inches off the floor, with a practical Velcroed apron, white cap, and short black veil. And even though Sister Mary Placida keeps her name in religion, others do not. Some who have been in religious life for more than fifty years take back the names they shed at the convent door. Liberation from the rule even prompts some Sisters of Mercy to leave their community and seek a new spirituality elsewhere. In the 1960s and '70s, upheaval is the norm.

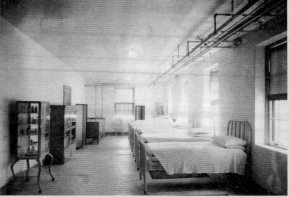

With the completion of the new six-story hospital in 1924, St. Joseph's became Mercy Hospital. Left, Mercy Hospital had a state-of-the-art dietetic lab. Bottom, left to right, the Sisters of Mercy kept detailed records in the record room, and the demonstration room was used to help train health care workers.

courtesy of Scripps Health

In 1925, The U.S. Navy Hospital Band played at Mercy Hospital. Most Navy dependents were treated at the hospital, resulting in it becoming one of the busiest hospitals in the nation during World War II. Today, Navy medical residents and nurses in San Diego receive emergency and trauma care training during rotations at the hospital. *courtesy of Scripps Health*

But to return to earlier days, even in the 1920s change was nearly constant, except for the steadying presence of Mother Mary Michael. The state of medical science was advancing rapidly and surgeon Dr. Clarence Rees (who later organized San Diego's first multispecialty clinic in 1923 with internist Dr. Clair Stealy) led staff development at St. Joseph's Hospital to its status as the first hospital west of the Mississippi to obtain accreditation by the American College of Surgeons in 1921. The Sisters of Mercy determined from the beginning to require the highest standards of their staff physicians. At the end of World War I, Dr. James F. Churchill arrived in San Diego as the city's first fully-trained internist; he gradually founded Internal Medicine Associates with physicians of the same caliber and served as Mercy Chief of Staff in 1925. Similarly, the first board-certified surgeon, Dr. A. E. Mills, established what would become Hillcrest Surgery in the next decade.

Meanwhile in 1921, the separate communities of Sisters of Mercy in Arizona and in San Diego, Los Angeles, and San Francisco, had voted to "amalgamate" under one rule—which ultimately explains why Mother Mary Michael's first successor did not last long in that role. When Mother Mary Michael died unexpectedly in October 1922, her shoes were filled temporarily by her nurse–assistant, Sister Mary Angela Cooney, who joined the San Diego community in 1901 and was among the first ten graduates (all nuns) of St. Joseph's School of Nursing in 1906. But as second administrator of St. Joseph's Hospital, she served only months. The following summer of 1923, the leadership of the amalgamated communities sent Sister Mary Angela to Oxnard to take over St. John's Hospital and brought Sister Mary Liguori McNamara to San Diego in her place. It was Sister Mary Liguori who established the corporate name Mercy Hospital and opened the welcoming new doors in 1924. (But Sister Mary Angela would be back.)

Mercy Hospital was built in the Mediterranean Revival style—a popular architectural style in the 1920s that reflected the Italian and Moorish influences of the Mediterranean coast. The 200-bed hospital opened in 1924 as a single central building. Two wings were added later in the decade.

courtesy of Scripps Health

The campus that evolved in the 1920s on what was then called 5th Street and Hillcrest Drive[3] (today's Fifth Avenue and Washington) was quite beautiful on its promontory overlooking Mission Valley. The six-story hospital with its back along a great slope was in the Mediterranean Revival style first popularized in the 1920s and reflecting the architectural influences of the Mediterranean coast—Italian and also Moorish themes from Southern Spain.[4] The baroque decoration can still be seen today in two historic buildings from 1926: the old Convent and the Mercy College of Nursing in peach-colored stucco with decorative tiles, twisted columns, and carved friezes of blossoms and shells, along the edge of Lewis Street overlooking the canyon. (The Chapel adjacent to the Convent is congruent in style but newer, 1950, and then the real outlier architecturally is the 1960s-era Mercy Manor apartments for interns and residents that were VERY popular during the thirty or so years the house staff lived there, according to senior physicians who were in training at the time.[5] After the last nurse graduated in 1970, the College of Nursing was used for a few years as offices, a senior center, and the medical library and is now empty, with historic property designation. But the other Lewis Street buildings have had a new lease on life: house staff departed the Manor in about 1990, when they were making enough money to rent elsewhere; the remaining Sisters moved over from the Convent, which needed renovation, to the Manor; and then the Convent was gutted and transformed into Mercy Gardens, a complex of 22 affordable apartments for persons living with AIDS.)

The villa-like 1924 hospital opened as only the single central building with 200 beds[6]—making it four times the size of Miss Ellen's new hospital by the sea in La Jolla—and it expanded as money came in. A north and south wing were part of the original design, built out in 1926 and 1929 respectively, the latter with a $300,000 bequest from John Spreckels. Formal lawns bordered all sides of Fifth Avenue, which was extended to curve along the canyon rim and terminate at the hospital entrance, so that the approach was similar to that of a fine hotel. Carefully tended roses, shrubs, and trees appeared through the first decades until eliminated by the insatiable need for parking.

Much of what we know about this era of Mercy San Diego comes from the nearly anonymous writings of a nun who went by the religious name of Sister Mary Aurelia until about 1970, when she returned to her given name of Rose McArdle. Sister Rose, then known as Sister Mary Aurelia, professed her vows in 1929 and was a history teacher and assistant principal of Marian High School, fifteen miles south in Imperial Beach, from 1960-69. It was during the decade at Marian High that Sister Aurelia/ Rose apparently made her way back and forth to Mercy Hospital to assemble the three separate documents called *The Sisters of Mercy in San Diego; Factual History of Mercy Hospital San Diego;* and a long untitled "Thermofax," which begins with Junipero Serra in 1769 and goes on to give us names and dates of the Sister administrators compiled at the beginning of this chapter. Mercy San Diego, like all the other houses of the order, assigned one Sister at a time to keep a memorable events log called *Annals,* which was apparently the raw material for Rose McArdle's work. Later, Sister Rose came to live at Mercy San Diego (1983-88)[7] and provided more living history by writing to prominent senior physicians and requesting their memoirs.

Until 1968, the Sisters of Mercy wore long black habits with white, half-moon bibs, long black veils, and leather cinctures. A rosary with an ebony cross was also part of the habit.

courtesy of Scripps Health

This letter is from "the genteel and soft-spoken"[8] surgeon Dr. Maurice J. Brown, who was President of the San Diego County Medical Society in 1956. It deserves to be printed nearly in its entirety and suggests why the elegant old hospital would eventually have to come down:

> Jan 2, 1988
> Dear Sister Rose McArdle:
>
> After St. Joseph's Hospital had passed its usefulness the first Mercy Hospital was built on the present site a number of years ago. This was soon outgrown and a wing was added at each end. This was the configuration of the hospital when I arrived in San Diego on August 1, 1941. At that time Dr. Brownell, a member of the staff, stabled his riding horses at the site of the present Mercy Clinic.
>
> The Old Mercy held a place of affection in my heart because it was here that I first began a surgical practice as an assistant to the late Dr. Clarence E. Rees. I had recently completed a five-year surgical residency at the University of California hospital, San Francisco, in addition to my year's internship. It was at the Old Mercy that I got

the real feel of the private practice of surgery. It was here that I had many surgical triumphs and some errors that haunt me to this day.

The old building was not ornate. In fact it was rather austere. It had one small central passenger elevator which served the lower level and seven floors above. A utility self-operated elevator large enough to hold a gurney or a bed was present at either end of the building.

The large wards had no bathrooms. Most of the private area had one bath placed between two rooms to serve each of them. Bedpans used by the ward patients had to be carried by the nurses along the hallways to closet-like areas where the pans were emptied and sterilized.

Operating rooms were devoid of x-ray equipment and monitoring apparatus… [and] until well after World War II most anesthesia was given by nurse anesthetists or general practitioners who had an interest in anesthesia.

During the late '30s and '40s Mercy Hospital was instrumental in raising the standards of surgical practice. With support of the sisters and primarily through the work of Dr. Clarence E. Rees and Dr. Joe O'Hara, unqualified doctors were prohibited from operating at Mercy. In addition, several doctors were dropped from the staff for questionable or unethical practice.

After World War II, tremendous strides were made in the practice of medicine. In this area Mercy was a leader… due in no small measure to the far-seeing cooperation of the medical staff and the Sisters, especially to Sister Alexine in surgery…[who] kept the nurses and staff under excellent control but maintained their respect and admiration. Much of Mercy's high standards in surgery are due to Sister Alexine.

Until the late '40s there was no blood bank. Those needing blood were serviced by friends or relatives who were brought to the hospital for matching. In this period much of the matching was done by the surgeon himself. Severe chills and fever was commonplace in those days during and after the transfusion.

There were no recovery rooms till the early '50s. Following surgery the patient was taken to the floor and attended by a private nurse if he could afford one. Otherwise he was watched over by a maid or student nurse during this critical period. Intensive care areas were not in existence in those early days.

Although the Old Mercy had many deficiencies compared with the Mercy of today, I look back on those days with a feeling of warmth and respect. Each floor was supervised by a devoted sister who held up high standards of care and maintained an atmosphere of "Reverence to God." The devotion of these women has been an inspiration to me over the years.

Sincerely, Maurice J. Brown, MD (Retired)

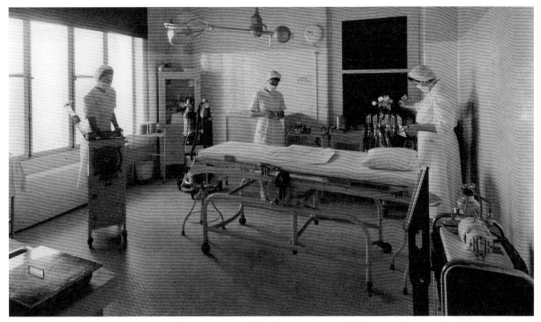

Nurses prepare the operating room for surgery in 1942. During the late 1930s and through the 1940s, Mercy Hospital was instrumental in raising the standards for surgery. *courtesy of San Diego History Center*

Sister Mary Alexine Shea was Operating Room supervisor for thirty-six years from the end of WWII (1945-1981) and had a legion of admirers who were all good surgeons by definition, because she did not tolerate any other kind. The former Katie Shea of Jerome, Arizona, was "feisty and fearless with deep blue sparkling eyes" and was tremendously intimidating, despite her average size; she would get a hapless doctor in the corner and "just give him what for."[9] Her reputation for being "tough and tolerating no nonsense" preceded her, according to the young Dr. Anita Figueredo, who came to operate on cancer patients at Mercy in 1948, but "once it was established that you were competent, she became your good friend."[10]

Among the Sisters of Mercy it was highly unusual to stay in one place for a whole career, and a directive came out at one point to transfer Sister Mary Alexine, "but the doctors made such a fuss, they left her there"[11] until her retirement in 1981—after which Sister Alexine continued to live at the Hospital Convent and volunteered at the information desk until her death in 1990.[12] (An excellent portrait of Sister Alexine by surgeon Dr. George Zorn, Sr., who operated with her through nearly his whole career, hangs in the Scripps Mercy Administration Conference Room.)

Sister Mary Alexine Shea served as supervisor of the operating room for more than thirty-six years. Intolerant of incompetence in her operating room, Sister Mary Alexine was a steadfast friend once a colleague earned her respect.

courtesy of Scripps Health

Top, officers of the USS Bennington, anchored in San Diego Harbor. Middle, in 1905, a boiler explosion on the gunboat caused San Diego's first catastrophic trauma emergency. Bottom, the explosion sent dozens of sailors to the then-named St. Joseph's Hospital, where the Sisters of Mercy signed them in for treatment, primarily of burns.

courtesy of San Diego History Center

From long before the Second World War, one of the great professional relationships in San Diego had been between Mercy and the Naval Hospital—two of the "three large hospitals which form a triangle around Hillcrest."[13] The first Naval Hospital in Balboa Park (1922) antedated Mercy by two years and was built in a similar grand style with an initial capacity of 250 beds. But the professional respect between the two authorities dated back to July 1905 when the gunboat *USS Bennington* exploded in San Diego Harbor, leaving 60 dead and 47 injured:

> On the following day an out-of-town newspaper (probably San Francisco) delivered an editorial which read in part: *Sisters of Mercy … have served on many a battlefield and are ever willing workers when the cry of pain comes from the men who guard the Nation's flag. St. Joseph's Sanitarium in San Diego did its full duty to the gallant jackies of the Bennington.*"[14]

As early as 1927, a formal arrangement began with the Naval Hospital to send house staff to Mercy for training. The founding rotation was six weeks in obstetrics and gynecology. This apparently transpired with the nod of a veiled head, because in 1929 Sister Mary Angela (who had taken over once again from Sr. Mary Liguori) reported that she had no written agreement with the Navy. Soon after, a letter arrived from Captain A. J. Geiger of the Naval Hospital appointing an officer who met with his counterpart, Mercy Chief of Staff Dr. Charles Fox, to define the internship program. (One of the instructions was that they were under the direct supervision of the Mother Superior.)

The arrangement expanded to a Mercy–Navy outpatient clinic and pediatric clinic under Commander John E. Porter, USN, with three other Navy doctors on duty. And the Sisters also traveled the other way. An entry in the *Annals* for 1932 reads:

> … the US Naval Hospital has 1200 beds divided into forty bed wards. It has no resident chaplain and the Sisters of Mercy are the only religious of any denomination that are allowed to visit the patients. The Sisters call weekly, stopping at each bed, cheering and encouraging …

In 1934, the Surgeon General of the Navy, Rear Admiral P. S. Rossiter, steamed into San Diego Harbor with a flotilla of twenty-eight ships, inspected the facilities offered at Mercy for the care of Navy dependents and stated that "the service at Mercy was highly pleasing and satisfactory to the Navy, and he hoped it was equally satisfactory to Mercy." The goodwill extended to landscaping, with a Navy gardener, Mr. Crofts, sharing a great many shrubs, plants, flowers, and trees with his Mercy friend, Sister Mary Gabriel.

The Navy-Mercy partnership continued during WWII when Mercy Hospital became one of the busiest civilian hospitals in America. According to one account:

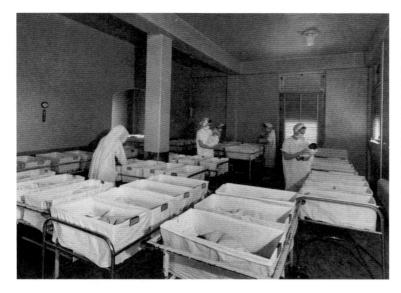

The nursery was busy at Mercy Hospital. By 1940, the hospital was delivering 250 babies a month and was caring for seventy-five newborns every day. Between 1946 and 1950, Mercy Hospital delivered 21,383 babies—more than any other hospital west of the Mississippi River.

courtesy of San Diego History Center

Mercy learned the meaning of the term "Baby Boom" long before the rest of the country. By 1940, the hospital was delivering 250 babies a month and caring for as many as 75 newborns a day. The March 28, 1942 issue of the *American Medical Association Journal* included the following assessment: "The organization and physical equipment of Mercy Hospital's obstetrical department is surpassed nowhere in the United States. Each nursery is a dream of cleanliness, efficiency and the latest equipment. In 1941, there were 2670 births and only four maternal deaths; in 1940, 2569 with two maternal deaths. The latter figure, in point of maternal deaths, is a national record."[15]

A leading Navy doctor wrote to the San Diego Board of Supervisors, "… without Mercy Hospital it would have been impossible for the Navy Medical Department to have granted medical care to Navy dependents."[16]

When the war ended, the Naval Hospital had become the largest in the world with more than 10,000 beds, and could now care for its own dependents;[17] its obstetrical program at Mercy came to an end in 1946, after nearly twenty years.

But before the war, the AMA had given Mercy Hospital approval for a civilian graduate medical education program, and in 1946, as Navy trainees left, the first civilian interns arrived. Residencies followed: pathology and OB-GYN in 1948; surgery and internal medicine in 1949, giving Mercy the oldest graduate medical education program in San Diego. (Anesthesia and orthopedics came later, in 1964 and 1965; and in 1967, the new UCSD Medical School began rotating students through Mercy.)

In the beginning, the program appears to have been run by the some of the most admired of Mercy's private physicians, including *Internal Medicine Associates* who mentored young physicians at the hospital and in their private offices. One of these,

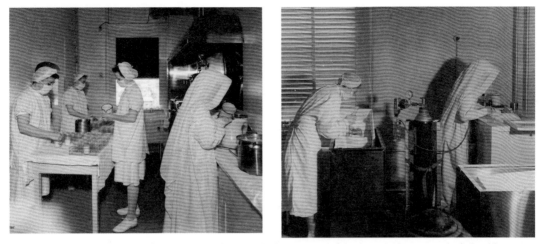

The obstetrical department at Mercy Hospital in the 1940s was one of the best in the nation. Left, health care workers, including the Sisters, prepare and mix formula for the nursery. Right, staff at Mercy Hospital provided individualized care for infants.

courtesy of San Diego History Center

Dr. Donald Landale, arrived in San Diego to stay in 1955 (after a detour through the Korean War) and was instrumental in setting up and steering the Internal Medicine Training Program.[18] He and pulmonologist Dr. Woodbury Perkins, who was director of Medical Education 1964-85, chose the first full-time program director in Internal Medicine, the superbly ambidextrous tennis player and endocrinologist, Dr. Jack Geller, who served from 1970-1993. Director of surgical GME for most of that same period, 1971-1988, was thoracic surgeon Dr. Max J. Trummer who had been Chief of Cardiothoracic Surgery at the Naval Hospital. Under these men and their successors and all of the dedicated attending physicians they chose, the GME program at Mercy became what it is today: annually at San Diego and Chula Vista, there are 79 residents (internal medicine, family medicine, "transitional" to surgery subspecialties, and podiatry) in three class years, as well as fellowship collaborations with the Navy, with Scripps Green, with UCSD, and a Palliative Care Fellowship with San Diego Hospice. The residencies at Scripps Mercy are famous for being "hands-on" and for turning out young physicians who are tremendously experienced and confident: the internal medicine residents have had a 100 percent pass rate on their Board examination for the past 16 years, the best in the nation.[19]

The current overall director of medical education at Scripps Mercy is Dr. David Shaw, who was a member of the cohort of top young cardiologists who came to San Diego in the early 70s as fellows under Dr. Eugene Braunwald at the University of California, San Diego; he "followed Skip Johnson by one year, and preceded Guy Curtis by two," before coming to Mercy under Dr. John Mazur. Dr. Stanley Amundson, who was himself a resident at Mercy from 1973-77, is successor to Jack Geller as internal medicine residency program director.[20]

Dr. Roy Tanaka with his wife, Nobu, c. 1979. Dr. Tanaka co-founded the Guadalupe Clinic in Barrio Logan in 1944, where physicians volunteered to provide care to underserved residents of the area.
courtesy of Tanaka Family

But to return one last time to World War II: Dr. Roy Tanaka was a respected general practitioner at Mercy Hospital at the time of the bombing of Pearl Harbor, and one of the sadder stories of the war was the "relocation" of San Diego's *Nikkei* community (that is, persons with any discernible degree of Japanese ancestry) away from the coast to internment camps in the remote interior. In San Diego, Order Number Four of the Western Defense Command authorized the removal of all persons of Japanese ancestry residing in the area from south of Del Mar to the Mexican border on April 8, 1942. Once rounded up, the first contingent traveled by rail to their initial "assembly center" at Santa Anita Racetrack in Arcadia, Calif. There they sat four months until August 26, when they "were once again lined up and loaded onto trains…with armed guards and drawn shades." Most were unloaded in the melting heat of Parker, Arizona—except for Dr. Roy Tanaka who was sent to the relocation center at Jerome, Arkansas, because of a shortage of doctors there,[21] along with his pregnant wife, young daughters, a sister, and her husband. Some months later, his son, Laurence, who would grow up to be a Mercy surgeon—was born at Jerome Receiving Hospital. (Francis Tanaka, Roy's brother and later partner in general practice, was the youngest of ten children and not a physician until the 1950s; he was in Hawaii with his parents.)[22]

In a 1979 interview, Dr. Roy Tanaka said that he had been forced to leave his practice and his position on the staff of Mercy Hospital but that "the hospital administrator"—presumably Sister Mary Beatrice Malone—"wrote to him at Jerome and informed him that [she] merely considered him to be on an 'extended leave of absence.'" Dr. Tanaka was welcomed back to Mercy as soon as he returned in 1944 and still had the energy and reserved goodwill to co-found the Guadalupe Clinic in Barrio Logan within months of his return.[23]

With Father Francis Kern of Our Lady of Guadalupe Church, Dr. Tanaka and Dr. Thomas O'Connell set up a single room clinic for the hard-pressed of Logan Heights under supervision of the Missionary Sisters of Our Lady of Victory.[24] Physicians from Mercy, including interns and residents, once the graduate medical education program was under way, donated their services.

Regarding charitable care, before the war, of course, there had been the stock market crash of 1929 and the onset of a grinding depression. Although the Sisters of Mercy had always provided care to the poor, need exploded. In 1935, a general clinic was organized, and that year two hundred indigent patients were admitted to Mercy

Hospital through the Clinic. All ethnic groups were served; the superintendent of the State Indian Agency said in a local address, "The biggest charity given the Indians anywhere in the State of California is given in San Diego by the Sister of Mercy."

The clinics served to organize the charitable care dispensed by the hospital and continued in one version or another through all the decades that followed. But there was really a need to get all patients closer to the hospital, and in 1961, when the voracious freeway system consumed Guadalupe Clinic, the patients merged in a new Mercy Clinic adjacent to the Hospital (where the elevator shaft still is. As Dr. Stan Amundson, says, "You see this thing that looks like it's pointing up to heaven out of the blue.")[25] By the 1970s, when several of today's medical leaders at Scripps Mercy arrived as young physicians, their "favorite nun" was Sister Mary Carmelita Padilla, a nurse at Mercy Clinic for most of that decade.

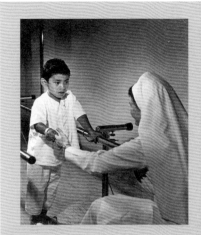

The Sisters of Mercy always provided care for the poor of all ages and ethnic groups. A young patient is helped toward recovery in the Guadalupe Clinic, which opened in 1944 to serve Logan Heights. When the Guadalupe Clinic closed in 1961, patients were served by the new Mercy Clinic that opened adjacent to Mercy Hospital.

courtesy of San Diego History Center

Sister Mary Carmelita (1926–1998) was born in San Diego to a "loving and generous" Mexican-American family and received her RN degree from Mercy College of Nursing in 1944. She entered the novitiate in 1948 and served professionally at Mercy San Diego twice: from 1953-1956 as nursing floor supervisor; then again from 1970-78 in the clinic. Sr. Mary Jo Anderson said of her:

> Sister Carmelita Padilla was a gem! She was an excellent nurse who guided the interns and residents through the Mercy Clinic. She "mothered" them spiritually and professionally. She could pass ethnically for a black, Indian and, of course, Latina. She was Jew to the Jews and Buddhist to the Asians. She would truly dance through life.[27]

And at her Memorial Service in 1998 it was said:

> She was always good for a hug, and because she was short, she was forced to look up. I remember her upturned face. She looked up to God and she looked up in optimism.[28]

Sister Mary Eucharia Malone served as the administrative leader of Mercy Hospital from 1956 through 1965. Sister Eucharia Malone supervised the building of the new eleven-story Mercy Hospital, which opened in 1966.
courtesy of Scripps Health

Senior physicians today, those arriving at Mercy in the early 70s, remember the last two religious administrators, Sisters Mary Placida (1965-77) and Mary Joanne (1977-83.) But their immediate predecessor was a remarkable leader. Sister Mary Eucharia Malone (1956-65) was a business woman rather than a nurse and highly regarded by her peers in the city. It was Sister Mary Eucharia who supervised the building of the new Mercy Hospital. A newspaper clipping from the *San Diego Union*, July 8, 1957, shows Sister Eucharia with Sister Angela (the nun who first took over the hospital after the death of Mother Mary Michael); the two are looking at an architect's sketch of the proposed multimillion dollar expansion for the hospital, "which will celebrate its 65th anniversary tomorrow," curiously shaving two years off the actual anniversary. The article goes on to say:

Sister Mary Eucharia, Administrator of the Hospital, [previously] supervised the building of a new hospital in Phoenix, Arizona. She said the expansion program would involve building to cost about $1.5 million next year. After that, she said, it would be achieved as fast as money can be provided. The program will start with the building of a road for ambulances and service vehicles from a widened Sixth Avenue extension. The first building construction will add a new wing on the east side of the present hospital and an outpatient and research building east of the College of Nursing. Sister Eucharia said that capacity of the hospital will increase by 75 beds [from its current] 372 beds and 80 bassinets. She explained that a large part of the building effort will be to modernize the Hospital. "It is not that we have failed to keep up with medical progress", she said. "We have installed new test equipment in many fields and as a result we are crowded. In the new building we [will have] more space and better facilities." The six story east wing to be built next year...will be the first major addition to the Hospital since 1928.[29]

By 1960, Mercy was bursting at the seams. In 1966, Mercy Hospital completed construction of a new, eleven-story facility on the foreground of the old hospital.   *courtesy of Scripps Health*

In 1960, Sister Mary Eucharia Malone was made fellow of the American College of Hospital Administrators at the annual ACHA Convention in San Francisco "in recognition of outstanding work as a hospital administrator." She also was on the lookout for good new talent, and when she learned in 1965 that she had been elected mother general of the Sisters of Mercy of California and Arizona and would have to return to Mercy Convent in Burlingame, she set her sights on a young teacher who was just opening the typewriter on her master's thesis in history at San Diego College for Women.

Mary Jo Anderson entered the Order of the Sisters of Mercy in Burlingame in 1956 at age seventeen, after being interviewed for admission by

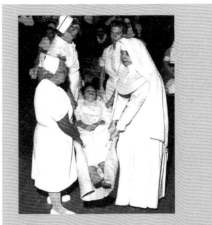

Mercy College of Nursing produced 1,550 graduates between 1903, when it opened as St. Joseph's Training School for Nurses, and its closing in 1970. Here, Sister Mary Clareta Doyle helps demonstrate how to lift a patient.
courtesy of Scripps Health

Sister Mary Eucharia. With the new name of Sister Mary Barbara, RSM (Religious of the Sisters of Mercy), she attended Lone Mountain College of the Sacred Heart and taught elementary school, sixth and eighth grade, for four years. Selected to teach history at Russell Junior College in Burlingame, Sister Mary Barbara proceeded to San Diego College for Women (precursor of USD) for graduate level courses in history, 1963-65. She lived on campus but would visit Mercy Convent on holidays and climb up ladders with Sister Mary Eucharia to the empty floors of the hospital under construction. And then Sister Barbara was literally just sitting down to begin her thesis when Sister Eucharia – who was short, slight and hard of hearing – took her hand gently and directed her toward her good ear. "Dear," she said, "I'd like you to switch to hospital administration." And fortunately Sister Barbara thought "it would be more exciting to work in a hospital than teach history the rest of my life."

So Sister Mary Barbara wrote her master's thesis in one month and earned her master's in history just in time to enter the University of California Berkeley School of Public Health in September of 1965. By 1968 she had completed a three-year program consisting of an internship at St. Mary's Hospital in San Francisco, where her mentor was Sister Mary Joanne De Vincenti; academics and an MPH at Berkeley; and residency at Alta Bates Hospital in Berkeley, after which Sister Mary Eucharia took pleasure in assigning her protégé to the new Mercy Hospital San Diego under Sister Mary Placida Conant.

Sister Mary Placida had been with Sister Eucharia in Phoenix in a building program there and—when the senior nun was called back to Burlingame—was the obvious choice to move to San Diego to finish the new Mercy Hospital here. In 1966 the doors opened to a modern eleven-story tower directly in front of the old, after

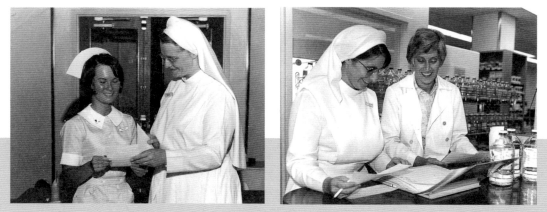

The Sisters of Mercy worked in various capacities at Mercy Hospital. Left, Sister Felice Sauers directs a nursing student. Right, Sister Edmund Pyke talks with a pharmacist. *courtesy of Scripps Health*

which the historically graceful, but obsolete, buildings behind were razed except for the elevator shaft. When Sister Mary Barbara arrived as assistant to Sister Placida, the new hospital was two years old. Sister Placida was a nurse, had taught in the schools of nursing, and was also highly regarded as an administrator.

But 1968 was the year of dramatic and visible change. The old ankle-length dresses of the Sisters disappeared - ironically, just as the Flower Children were putting them on. The habits obscuring the whole person except for face and hands gave way to a style that was not exactly *au courant* with the 60s but at least more like street clothes. Hair reappeared to frame the face. Many Sisters took back their original names: Sister Mary Barbara reverted to Mary Jo Anderson and her friend from the novitiate, Sister Marie Antoinette, was once again JoCeal Young. For four years, Sister Mary Jo worked at her superior's side, and later said of her:

> Sister Mary Placida was maybe about 5'5" and sturdy, sort of a farm girl with a round face and rosy cheeks. And Sister Placida could be very serious and stern with the doctors when she was worried about something, but she was also down to earth, very gentle and oh, so good with me.

The Sisters of Mercy worked closely with the nursing staff Sister Mary Placida is second from right.
courtesy of Scripps Health

I was, of course more liberal than she, and she never scolded me for
any of that. She gave me a lot of leeway.

During this time period, a commercial mortgage banker from La Jolla by way of
Des Moines, Iowa, named Daniel Mulvihill[30] got acquainted with Mercy Hospital
when Sister Placida asked him to join a committee on real estate. Mr. Mulvihill said:

> It was basically she just wanted to have a conversation with people in
> the community. And so we would have monthly meetings and she'd
> tell us what they were doing at the Hospital, what she'd like to build
> and her vision of the future. And after several months she told us she
> wanted a medical office building developed across the street from
> the Hospital at 4060 Fourth Ave. Then she asked me to be on the
> committee to select the developer.
>
> So I went to the first meeting and listened to all these people talking
> about Sister giving them the land, or a 99-year lease so they wouldn't
> have the expense of buying the land, and it didn't make any sense to
> me. So I went back to Sister Placida and told her I wanted to resign
> from the committee. She said, "Why?" and I told her, "I'd like to bid
> on this myself." So she said, "OK, you're fired," and we went to work
> together building those offices.
>
> We arranged a fair price for the land of $675,000 and Sister agreed to
> lease back one third of the space in the building if it didn't fill up –
> but I got most of it leased before we broke ground. I enjoyed working
> with her very much. She had a good mind and she was practical. And
> she prayed for me.

And it was fortunate that Sister Placida prayed and was understanding because in
January 1972 Sister Mary Jo Anderson left the Sisters of Mercy and made vows the
same day in her new order, the Community of the Holy Spirit. She was joined in this
by friends who were Dominican nuns and, as radical as it sounds, the new community
was blessed by the Bishop of San Diego.[31] However, Sister Mary Jo Anderson, CHS,
also took leave of Mercy Hospital and was out of work for six weeks before she was
hired by the Comprehensive Health Planning Agency of San Diego. The following
year she accepted the post of assistant administrator at Children's Hospital and
remained there six years, from 1973–79.

Back at Mercy Hospital, Sister Placida had seen the handwriting on the wall
and hired the first secular administrator in 1972, a man named Ed Hertfelder from
Birmingham, Alabama, who was "a social kind of person and a problem solver,"
often seen with donuts and cigarettes; his wife was a nurse at Scripps La Jolla. In this
arrangement, Sister Placida became executive director, and in 1977 that title transferred
to her successor, Sister Joanne DeVincenti.[32]

The students at the Mercy College of Nursing were among the most skilled in the country by the time they graduated from the three-year program. The 1969 class was one of the last to graduate before the school closed in 1970.
courtesy of Scripps Health

Another end of an era was the closing of Mercy College of Nursing, more than six decades after it was opened in 1904 by Mother Mary Michael on the campus of St. Joseph's Sanitarium. Mercy College was a three-year diploma school, meaning that the prerequisites for entry were "willingness and a good grade point average in high school." As Sister Mary Jo describes it:

> The girls had superb experience. By the time they were seniors in their three-year program they were oftentimes night supervisors on the floors. That was the benefit of diploma school I think. They got a great deal of clinical experience.[33]

And graduates excelled on the Board of Registry exam for the RN. But the times were changing, and the trend was toward four- and five-year baccalaureate programs.

> And it was very expensive to maintain a school of nursing. The professors felt that perhaps they were doing the nurses a disservice by not turning them out with an academic degree.[34]

So, despite that fact that the 1,550 graduates of Mercy College of Nursing were among the most skilled anywhere in their time, the last graduates dispersed into the hospitals of the city and country in 1970.

Dr. John H. Mazur was the first medical director of cardiology at Mercy Hospital.
courtesy of Scripps Health

Meanwhile, of course, medical science was evolving rapidly, especially in the great arc of cardiology. The first medical director of Cardiology at Mercy Hospital was Dr. John H. Mazur in 1963. He served thirty-three years in that role until his retirement in 1996 from a career spanning all of the extraordinary eras from the stethoscope and EKG to the Palmaz-Schatz stent. Dr. Mazur was a graduate of Jefferson University Medical School in Philadelphia and, like many of the great physicians at Mercy, arrived there after postgraduate training in the Navy. While at Mercy he also served as director of the Cardiopulmonary Laboratory at the San Diego Naval Hospital—and he did it all as a pediatrician. Mercy's current Director of Cardiology, Dr. Jerrold Glassman, was first at

Mercy as a medical school extern under Dr. Geller, and then a cardiac fellow with Dr. Mazur in the late 1970s. Dr. Glassman said:

> Dr. Mazur was a pediatric cardiologist running the adult cardiology program at Mercy—and they made a terrific choice. He basically taught himself adult cardiology. He was a very smart man. And John had a wonderful way of allowing you to do all the work, up to the point of making mistakes, so we had a tremendous experience here.[35]

Early on in Dr. Mazur's career at Mercy in 1966, the newspaper reported the case of a three-year-old girl with a "very rare and nearly always fatal heart condition"—a second left atrium that was causing her heart to fail. The child's life was saved by "very delicate" surgery, and the paper also commented:

> The most remarkable accomplishment in Jennifer's case was the diagnosis. It ranks as a major medical triumph. But the modest cardiologist who did it requested anonymity and down-play of his part as he described the procedure: "By using catheters (flexible tubes inserted in blood vessels) to measure heart chamber blood pressures, and angiograms (X-ray movies) we were able to make a conclusive diagnosis."
>
> The procedure is highly complex, requiring precise comparative measurements, exacting placement of tubes and needles and exhaustive analysis of electrocardiograms, films and other findings.[36]

And this was all accomplished in a setting even more primitive than the one Dr. Glassman found when he arrived at Mercy a decade later: a cath lab with the patient in a cradle being rocked back and forth to get different views because the X-ray arm was fixed and didn't move at all. About his chief, Dr, Glassman said:

> Dr. Mazur was a small man, clearly brilliant, but an absent-minded professor. In the old days, X-rays were put on little 35 mm films. So we had a darkroom with a viewer in there. Often he'd go in and we'd wait for him to come out. And every now and then he'd go in and never come out. He was like a phantom at times. He would just disappear.

And Dr. David Shaw said:

> He was good with his hands and inventive. When I started at Mercy I was in the cath lab doing a *cut down* (a surgical dissection over a major vein in order to insert a catheter) and John Mazur walked into the room and said, "What barbarian taught you to put in a central line that way?" Of course, it was standard procedure at the time.

> He was the first in San Diego back in the 60s to do *subclavians* (inserting a catheter into a large vein in the neck just by piercing the skin above it). Everybody else was still afraid of puncturing the lung.

As we've seen elsewhere in the Scripps Health story, cardiology in the 1970s, however brilliant, was still mostly diagnostic. There was no intervention by cardiologists. Patients were referred out to cardiac surgeons for an ever-growing list of spectacular procedures: at Mercy's Heart Care Center, open heart surgeries grew from twenty-four per year in 1963 to more than 300 in 1982, and the busiest cardiac surgeon was Dr. Leland Housman. A list of firsts in San Diego at Mercy include the first triple valve replacement (1968), cardiac pacemaker (1969) and coronary bypass (1970.)[37] But then Andreas Gruentzig gave his famous first Interventional cardiology course in America in 1981, and things began to shift. The first coronary angioplasty was done that same year at Mercy.

Sister Joanne De Vincenti served as the executive director of Mercy Hospital.

Sister Joanne De Vincenti hired Sister Mary Jo Anderson to be her assistant at Mercy Hospital. Sister Mary Jo had previously worked at Mercy under Sister Mary Placida.

courtesy of Scripps Health

Sister Mary Joanne De Vincenti was by this time the new executive director with Ed Hertfelder as administrator reporting to her, along with several male assistants. But things were a bit rocky. So Sister Joanne called on the former administrative intern she'd coached in San Francisco and offered her her job back at Mercy after an absence of seven years. And Sister Mary Jo Anderson accepted, returning in 1979 to act as Sister Joanne's assistant, helping deal with the increasing complexity of running a modern hospital. The new administrative wing opened at Mercy in 1981 to a design approved by Sister Joanne, and things were somewhat easier, and then, finally Sister Joanne was getting older and wanted out of management. But she had two major contributions left for Mercy.

One was her full-bore support of a trauma center under former Navy surgeon Dr. Dick Virgilio and a remarkable trio of young surgeons who had come "home" to Mercy: Drs. Eugene Rumsey, Jr, George Zorn, Jr, and Laurence Tanaka—all sons of Mercy physicians and partners to one another.

Family Medicine at Mercy

The senior Eugene Rumsey and George Zorn were surgeons; Laurence Tanaka's father was Roy, the much-admired general practitioner who founded Guadalupe Clinic.

Eugene Rumsey, Sr. (1918-2007) was born in Marbleton, Wyomying, a dot on the map north of Big Piney, and rode the train one way to San Diego with his family in 1924 when he was six years old. Young Gene grew up in Mission Hills and was in medical school at the outbreak of WWII. He served as ship's surgeon later in the war and then returned to San Diego in 1952 as a fully qualified surgeon. In solo practice for several years, he joined George Zorn, Sr. and partners in the late 1960s at Hillcrest Surgical and was an ardent supporter of Mercy Hospital throughout his career.

In 1994, Drs. Eugene Rumsey, Sr.; left, and Eugene Rumsey, Jr., volunteered their medical expertise during a Mercy Outreach Surgical Team (M.O.S.T.) mission in Mexico.
courtesy of Scripps Health

George Zorn, Sr. (b. 1922) was also in medical school at the outbreak of WWII; he enlisted in the Navy, but was told to stay in school. After the War in 1946, he was sent first to Long Beach (where his son George Jr. was born), then to Balboa Naval Hospital San Diego in 1949. After transfers with his family to Panama and the Great Lakes, he returned to San Diego permanently in 1955 and into private practice at Mercy in 1957 with A.E. Moore and John Steelquist, and later Eugene Rumsey. Dr. Zorn was chief of staff at Mercy in 1980 and was also an accomplished, self-taught painter. He retired in 1981, two years after Sister Mary Alexine Shea, and painted her wonderful portrait when he was in his early seventies.

Laurence Tanaka (b. 1944), Eugene Rumsey, Jr. (b. 1947) and George Zorn, Jr. (b. 1948)

are all members of Hillcrest, as well as Pacific Bariatric Surgical Groups. Eugene Rumsey, Jr. served as chief of staff at Scripps Mercy 2003-04.

The inside of the new emergency department at Scripps Mercy, which opened January 2012, is dedicated to the senior Eugene Rumsey and George Zorn.

The new emergency department at Scripps Mercy Hospital, San Diego, is dedicated to Drs. Eugene Rumsey, Sr.; and George Zorn, Sr. Left to right, Dr. George Zorn, Jr.; Dr. Zorn, Sr.; Dr. Eugene W. Rumsey, Jr.; Dr. Rumsey Jr.'s grandson, Caleb; and Robert Price with his wife, Allison Price. The Price Family Charitable Fund had the naming opportunity for the Scripps Mercy Hospital Emergency Department and honored the physicians for their dedication and service. *courtesy of Scripps Health*

Mercy Hospital was formally designated a trauma center in 1984 after surgeons arrived at Mercy Hospital who were trained in the care of the seriously injured patient. Dr. Dick Virgilio served as head of the trauma center.

The three younger men had all come from surgical training programs with high volumes of trauma and much hands-on experience for residents. But, when they all arrived at Mercy in 1979 they found Dr. Virgilio struggling to find help in trauma—which had not been part of the training or interest of most of the older surgeons. Care of the seriously-injured patient was time-consuming, high-adrenaline work and no respecter of night hours or office schedules. So everyone at Mercy was delighted with three more willing general surgeons to take up the challenge, as well as the two vascular surgeons who joined them, Drs. Joe Devin and Gordon Sproul.[38] With this group taking round-the-clock call, Mercy Hospital was formally designated a trauma center in 1984, along with Scripps Memorial La Jolla in the new San Diego Trauma System.

And it was the Trauma System that brought the Navy back to Mercy after an absence of forty years. In the new system, Balboa Hospital did not have a trauma center of its own. So Dick Virgilio at Mercy worked with his former protégé at Balboa, trauma and vascular surgeon Michael Sise, to bring the first Navy surgical resident onto the trauma service at Mercy in 1986. Mike Sise himself began moonlighting for Dick Virgilio in 1987, joined the staff at Mercy five years later and succeeded his mentor as Director of Trauma in 1994. Mike says:

The welfare of the patients always came first for the Sisters of Mercy. Left to right, Sister Mary Freda, Sister Mary Imelda, Sister Mary Joanne De Vincente, Sister Mary LaSalette Trevillyan, Sister Mary Alexine, and Sister Mary Cornelia.
courtesy of Scripps Health

The first Mercy Hospital Foundation Board was established in 1985. Members included Sister Joanne De Vincenti, seated left, and mortgage banker Daniel Mulvihill as chairman, third from right, standing.

> The Navy has been a continual presence here for twenty-six years… and now includes junior and senior surgical residents, anesthesia and emergency medicine, nurses and physician assistants. In 1998 we formally integrated the Navy residents into our own GME program, now under the direction of nationally-known trauma surgeon, Dr. Steven Shackford[39], as Navy Medical Center San Diego and Scripps Mercy Hospital. They get a fabulous experience.[40]

Sister Joanne De Vincenti's final contribution to Mercy was to call upon Daniel Mulvihill,[41] who describes the conversation this way:

> She called me one day and said she wanted to see me. And I went up to see her, and she said, "Dan, I want a Foundation for Mercy. I want to get it started. And you're the Chairman."
>
> I said, "Sister, I don't know anything about Foundations. I don't know how to do that. Get Jim Mulvaney because he knows all about that stuff." She says, "I'll get Jim Mulvaney, but you are the chairman."

She did get Jim Mulvaney who, Dan says, "was a very good attorney and the guy who got us going properly—and he taught me one thing about philanthropy which is that the thing you have to do is to ask." So the Mercy Foundation was established in 1985 with a board that was willing. But they struggled at first until Jim Mulvaney suggested they ask Norman Seltzer, one of San Diego's premier real estate and land-use attorneys, to bring in all his contacts and know-how—and "after that things really took off."

In 1985, Sister Mary Joanne De Vincenti moved into the little Victorian house across the street which was the home of her new foundation and served another two years until she returned full circle to St. Mary's in San Francisco to work with the foundation there. She was the last religious chief executive for Mercy. But there is one last nun whose dates at Mercy San Diego (1979-95) skirt the outside edge of this chapter, but who was a beloved icon, and that is Sister Mary La Salette Trevillyan.

Sister Mary La Salette Trevillyan kept
the spirit of Mercy Hospital alive after
Sister Joanne De Vincenti retired as chief
executive. Much beloved, Sister La Salette
wore the white habit throughout her career
and offered a smile to all.
courtesy of Scripps Health

Sister La Salette (who took her name in religion from a mountain village near Grenoble, France, where the Virgin Mary was seen by two shepherd children[42]) came to Mercy at the age of fifty-five as Chaplain. Sister "La" was impressive in the role—impressive physically, at over 6 feet tall, gliding through the rooms in a snowy white habit (after most of the remaining Sisters had moved on to street clothes) and apparently radiating comfort wherever she went. In 1983, when Sister Joanne De Vincenti walked out of her office in Administration for the last time and turned the keys over to a layman named Richard Keyser, there was reasonable anxiety on campus about how to keep the spirit of Mercy alive. One of the answers was Sister La Salette as "Mission Services Director," a mandate she would fill with her ethereal presence until 1995 and the merger with Scripps Health. Her post was the precursor of what would come to be known in the twenty-first century as "Director of Mission Integration."

Tremendous challenges still lay ahead for Mercy Hospital as they did for every hospital in the city. It would not be long before the new lay leadership would be called upon to make a transforming decision for the decade and century ahead.

CHAPTER TWELVE
Change and Unrest
1990 - 2000

WHEN DR. CHARLES EDWARDS AT SCRIPPS CLINIC began looking around for another partner, he was joining a sort of courtship dance with virtually every other health care executive in town. Managed care—meaning controlling costs for health care by transferring risk to the providers—had slammed into San Diego like a freight train, and San Diego was one of the earliest-hit and hardest-hit areas in the country.[1] Physicians in their private offices were buried in regulations for programs with acronyms they didn't understand, and hospitals were struggling to stabilize the bottom line. About Scripps Memorial in that era, Ames Early said:

> "Managed care" is a good proxy for a whole welter of interacting elements that joined to make the 1990s a very, very difficult decade.
>
> I loved the '80s at Scripps. You know, I was around the hospital; I liked that and you're in touch with what an institution like that is there for and what it's about. And then during the '90s you get caught up in all of the things that take away from that.[2]

The era of mergers and acquisitions was driven by what was driving managed care, as Charlie Edwards described:

> Competition had increased, and proprietary hospitals had come under enormous pressure to improve profitability. Government and the insurance industry had become increasingly important players in health care delivery. And fixed fee for service was the model for payment.
>
> We began to consider a merger.
> It could give us new economies of scale, spreading the costs of administrative staff and expensive technology among a larger patient base – you had to have the latest technology—and also provide access to capital not available to us as a freestanding clinic.[3]

So Scripps Clinic (Charlie Edwards) began confidential merger talks with Sharp HealthCare (Peter Ellsworth) in 1989, and Mercy (Richard Keyser) with Scripps Memorial (Ames Early) at about the same time. By then Mercy was one of the thirteen original hospitals of Catholic Healthcare West which:

> was founded in 1986 when the Sisters of Mercy Burlingame Regional Community and the Sisters of Mercy Auburn Regional Community merged their health care ministries into one organization. The Sisters forged this union to enhance their charitable capabilities, expand the Catholic health care ministry, and promote social justice.[4]

But all the other "Mercies" were more geographically connected, and San Diego was a very tough market. As Sister Mary Jo Anderson said:

> We could see the way systems were going. Mercy was part of a large system of hospitals in California and Arizona and Nevada. But it was isolated in San Diego. And we saw that there were contracting agencies now with the insurance companies.
>
> And to really be competitive in San Diego, as the insurance companies would say, "you had to have an S in your name." You either had to be part of the Scripps system or the Sharp system to get the best rates. At that time they weren't negotiating rates on a California statewide basis. And so that was the thing that caused people to say we should look around for a local partner.[5]

But Scripps Memorial was completely blindsided in June of 1990 by a headline in the *Los Angeles Times* that read, "Scripps Clinic, Sharp Discussing a Merger: The joining of the biomedical research facilities and non-profit hospital chain would create a $750-million-a-year medical giant."[6] Ames Early says:

> We had been thinking "We'll compete as a hospital system, and the Clinic will do what they're going to do, and our main competition will be with Sharp." But the world looked a lot different to us when the Clinic was included in the Sharp system.
>
> And the roots of our two organizations were identical. There was all our Scripps history, and to see that go out the window, just like that, did not seem right. It did not have poetic symmetry.[7]

Just after the announcement came out about Sharp and Scripps Clinic, and Ames Early and his team had a little time to talk about it without coming to any conclusion, Mr. Early ran into Bill Nelson standing in the morning sunshine on the steps of an accounting office. Mr. Nelson was the erstwhile builder of office buildings at Scripps Memorial and now Chairman of the Board of Scripps Clinic. And Ames says:

I had to say something, so I said, "It's kind of too bad that the organizations are going the way they seem to be going. It would seem that there would be a lot that could be gained if it were otherwise." But I also said that any change in direction wouldn't come from the CEOs.

And when we parted I think Bill had the impression that if overtures were to come from Clinic trustees in the direction of Scripps Memorial trustees, that they would be well received and something might happen.

And shortly thereafter, exactly that did begin to occur.[8]

Bill Nelson's recollections add details behind the scenes. He says:

I had known Pete Ellsworth a long time—as lawyers, we were both active and friendly—and while he was CEO at Sharp and I was on the board at Scripps Clinic we made a number of trips to find out more of what was happening in Washington and also investigate other health groups. Out of those discussions arose the possibility of combining the two. Because frankly, both institutions were having financial trouble and looking down the road to even deeper financial trouble.

At the same time I was chairing a fund-raising campaign for Scripps Clinic and called on many long-standing donors who gave to both the Clinic and Scripps Hospital and I got a fair feeling in talking to them that their general attitude was we really ought to look again at [merging with] the Hospital. These were people who really cared a lot about the [whole] Scripps organization - old time people like the Black family, and so forth.

I had also been talking to board members during that fund-raising campaign and many of them were donors to both institutions and knew there were real concerns about both... That produced some discussions about a possible merger with SMH, which I was designated to lead.

I don't want to say the Board leapt into the boat and upset the rowers, but they were ready.[9]

After that, things moved very quickly. Board members Ed Danenhauer and Dick Hibbard for Scripps Memorial, and Ernie Hahn and Gordon Luce (with the encouragement of Cecil Green) for the Clinic were constructive in negotiations. Seven weeks after the original announcement, the same reporter for the *LA Times* wrote that "whirlwind secret discussions between Scripps Clinic and Scripps Memorial Hospitals would lead to a merger on January 1, 1991."[10]

Sharp turned to Grossmont, and the talks with Mercy were put on hold.

Left to right, Ed Danenhauer, Bill Nelson, Ames Early, and Dr. Charles Edwards were focused on making the new Scripps Institutions of Medicine and Science successful.
courtesy of Scripps Health

The remarriage of what came to be called the Scripps Institutions of Medicine and Science (SIMS) was big news,[11] but not without the frictions and readjustments one might expect after forty-four years apart. Most of the parties were intent on making it work, though Richard Lerner at the Research Institute was unenthusiastic from the start. And although Bill Nelson said:

> Richard Lerner understood that people don't give money to Petri dishes, they give money to doctors who save their lives,[12]

Dr Lerner's feeling was:

> We are an international organization, right? And they are, in our worldview, a local caregiver.[13]

Not long before the merger, Scripps Memorial had purchased for its new administrative offices the former headquarters of a bankrupt moving van company called Four Winds.[14] The red-tiled building on Campus Point Court, visible across the road from the La Jolla Hospital, became the new house of SIMS. Charles Edwards was installed as president and CEO and Ames Early as executive vice president and chief operating officer. Under the SIMS umbrella were four divisions:

Left to right, in 1991, Ames Early of Scripps Memorial Hospitals and Dr. Charles Edwards of Scripps Clinic signed the merger to reunite the two organizations
courtesy of Scripps Health

1. Scripps Memorial Corporation, headed by Ames Early, with four hospitals (La Jolla, Encinitas, Chula Vista and now Green), two skilled nursing facilities (Encinitas and Torrey Pines), medical office buildings, The Whittier Institute and the Scripps Memorial Hospital Foundation;

2. Scripps Clinic and Research Foundation (SCRF), then headed by neurosurgeon Tom Waltz and consisting of Anderson Outpatient Pavilion, Shiley Sports Center and other clinical facilities on Torrey Pines Mesa, plus satellite clinics throughout the county;

3. The Scripps Research Institute (TSRI), under Richard Lerner; and

4. The Scripps Foundation for Medicine and Science, under director James Bowers, which raised funds for the other divisions.[15]

But Ames Early said:

> We actually referred to ourselves as ScrippsHealth from the beginning. We needed a name to start going out in the world with.
>
> In 1990, I met with Charlie Edwards and Paula Dean who was head of human resources at the Clinic and kind of "general right hand" to Charlie – and the three of us put our heads together and picked out the name ScrippsHealth. We spent some time discussing should it be Scripps Health, should it be Scripps Healthcare, should it be one word or two words or three words? And at one point I said, "Well, you know, let's just go clean as a whistle and make it one word ScrippsHealth." And so they said, "Okay, let's do that."
>
> And even though the corporation, the overarching umbrella, was SIMS, when we talked about ourselves in public it was ScrippsHealth from very early on.[16]

The coalition was at that point the largest health care concern in the county with 1,600 physicians and 6,200 employees and continued to forge ahead. And it was certainly as ScrippsHealth that the company purchased a fifth hospital, Valley Medical Center in El Cajon, from Epic Healthcare Group, one of the largest for-profit hospital companies in the nation, in February 1993.[17]

Epic had approached Scripps through Robin Brown (current Chief Executive at Scripps Green), who was at that time head of "Affiliated Business Services"—meaning all the non-hospital units; Robin had previously bought Epic's local home care business. Valley Medical Center was "a teetering institute that needed capital, and Epic didn't have a strategy that was viable and were extracting themselves from the market."[18] So Lauren Blagg, President of the Scripps Memorial Hospital division, collaborated with his usual outside consultant Bob Gregg to make the deal. Robin Brown said:

> Bob Gregg was a really outstanding guy and instrumental in working with Lauren and Ames in most of the acquisitions we have today. He was involved with Lauren in buying Encinitas Hospital, in Chula Vista Bay General and was also involved in Mercy.[19]

In a press release, Charlie Edwards said that "The ScrippsHealth network includes facilities in all parts of [San Diego] except East County" and "access to this system for that large population… meets an important Scripps goal."[20] And Robin Brown was sent out to the new 172-bed Scripps Hospital – East County as Administrator.

By June of 1993—two years in—Dr. Charles Edwards had had enough and announced his decision to retire at the age of 69.[21] In essence, he took The Scripps Research Institute with him, because Richard Lerner – who had a good relationship with Charlie Edwards – ultimately refused to stay in SIMS without Dr. Edwards in charge. The statement released to the press about Dr. Edwards' retirement quoted Richard Lerner as saying:

> It is very unusual that a group of research scientists would be so fond of any boss, but the fact is we have nothing but admiration for Charlie Edwards' leadership.[22]

Soon TSRI's connection to SIMS hung by the threads of The Scripps Foundation for philanthropy, and a hundred-year, rent-free lease on the ground under all those labs. [23]

Meanwhile, the program for filling Dr. Edwards' shoes was that Bill Nelson, chair of the SIMS Board, would act as interim CEO for an unspecified term while a permanent replacement was sought. J. Frank Mahoney, chair of the Board of ScrippsHealth, moved up to chair the Board of SIMS. This situation lasted for a year during corporate restructuring that legalized the corporate name that had been used informally since 1991. General Counsel Richard Sheridan said:

> In anticipation of upcoming mergers we began to refer to Scripps Memorial Hospitals as ScrippsHealth. Effective over a several month period ending in early 1994, we merged Scripps Memorial Corporation and Scripps Memorial Hospital Foundation into Scripps Memorial Hospitals; and then in March of 1994 also merged SCRF into Scripps Memorial Hospitals.
>
> That aggregation of corporations is the unified ScrippsHealth.[24]

The executive officer of SIMS—in this case, the interim Bill Nelson—was technically CEO of both SIMS and ScrippsHealth, but this changed shortly. In May 1994, the board considered that the ScrippsHealth component was "primarily a large hospital system requiring the management of an individual skilled in institutional governance" and unanimously elected the steady Ames Early president and CEO. The

ScrippsHealth Board went on to thank William Nelson for his "extraordinary and most valuable contribution" as interim CEO, to name as new interim CEO former Scripps Memorial Trustee Edwin Danenhauer, and finally to send a pointed recommendation to the SIMS Board of Trustees:

> That we actively pursue new and permanent leadership in the position of CEO of SIMS and that a search committee, with participants recommended by Trustees, carry out that search in an expedient manner.

As it happened, there were actually two different search committees in the two and a half years from May 1993 to November 1995.[25] The first, chaired by Bill Nelson, was officially the "Search Committee for CEO of SIMS/ScrippsHealth," but was undermined by frequent changes in ideas about what the top position would be or even be called. Nevertheless, this committee did get one candidate actually to accept the challenge, and that was Ron J. Anderson MD, president and CEO of Parkland Hospital in Dallas, then considered the premier public hospital in the United States. But Dr. Anderson no sooner agreed to come to La Jolla than his board at Parkland made him a superior offer, and he withdrew.

The second was inaugurated as the "Search Committee for Chairman, Office of Presidents of SIMS" on May 22, 1995. In a letter to the entire Scripps community, Ed Danenhauer explained the Office of Presidents as:

> a group established to deal with issues of joint interest and concern to ScrippsHealth, The Scripps Research Institute and the Scripps Foundation for Medicine and Science.

> The individual selected as Chairman, Office of Presidents…will serve as Scripps' chief institutional advocate and spokesperson [and] be responsible for guiding relationships and activities involving the entities which comprise SIMS.

This 16-member search committee was chaired by philanthropist Deeda Blair of the Albert and Mary Lasker Foundation for Biomedical Research. Members included Ames Early, Richard Lerner, Ed Danenhauer, and Bill Nelson; the three chairs of the organizational boards; and physicians Clifford Colwell, Brent Eastman, Carla Stayboldt, and John Trombold, as well as emeritus trustee Burl Mackenzie. The very capable staff coordinator throughout the whole process was Janet Colson, whom Charlie Edwards had hired from Ronald Reagan's White House where she was Special Assistant to the President for National Security Affairs. (Ms. Colson had been among the shocked crowd of White House personnel in the office of Chief of Staff James Baker on March 30, 1981, when the news came in that President Reagan had been shot.)[26] But ultimately no outside leader for SIMS could be found.

Now that ScrippsHealth was formally organized, recognized, and managed, the whole reason for the continuing existence of The Scripps Institutions of Medicine and Science was the *science*—and the persistent hope that a national leader with impeccable credentials, another Charlie Edwards, could persuade Dr. Lerner and The Scripps Research Institute to return to the fold. There was what Ames Early called:

> a divergence of aspiration—on one side with Richard Lerner and TSRI, and the other with the residual leadership from Scripps Clinic who weren't going to give up totally on TSRI separating further. There was still a hope among long time supporters of the Clinic that the Research Institute would remain part of the family.[27]

Excellent candidates were approached, of the caliber of former U.S. ambassador to Russia Robert Schwartz Strauss and former Director of the National Cancer Institute Dr. Samuel M. Broder. Finally, after a discouraging six months, Chair Deeda Blair sent a letter to the search committee declaring that:

> Conventional wisdom has caused some of us to reconsider that the various constituencies of this organization are functioning effectively under strong, competent leadership.
>
> And, as many of you have wisely pointed out, a person of the caliber we sought would undoubtedly have wanted a stronger job description and far more involvement in the institution's day-to-day operations, and could very well have upset the balance that has now been achieved.[28]

With that, the search for a new head of SIMS was discontinued, and ultimately SIMS itself faded away.[29]

Dr. Thomas Waltz served as president and CEO of Scripps Clinic.
courtesy of Scripps Health

As it turned out, the whole coalition with the institutions west of highway 5 was once more under siege. Now the outpatient division of Scripps Clinic was actively negotiating with ScrippsHealth to have itself bought out by venture capitalists. The then–President and CEO of Scripps Clinic, Dr. Thomas Waltz, had been hand-picked by Charlie Edwards to succeed him within the SIMS structure. Tom Waltz was a highly respected neurosurgeon and "wonderful human being" who—according to Tom's successor, Dr. Robert Sarnoff:[30]

> basically was charged with the growth and the expansion and change in business direction of our Clinic. Prior to Tom, this was really kind of a sleepy little place that basically catered to people with insurance, the rich, the famous, and so on.

What Tom attempted to do was bring the Clinic into the mainstream of medical practice. And what Tom would say is, "The way that we're going to grow, the way that we're going to develop, is to bring in the patients." At the time, the way we'd bring in more patients was to get involved with what we knew then as "managed care, capitated care." And Tom struggled valiantly to try to transform this very specialized Clinic into a care machine more akin to Rees- Stealy, more akin to Kaiser.

And unfortunately we didn't have the infrastructure. Unfortunately we didn't have the capacity to succeed.

It wasn't part of our tradition to nickel and dime things. I mean, you know, we were attempting to do liver transplants. We were attempting to put in hips. We were doing a lot of very, very specialized things, expensive things that really didn't fit well with the challenges of managed care at that time. And we weren't good at it. It really wasn't part of where we were and it didn't garner much enthusiasm from the people who were working here.[31]

So, money became a huge issue at the Clinic and, acquiescing to persistent demands, ScrippsHealth contracted in January 1996 to sell the outpatient Scripps Clinic business to Scripps Clinic Medical Group (SCMG), Enterprise Partners and Westar Capital. The sale price was the assumption of liabilities; leases for all space; overhead services at market rates; and the name "Scripps" licensed under agreement. (But even with infusions of cash, the enterprise was doomed. Dr. Sarnoff said:

By the year 2000, despite Tom's best intentions, despite his valiant efforts and everything that he and his team were trying to accomplish, it was apparent that we were failing and we were beginning to lose physicians. We were having difficulty not only recruiting new physicians but retaining the ones we had.)[32]

At Mercy Hospital, meanwhile, a "brilliant tall blonde and superb ICU nurse"[33] named Mary Yarbrough had succeeded Richard Keyser as CEO in 1992 after serving first as chief nurse executive and then chief operating officer. The pressures that had led to the first talks with Scripps in 1989 had not gone away. Mary Yarbrough approached Ames Early again about an affiliation, and this time the response was welcoming. Sister Mary Jo Anderson said:

We looked around to see who we wanted as a partner and clearly Scripps was the one with whom we thought we were most compatible geographically as well as ethically and culturally.

There was good will on both sides and I think that's why it was able to happen, because we had respect for one another and appreciated one another.

Mercy Hospital became part of the Scripps system in 1995. Under the new structure, the hospitals would have the same board of trustees and one executive team, with Mercy remaining a Catholic hospital.

courtesy of Scripps Health

Bill Nelson was involved in complex negotiations stretching into the next year with Catholic Healthcare West, and Ms. Yarbrough, Bishop Robert Brom of San Diego, and the Vatican. One of the most fascinating documents in ScrippsHealth archives is the faxed "Indult" from Rome, permitting the transfer of CHW's membership in Mercy San Diego to ScrippsHealth as an "alienation of church property."[34]

The new affiliation called for the two hospitals to be governed by the same board of trustees—with 20 percent of members nominated by Catholic Healthcare West—and operated by a single executive team. Scripps Mercy would continue to operate under the *Ethical and Religious Directives (ERDs) of Catholic Healthcare Services.*[35] The transition to Scripps became official on August 20, 1995, at which time Mary Yarbrough left to take up another chief executive post in Phoenix—but Mary also left to ScrippsHealth a tremendously experienced strategic planner named June Komar, whom she had brought to Mercy just the year before from San Diego County government; there June had been in charge of multibillion dollar budgets and thousands of employees, but was ready for a career change from the public sector. Fortunately, she was intrigued by health care and also by the new affiliation with Scripps Health, where she would play a key role as director of strategic planning in the new millennium.

Meanwhile, Mary Yarbrough was replaced by a much-beloved physician, Dr. Ralph George as senior vice president and first administrator of the new Scripps Mercy Hospital.

Ralph George, MD (1936-1996), was a hematologist-oncologist who joined the Mercy Medical Staff in 1971 and moved easily through leadership positions as chief of Internal Medicine, chief of staff and then the first (and only) chief medical officer before accepting the top post at Scripps Mercy. Dr. George was small and trim, a runner, humorous, gifted with people, and admired by his peers, interns, and residents, and apparently everyone else. Sister Mary Jo said:

> We called him "St. Ralph." He was just a great administrator and, with his partners and the wonderful office nurse we called "Amazing Grace," he was able to go on seeing patients. Everybody loved him. They would do anything for him. And then he got renal cancer.[36]

The beloved Dr. Ralph George became senior vice president and first administrator of Scripps Mercy Hospital.
courtesy of Scripps Health

In retrospect, Dr. George was already ill at his first meeting at ScrippsHealth Campus Point and died within the year, just when his skills were perhaps most sorely needed for what lay ahead.

In the spring of 1996, with the search committees for a new leader abandoned, Ames Early was dealing with a health care management environment that was ever more complex. He said:

> The half life of what you were taught about management and about how things work, became shorter and shorter, the longer I went on. A management group we hired concluded that we needed to find some strategic approach to the very dynamic landscape—so that we didn't become inadvertently the dinosaur…
>
> So we were talking to consultants, and one was Dr. Stan Pappelbaum. I learned about Stan through our membership in VHA, Voluntary Hospitals of America, which is a large collective to do purchasing and facilitate best practices; Stan had been working for one of the member hospitals in Hawaii. And I thought, "Stan's here in town, well, we should talk to him, too." So Stan did come and he presented to the management group. And we agreed then on a consulting arrangement.
>
> Up to that point, we, as a management group, had always been adhering to the view that *incremental change is the only lasting and effective change*. But part of the reason we chose Stan is that I kind of reached the conclusion that *incremental change wasn't going to be sufficient and we had to take a different game approach. We had to go for radical change*.[37]

Dr. Stanley J. Pappelbaum became chief transitional officer in 1996 and then president and CEO in 1999.

courtesy of Scripps Health

Stanley J. Pappelbaum, MD, MBA, was Canadian, a graduate of McGill University and the University of British Columbia School of Medicine, and did a pediatric residency at Montreal Children's Hospital and fellowship in pediatric cardiology at UCLA. From 1969-84, Dr. Pappelbaum taught and practiced pediatric cardiology at UCSD and at San Diego Children's Hospital, where he was chief of that section from 1972-78 and in partnership with Dr. Searle W. Turner. Then Dr. Pappelbaum earned an MBA (health option) from Massachusetts Insitute of Technology, while Dr. Turner acquired an MHA (Masters in Health Administration) from the University of Colorado. Together in 1985 the two established Professional Health Consulting Group, a company which "analyzed and managed change for complex not-for-profit healthcare systems"[38]— which was exactly the expertise ScrippsHealth was looking for.

On March 27, 1996, Stan Pappelbaum was introduced to the ScrippsHealth Board of Trustees as "a physician/consultant/leader who understands how business thinks and acts." The new consultant went on to present details of a proposed strategic plan called *Project Scripps,* which was appealing and seemed to make excellent sense. The minutes of the board meeting include Dr. Pappelbaum's *Exhibit 1: Guiding Principles*:

- The vision begins with what is best for the patient.
- The system is physician and hospital driven; by partnering it will become a "virtually" integrated healthcare network.
- Quality of care, quality of life, quality of service, easy access, cost and utilization are primary considerations—optimal care must be provided with the available resource constraints.

And there were the *Core Strategies:*

- Effective partnering with medical groups/IPAs.
- Strategic alliances with other healthcare entities and businesses.
- Maximizing value for the community (cost/quality/service).
- Optimizing the decision making processes (governance and senior management).

The board voted to "affirm their support of management to move forward with Project Scripps." Dr. Brent Eastman said:

> I had just finished four years in a national post as Chairman of the Committee on Trauma for the American College of Surgeons, and was Trauma Director at Scripps La Jolla. Ames Early called on me to be a physician leader working with the new consultant, and I agreed to serve because I agreed with the *Guiding Principles and Core Strategies*.[39]

Six months later, Ames Early told the board that Stan Pappelbaum had been asked and agreed to shift from consultant to employee as a member of the management team. His appointment as chief transitional officer was effective October 1, 1996. This was the most remarkable of all the stunning makeovers of ScrippsHealth management since the decade began. Dr. Stanley Pappelbaum, who was certainly an adept physician and consultant, but who had never run a business larger than his partner and himself, now had the entire Scripps organization reporting to him, "with the exception of legal and finance, which still reported to Ames."[40] Ames Early retained the title of President/CEO for nearly another three years until his retirement in July 1999; but Stan Pappelbaum was directing the future.

Central to the strategy of *Project Scripps*, according to Dr. Eastman:

> was that physicians needed to be organized in a way in which they could collaborate with administration. But California is one of a handful of states with a prohibition against the corporate practice of medicine.
>
> So Project Scripps required the formation of a physician group which could function as partner. The group was called Scripps Physicians, and I was asked to lead it.[41]

Within Project Scripps, a central part of the strategic plan was creating what were called Systems of Excellence (SOE). Each SOE was a triad of leadership: physician, nurse, and administrator. There was one System of Excellence for each clinical field.

> For example, there was the cardiovascular SOE, oncology SOE and women's and children's SOE.
>
> The problem was not in the concept. The problem was in the execution – especially in how the physician leaders were chosen. They were selected by Dr. Pappelbaum in a top-down process which, fatally, bypassed the elected medical staff leadership.[42]

Over the next three years, this visionary plan was unfolding and unraveling simultaneously.

There was a second problem. To manage the whole insurance and contractual side of the strategic plan, Dr. Pappelbaum recruited Joseph Sebastianelli, retired president from Aetna "with 25 years of high-level experience in the health care field."[43] In April 1999, Mr. Sebastianelli was appointed executive director of Scripps Care, a joint venture between Scripps Physicians and Scripps Health[44] which would have had the hospital managing all contracts.[45]

According to Dr. Kevin Glynn, Chief of Staff at Scripps Mercy 1999-2000:

> Many of the nearly 2,000 physicians who practice at Scripps embraced the vision as a way to enhance collaboration with the hospitals. But while acknowledging the vision, many also foresaw having to turn over control of their practices to the hospital system, so they resisted.
>
> The first year, the system coasted through with a 5% return on investment. The second year, however ROI dropped to 2 percent, and in the third year, serious difficulties became visible when health plans angry about having their contracts canceled retaliated by reducing payments to the various physician groups and IPAs within the system. The picture darkened when the census dropped at the largest hospital in the system (Scripps Mercy) since managed care patients were being diverted elsewhere. In addition, surgeons took cases to other hospitals and freestanding surgi-centers to demonstrate their independence...
>
> Coincidentally, the CEO of the system was about to retire [and] the physician consultant...to succeed the departing CEO.[46]

After 23 years at Scripps, Ames Early retired in 1999.
courtesy of Scripps Health

After twenty-three years at Scripps through a barrage of past and present change, Ames Early retired in July 1999 at the age of 63. And Ames said:

> The board did something very wise when I was retiring and recommending that Stan step in – which they agreed to because we didn't want to seem like we were turning Project Scripps around or dropping it. They recognized Stan's strengths but they also recognized his lack of hospital operating experience and they insisted that the first thing he do is hire a strong operator. They said, "Stan, you've got to get somebody."

And that somebody turned out to be Chris Van Gorder.[47]

Chris Van Gorder was then CEO of Long Beach Memorial Medical Center, 700-bed flagship of a hospital system called Memorial Health Services.[48] Before coming to Scripps, Stan Pappelbaum had consulted on a cancer plan at Long Beach Memorial; and when Dr. Pappelbaum was looking for his new COO, a mutual friend recommended Chris Van Gorder.[49] Dr. Pappelbaum sought out Mr. Van Gorder himself after exhausting a whole list of other applicants supplied by a national recruiting firm—which specifically did *not* offer Mr. Van Gorder as he was in the process of being placed by the same firm in another health system in California. As it turned out, it took too long—five months—to bring Mr. Van Gorder on board, and by that time the situation was irreversible.

Dr. Kevin Glynn wrote of those intervening five months:

> Once ensconced as president of the system, the new physician-CEO forged ahead. He created a medical group, renegotiated contracts with health plans, and began constructing the infrastructure for the grand design. But as he fleshed out the concepts, the mistrustful doctors became more vocal. Nurses began to question the strategy, as well.

> Determined to make the plan work, he tightened his hold. He orchestrated monthly presentations to the board extolling the benefits of his plan and implied that the farsighted doctors were behind him, with only a vocal minority of reactionaries in opposition.[50]

But, in truth, a palpable sense of unrest was rising on all the Scripps campuses. At La Jolla, the most visible sign of rebellion was the white board in the doctors' lounge—the 1990s version of Twitter, perhaps—where increasingly angry messages were scrawled daily through the latter half of 1999 and spring of 2000 in a naming names and taking no prisoners style. The medical staffs of the newer Scripps hospitals, which were still feeling their way in the Scripps system, were baffled. Out at East County, Robin Brown had worked hard for four years to build an Independent Practice Association (IPA) called Scripps Medical Associates (SMA); he said:

> These people wanted to be with Scripps. They liked being involved with Scripps. And for us to essentially say, "No, it's not that. We're going to create something new –that's not what we had in mind…"

> It's like they couldn't believe it because they had spent all this time and effort doing what we asked them to do. And it eventually caused a big rift between Scripps Medical Associates and Scripps Health.[51]

Chris Van Gorder was to take on the enormous task of creating a viable and fiscally sound Scripps Health.
courtesy of Scripps Health

Similarly, relations deteriorated to the breaking point between Mercy Physicians Medical Group and Scripps Health, such that Mercy Foundation feared for the mission of the Sisters; both the Mercy chief of staff and the chairman of the Foundation wrote Dr. Pappelbaum and the Board of Trustees requesting outside mediation.[52]

Meanwhile in December 1999, Chris Van Gorder arrived at Scripps to take up his post as Chief Operating Officer of Scripps Health. He describes his first day on the job:

> Stan said, "Would you go over to Scripps La Jolla where they're having a general kind of medical staff meeting, and introduce yourself to the medical staff?"

So all the docs are sitting in the auditorium by the dining room and I get in there and I say, "I'm Chris Van Gorder, I'm from Long Beach Memorial, and I've read the strategic plan and, wow, that's what attracted me here." Of course, I didn't know they hated it.

And so I get done talking, and in walks Dr. Harold Shively, chief of the medical staff, with Joe Sebastianelli—they'd had a furious confrontation in another room about the status of contracts, a misunderstanding which led Dr. Shively to call Mr. Sebastianelli a liar —and Dr. Shively says to the crowd, "Joe's back again to talk about the contracts." Joe says, "Look, I was going to explain the contracts, but I'm not going to do that now. I'm quitting my job right now, so I can sue this guy for slander and libel." And out he walked.

One of the doctors leaned over to me and said, "You're on."[53]

When he took over as CEO of Scripps Health in 2000, Chris Van Gorder toured the hospitals, including Scripps Memorial Hospital Encinitas. Left, Mr. Van Gorder discusses the needs of the Rehab Services Department at Scripps Encinitas.
courtesy of Scripps Health

And that was the beginning of the end. The documents of the first five months of 2000 reveal a board of trustees[54] with a background of countless volunteer hours to Scripps Health, grappling with ever more implacable assaults on their decisions. Chair Frank Panarisi had first been chair of the Mercy Board of Trustees, shepherding the 1995 affiliation with Scripps that had seemed such a triumph; now he was waking up to newspaper headlines such as "Despite physicians' unrest, Scripps board backs CEO,"[55] and "Scripps Health quality under fire."[56] Individual trustees were notified by letter that the CEO "has lost the capacity to command trust and respect in the Scripps community [and] we need action to stanch the loss of patient base and employee morale."[57] The final events began with a series of unprecedented votes between April 24 and May 17 of *no-confidence* in Scripps Health senior management by the medical executive committees of the Scripps Hospitals; when the CEO stood his ground,[58] the last straw was notice to the board by major donors that they would withhold further philanthropy. On May 26 the Scripps Health Board of Trustees accepted Dr. Pappelbaum's resignation, and it was all over.

It was also a new beginning, with Chris Van Gorder. He was on.

Chief Executive Officer Chris Van Gorder would transform Scripps Health with his dedication to inspiring trust, developing transparency, and building relationships. *courtesy of Scripps Health*

CHAPTER THIRTEEN
The New Millennium
2000 - 2012

The interim chief executive for Scripps Health who took the reins on May 26, 2000, was the fifth in seven years. With an initial contract for ninety days and clear notice that a national search was under way, he won the permanent position in a single month. And he did it so convincingly that, within that month, the chiefs of staff of all five Scripps hospitals—who had voted no confidence in his predecessor—took out a full-page newspaper ad expressing their support.[1] "That month," Chris Van Gorder said:

> I met with every single Board member. And I asked them one-on-one, "What would you like me to do? Do you want me to be a caretaker or to act like a CEO?"
>
> And every single one of them said, 'You are the CEO—act like it. Do what you need to do. Keep the Board informed.'
>
> And that's when I came up with the idea of the Physician Leadership Cabinet.

CEO Chris Van Gorder and Chief Medical Officer Brent Eastman co-chaired the game-changing Physician Leadership Cabinet. Left to right, Todd Hoff, Dr. John Romine, Dr. Peter Walther, · Dr. David Shaw, Dr. Davis Cracroft, Gary Fybel, Chris Van Gorder, Dr. Brent Eastman, Dr. Luis Sanchez, Dr. Ed Cohen, Dr. Dana Launer, Dr. Sabina Wallach, Tom Gammiere, and Robin Brown
courtesy of Scripps Health

The Physician Leadership Cabinet (PLC) was a game-changing construction made up of the chiefs and vice-chiefs of staff from each hospital, along with their hospital chief executives and a representative chief nurse. It was co-chaired by Chris Van Gorder and Chief Medical Officer Brent Eastman, and based on the concept that *a gap of information leads to dissent and anger and divisiveness. But sharing information in a spirit of transparency leads to alignment around the same decisions.*

"I learned that," Chris said, "in my first senior administrative job, as a vice-president at Anaheim Memorial Hospital.

> Our Board at Anaheim was 49 percent physicians, the maximum allowed by law, and historically the medical staff elected their more negative members, to 'take on' the administration. And I watched what happened when those physicians had the same information the Board had—which was that they supported the board and administration, and we never had less than a unanimous vote.
>
> And I realized doctors are very smart people and administrators are pretty bright, too. The only reason for an adversarial relationship is a gap of information.

At Scripps Health in those first crucial days, Chris set the stage for nearly all the progress of the coming decade with an approachable transparent style that defused tension—a style he learned first as a working cop.

Chris Van Gorder has always believed in serving his community. Left, Mr. Van Gorder served as a Monterey Park Police Officer in 1976. Right, Mr. Van Gorder is currently a reserve commander for the San Diego County Sheriff's Department in command of the Search & Rescue Team. *courtesy of Chris Van Gorder*

Chris Van Gorder grew up with a twin in the western San Gabriel Valley of Los Angeles, in the small city of Alhambra, to parents who emigrated from Canada after dropping out of school for jobs during World War II. Both parents earned their high school diplomas at night while working full-time; and the family understanding was that you worked hard, earned your own education, and gave back to the community as soon as you could. Chris went to work as a thirteen year old in a bookstore managed by his mother, and was never unemployed again.

It was in freshman year at Cal State University, Los Angeles that his interest in law enforcement was sparked by a poster on the corkboard next to the student employment office—a broadside from the Los Angeles Police Department recruiting "student officers" for good hours and good pay. Chris was hired forthwith and spent some fascinating and sometimes wrenching months on the "missing persons" desk and then with the tough west side "Rampart Division," until he took over his brother's job as emergency room clerk at Huntington Memorial Hospital, Pasadena, and began his singular alternating career in law enforcement and health care. By the end of three years at Huntington Hospital, he had moved from clerk, to security guard, to full-time laboratory office manager, all purely on the basis of work ethic and performance, and all while still in college—and then left the hospital for the Los Angeles County Sheriff's Academy, graduating as a California Peace Officer in 1976 when he was twenty-three years old.

Chris Van Gorder liked the force, became a good judge of people as a policeman, and learned to make quick decisions. He was an active police agent for the City of Monterey Park for a little over two years, until his career was derailed by an injury in the line of duty. In November 1978, he answered a domestic dispute call—one of the most dangerous for any officer—and a distraught mother carried out her threat to ram her car into any police vehicle that tried to stop her fleeing with her child. Chris's patrol car was hit head-on at 55 mph. Crushed by the steering wheel, saved by his bullet proof vest, and extricated from the car, he suffered fractures of his cervical and lumbar spine, among other injuries, which had him hospitalized—first, in the absence of a trauma system, at the closest community hospital—and then after a week, at Los Angeles Orthopaedic Hospital where he returned for reassessment and physical therapy repeatedly over the next year.

Over that long year, Chris had time to study how Orthopaedic Hospital was run and also to get to know the people in charge. When it was clear by 1980 that he would be placed on the disabled-retired list by the police department, he applied for a job at Orthopaedic as director of Security and Safety and was hired, and first saw the dark-haired Rosemary Treiger who was Director of Child Life (a program designed to ease the emotional and physical pain of hospitalized children).[2]

Further intrigued, he enrolled in graduate studies at the University of Southern California, persuaded Rosemary Treiger to marry him, and earned an MPA in Health Services Administration (with honors and first in his class) in 1986 after returning to Orthopaedic Hospital for his mandatory year of administrative residency. After that it was onward and upward, from Anaheim Memorial Hospital to Little Company of Mary Hospital in Torrance as COO, back to Anaheim Memorial as president and CEO, while Anaheim was a stand-alone hospital and also after opening up a process to merge the hospital with a system called Memorial Health Services; and finally as CEO of the flagship Long Beach Memorial Hospital until the fateful call to Scripps. And Chris said:

> I'm very grateful Stan brought me here, because—although I was a good candidate for Chief Operating Officer—I never would have been recruited here as CEO since I hadn't run a system. I'd run a big hospital, but not a system.
>
> And then I was here just long enough for the board members and physicians to get a chance to see what I could do, but not long enough to be blamed for what happened.

And although Chris Van Gorder was determined to regain trust going forward, he could not say yes to every demand. One of his first official acts, nine days after taking office, was the painful business of closing Scripps Memorial Hospital, East County. Ironically, the closure was not much related to the turmoil of previous months. Chris himself, while still chief operating officer, had made a straightforward assessment that the community theoretically served by the hospital was not using it in sufficient numbers to keep it open, but was essentially bypassing it for bigger institutions further west—including other Scripps hospitals. After seven years of work and a net loss of $10 million, occupancy at Scripps East County held at a stubborn 30 percent. Closure was inevitable, but the wash of new negative publicity[3] drained away with Chris's pledge of jobs on other Scripps campuses for all East County employees.

Then came the third fraught marriage of Scripps Health and Scripps Clinic.[4]

The latest four-year separation had been very hard on the physicians of Scripps Clinic Medical Group, whose leadership was pursuing a strategy of making up potentially fatal losses in the managed care market by trying to become a publicly traded company. But SCMG physicians had taken a serious pay cut and invested in a management company just as other such arrangements around the country were collapsing. Health care consultant Bob Erra said:

> It didn't make a lot of sense for the doctors to keep investing in an independent medical group with no real exit strategy because they couldn't do the kinds of things that they wanted to do to be a premier medical group. They couldn't invest in research. They couldn't invest in education. All they were really investing in was trying to stay afloat as a group.

Re-affiliation would be the financial salvation of the Clinic and restore to Scripps Health this prestigious integrated, multispecialty medical group that constituted nearly the entire admitting staff to Green Hospital—owned by Scripps Health.

But negotiations were so super-charged and volatile that Chris Van Gorder finally requested the two sides keep to separate rooms while a trusted mediator carried out shuttle diplomacy between them. The mediator, Bob Erra, had been chief financial and then chief operating officer of Scripps Clinic under Charlie Edwards and helped to engineer the 1991 merger with Scripps Health into SIMS. Mr. Erra said that Dr. Brent Eastman for Scripps Health and Dr. Phil Higginbottom for the Clinic were trustworthy voices of calm in the negotiations; but also that:

> Chris Van Gorder was in a very tough position, having to decide as the brand new CEO whether to pursue affiliation. He had to persuade the independent physicians in his other four hospitals, "I'm not going to try and make you look like Scripps Clinic. We'll have a pluralistic approach on how we affiliate with physicians."[5]

And Chris said,

> I asked the independent doctors to give me time to turn around the Clinic and Green Hospital.
>
> And I told them we had three solid reasons for buying back the Clinic: the first was that Clinic doctors were responsible for roughly a quarter of a million patients, and if they went bankrupt, all those patient/doctor relationships would be disrupted; second, they share our name - and the community wouldn't know whether it was Scripps Clinic or Scripps Health that failed; and then they were responsible for sixty percent of our philanthropy.[6]

Robin Brown worked in a variety of roles at Scripps before becoming chief executive of Scripps Green Hospital in 2000. Since his appointment, Mr. Brown and his team have achieved outstanding success in clinical outcomes, financial performance, employee satisfaction, and customer service.

courtesy of Scripps Health

On July 14, 2000 (Bastille Day), the Clinic was repurchased by Scripps Health with payouts to capital partners and assumption of liabilities, leases canceled, and a 25-year, renewable, professional services agreement with the Medical Group. After his final collaboration with Chris Van Gorder, Dr. Tom Waltz retired from management and returned full time to the practice of neurosurgery.[7] The combined duties previously shouldered by Dr. Waltz were divided in two. The newly elected President of Scripps Clinic Medical Group was pulmonologist Dr. Robert Sarnoff who came to the Clinic from UCSD in 1980, at "the dawn of the era of critical care medicine" and within months was made Director of Critical Care.[8] And on August 1, Chris Van Gorder chose Dr. Hugh Greenway, chairman of Mohs and dermatologic surgery and a physician leader and protégé of Dr. Edmund Keeney, as CEO of Scripps Clinic—meaning the newly named Scripps Medical Foundation, which replaced the former Scripps Clinic and Research Foundation for the purpose of conducting business.[9] Already in place for several months as Green Hospital Chief Executive was the highly experienced Robin Brown.

With time the die-hard discomfort between independent and integrated physicians—and between the integrated physicians and the leadership at Campus Point—would slowly give way to respect and an understanding of everything to gain by collaboration. But that was still years away and would require leaps of faith and diplomacy on both sides.

After that difficult early summer, the trajectory of recovery was slowly but steadily up—despite the huge challenges of system wide disaffection and a negative bottom line. In essence the Physician Leadership Cabinet was the precursor of what is now called horizontal co-management. Chris said:

> We learned to trust each other. I got to know the doctors, they got to know me - and the leaders of the revolt on each campus became leaders in the calm that followed chaos. They realized we really do have a common vision. We want to do the best we can for our patients, but we also want to have a successful organization. And the only way we can do that is to trust each other and work together.

After the PLC came the equally remarkable Scripps Leadership Academy (SLA) in 2001—a year-long program for managers from across the system who meet with Chris Van Gorder for a whole day, eleven times a year. The SLA was developed by Chris in conjunction with his long-time friend Elliot Kushell, organizational consultant and professor of management at Cal State University, Fullerton. Chris and Elliot Kushell had by that time known each other fifteen years, from the early days at Anaheim Memorial when Chris was a new VP and Elliot a fresh young consultant who rose quickly to the notice of senior management. Elliot said:

> Chris got the idea for Leadership Academy from a similar program at Memorial Health System when he was CEO of Long Beach Memorial. However, his vision was quite different in that he wanted Scripps Leadership Academy to be much more interactive—to include a no-holds barred, transparent Q & A session with him as a way to align and engage the participants and give them insight into how and why decisions are made at top levels.[10]

"Because," Chris said:

> I knew that we were going to have to change the culture of this company, and I can't write a memo to change culture. The senior leadership can't be visible enough, and the rank and file don't have the power. So I said, 'You know it's this middle management group. I think the power of changing this company comes from the middle.'

The application process requires writing an essay on why the individual wants to be part of Leadership Academy. Chris reads all the essays and is looking for people "who talk about wanting to get to know how other people work at other campuses"—the whole idea of what he calls "breaking down the silos." And, once in:

> the first two and a half hours of every session is wide open Q & A with me. There are only three things we won't talk about: a personnel issue as it relates to an individual, because that would be breaking the law and violating a confidence; patient-specific information; or a business transaction with another organization that has a confidentiality agreement.

> Otherwise it's wide open. We give them the financials. We give them the balance sheet, our CFO Richard Rothberger comes and reports. They get strategic planning from June Komar, legal with Richard Sheridan, HR with Vic Buzachero and clinical insights from Brent Eastman and other physician leaders.

> Sometimes I chide them for not asking tough enough questions. Eventually that builds the courage to ask about anything and everything.

Johan Otter, now Senior Director Occupational Health and Wellness, is an alumnus of the first Scripps Leadership Academy. He said:

> After the first and then the second Scripps Leadership Academy ended, we realized how much we had come to value the monthly updates with Chris, and we missed the sessions. Alumni of the first two classes met as a small group and agreed the organization needed more communication and continuity after this year of intense immersion. I was not shy, so I asked Chris, "Now what?" during a meeting where we were describing our withdrawal symptoms.
>
> Chris welcomed the spirit of the question and answered that the Leadership Academy's Alumni mission was to act as seeds for positive change at Scripps, scattering and taking root across the organization, to grow a forward-thinking, transparent culture.[11]

Johan Otter collaborated with Corporate Communications Senior Director Mike Godfrey, another early graduate, to establish the official Scripps Leadership Academy Alumni (SLAA). In the eight years since, the Alumni have spearheaded a host of projects including the HOPE (Helping Our Peers in Emergencies) Fund, staff support for an annual system wide Quality Summit and the hugely popular summer family extravaganza, Scripps Night at the Ballpark. Most important of all, they are back to meeting monthly with Chris.

With this crucial first order of business—regaining trust—under way, Chris could begin to make progress with the battered finances. For one thing, physicians who had reacted against the prior administration by sending their patients elsewhere returned to their ordinary practice; at Scripps Mercy alone, the occupancy rate was up 40% in the first year. Chris began attending to the deferred cleaning, painting and repairs on all campuses which had added fuel to the fire, and also engineered a pay raise for nurses. He made his first executive hire in the summer of 2000, of Gary Fybel as chief executive for the "legacy hospital" Scripps La Jolla. Gary came to Scripps from twelve years at Mission Hospital Orange County and immediately focused on "elements of

Left to right, Cliff Robertson, Betty Knight Scripps, and Gary Fybel. Betty Knight Scripps continues her family's legacy of supporting Scripps Health by serving as General Chairman of the Candleight Ball since 2004.

courtesy of Scripps Health

honesty and mutual respect and the notion that we are all here to provide the most exceptional care possible to our patients."[12] (One indicator of the success of this approach would be the 2005 designation of Scripps La Jolla as the first facility in San Diego to be awarded "Magnet Hospital" status for excellence in nursing. Another is the delightful Wolfstein Sculpture Park, devoted to the premise that *art enhances the healing environment*.)[13]

Chris was fortunate to have in-house already his own "Jacob Harper"—general counsel Richard Sheridan who had been serving Scripps Health with a clear eye on ethics and the law since 1988. Richard arrived at Scripps after a fascinating early career as midnight reggae disc jockey (Lawrence University, Appleton, Wisconsin) and bicycling part-time carpenter in Boston—until one day the girl he loved informed him she had registered him for the Law School Admissions Test to be held in two days time. With scores on the LSAT in the 99th percentile, Richard attended Boston University School of Law two years with a third year at Stanford (and also got the girl, his wife Nancy). Appointed counsel to Scripps Memorial by Ames Early, Richard was the only top level executive for the Hospital who kept his position in the creation of SIMS;[14] and through all the turmoil of the 90s he was a constant voice of reason, and also of history. He had majored in history in college; he had read the legal archives. He knew Miss Ellen's intentions and was not afraid to speak in her behalf.

And Chris was also blessed with the talent and almost 30 years of management and strategic planning experience of June Komar, who had come to Scripps from Mercy five years before, by way of Ann Arbor, Michigan, and San Diego County Administration. In 2001, Chris made June his Corporate Senior Vice President for Strategic Planning and Business Development. That same year, Berkeley MBA Barbara Price was recruited from the corporate office of Kaiser Permanente in Oakland. There, Barbara had led internal consulting services across several regions of the United States, and set up a similar Project Management Office at Scripps to eliminate reliance on outside consultants and their sizable fees, and to develop internal analytical capabilities of a national caliber consulting organization. (Barbara, in her current role as corporate

As Corporate Executive Vice President of Strategy and Administration, June Komar oversees strategic planning and business development, government and community relations, marketing and communications, information services, and Scripps Home Health Care. Her strategic planning has yielded unprecedented recognition and results for Scripps, including recognition by *USNews & World Report*.

courtesy of Scripps Health

senior vice-president for business and service line development, reports to June Komar, as does marketing and communications. Over the years, June would take on the vast intricacies of Information Services; and Chris would speak of her as "the quiet rock of our team.")

But now, in 2001, Chris was searching for a new financial officer who could engineer a turnaround, as well as a head of human resources who could build on the momentum of fragile good will that was opening around the system. He was specifically looking for leaders who were "operations oriented and experienced," who really understood how health care systems worked, and "believed in the intellectual capital of people."[15] And in this endeavor he was much helped by the weather in San Diego.

In the spring of 2001, both Richard Rothberger[16] and Vic Buzachero[17] were looking for climatic improvement—Rich Rothberger to avoid a move to the heat of Arizona, and Vic Buzachero to escape the gloom of the Pacific Northwest. Both were highly experienced in their fields of finance and human resources and understood the recent difficult history at Scripps Health and the commitment of Chris Van Gorder to turn things around; neither wanted to join a troubled system just to watch it be handed over to *someone else* who could make it work. So Rich Rothberger came to visit La Jolla at nearly the same time Vic Buzachero and his wife were enjoying the sunshine in Coronado, and by the end of the summer of 2001 they had both joined the turnaround team at Scripps Health.

Vic Buzachero joined CEO Chris Van Gorder's leadership team in 2001 in human resources. Under his guidance as corporate senior vice president for innovation, human resources and performance management, Scripps regularly achieves high marks for employee satisfaction.

courtesy of Scripps Health

By 2003, Corporate Executive Vice President and CFO Rich Rothberger had turned the financial health of Scripps around so the organization could continue to provide high quality care to the San Diego community.

courtesy of Scripps Health

Rich Rothberger's entry into health care was through applied mathematics, when he followed up a college degree in math with a master's in "industrial engineering with an emphasis in health systems" from Northeastern University. Rich said:

> I knew health care was going to be around forever and was looking for a place where I could meet my social service needs as well as apply my mathematical skills in a way that I could make a difference. My college counselor told me about this program that was heavy math with a finance twist and applied in a social service field. And I said, "This sounds perfect."

After internship as an industrial engineer at the Massachusetts General Hospital, Rich made his way from a Midwest consulting firm to Mercy Healthcare Sacramento in 1978. All told, he worked with the Sisters of Mercy for twenty-three years, as director of management engineering and then as CFO. And Rich said:

> I respected and liked physicians and became known for win-win solutions with medical groups.

> And it was wonderful working with the Sisters. There was a spiritual piece that was always there, a caring piece. It permeated through the organization and gave you a sense of purpose and mission.

But, in 1987 Mercy Sacramento became a division of Catholic Healthcare West. And eventually CHW centralized senior management and invited Richard Rothberger to Phoenix, Arizona— in August—to head consolidated financial operations for their forty-eight hospitals. He and his family declined that job; and ultimately Rich Rothberger left his own top-performing division in Sacramento for Scripps Health and Chris Van Gorder.

Just how poor the financial situation was at Scripps Health in August 2001 was hard to find out. There was very little published data by the prior CFO, no bond rating, no leadership for the revenue cycle (meaning billing and collections), and the supply chain (purchasing) was outsourced. On top of all that, health plans had shifted all risk to the hospitals, with contracts that paid a flat rate but did not cover costs, so that "we were heavily in managed care, but not managing care."

As Corporate Senior Vice President of Supply Chain/Facilities, dedicated Scripps employee John Armstrong oversees surgery, pharmacy and supply chain management, facilities design and construction. Under his leadership, supply costs as a percentage of net revenue have continuously decreased.

courtesy of Scripps Health

So Richard Rothberger's first hire was Dave Cohn—an Arthur Anderson consultant who worked for Rich in Sacramento—to manage the revenue cycle, meaning:

> making sure that we don't leave money on the table with the insurance companies and that we're billing appropriately and compliantly and we're collecting appropriately and we're documenting. And Dave had a broader vision in terms of revenue cycle that included not only billing and collections but admitting, registration, coding and documentation and case management. It was pretty nuovo ten years ago to do that.

Long-time Scripps employee John Armstrong was asked to bring the supply chain back in house and under control—a sometimes thankless, always laborious task that would finally come into its own through horizontal integration with John as Corporate Senior Vice President, Support Services Division.

Skilled nursing facilities (SNFs) in La Jolla and Encinitas were sold off in 2002. Torrey Pines Convalescent and Ocean View Convalescent had been acquired by Scripps in the 1980s when the mission was to provide the continuum of care from birth to end of life. It was also at a time when Medicare started paying hospitals a fixed amount for a patient's condition, the so-called *Diagnosis Related Groups*, or *DRGs*. "So it was really wise," said Mary Lou Carraher,[18] Chief Executive of Scripps Home Health, "for the two Scripps Hospitals [La Jolla and Encinitas] to start reducing their length of stay and moving patients to convalescent homes, because they didn't get paid for those extra days.

> I was working in Home Health in New York at that time, as Head of Operations for Visiting Nurses. And I remember we were getting patients "quicker and sicker." Those were the words they used.

Mary Lou Carraher arrived at Scripps in 1998, and in 2001:

Chris asked me to oversee the skilled nursing facilities in addition to Home Health. And I didn't have them under my wing for more than a month or two when Chris told me that we were going to sell them. You know as we looked at it, there were three compelling reasons to sell: one was that our mission was changing from "providing" to "collaborating" with the continuum of care; then the SNFs were a very, very capital intensive need, requiring major modernization and renovation; and finally, running nursing homes was not our strong suit.

By contrast Scripps is providing superb post hospital care through Home Health, which began twenty-seven years ago at La Jolla and after 1995 merged with a similar big operation at Mercy. And in fact, prior hospitalization is not a requirement, as long as the patient is housebound with "maximum assist" and is referred by a physician for a medical need. Census in Scripps Home Health on an average *daily* basis is an astonishing 450-500 patients served.

So by 2003, Rich Rothberger had gotten enough control of finances that Scripps Health was making $10 million a year instead of losing that amount, which was the case when he arrived. For a nonprofit institution, that meant having funds to *begin* to cover charitable care and reinvest for capital needs. But now Rich and the team took an enormous step and got out of managed care, moving the company away from risk contracting to fee for service.

This was one of the leaps of faith required of Dr. Robert Sarnoff and Scripps Clinic Medical Group, which had something like 130,000 "lives," meaning patients under contract (in the only permissible business arrangement between hospital corporation and physicians in the state of California, which is the foundation model. In 2003 Larry Harrison, with an MBA from the University of Southern California and Master of Health Science from Johns Hopkins University, had succeeded Dr. Hugh Greenway as chief executive of the Scripps Clinic Medical Foundation).[19]

And now Rich Rothberger said:

> I went to talk with Dr. Sarnoff about dropping the contracts because the risk was that if I misjudged and we lost half the patients, what would Bob do?

> We were in financial straits with the Clinic because they were still losing money, and we were still on the hook for their salaries after bailing them out. And so I had a heart to heart with Bob and the group and said, "Look. We are on the edge. This company will not survive with the model that we're in."

> And he said, "I agree." And I said, "You're going to have to trust us. If I can get the rates that I think we can get, you'll be better off than before and have a sustainable business plan."

So in 2003 with agreement from Scripps Clinic Medical Group, Rich Rothberger had Marc Reynolds—"a magician in terms of working with payers"—cancel all contracts; and Marc Reynolds told the insurers, "Our goal is not to NOT do business with you; but to do business with you on a fee for service basis."
And Rich said:

> We went all fee-for-service and did have to give up some 30,000 patients at first. But even with losing those "lives" we were ahead of the game on revenue. And as the momentum picked up when these contracts were renewed, it just started multiplying; and when all insurers were finally on board, the volume went through the roof.

While Rich Rothberger was working this financial magic, Vic Buzachero was doing something similar with employee relations, building on the transparent foundation set by Chris Van Gorder. Vic—whose title of Senior VP of Innovation, Human Resources and Performance Management speaks to the scope of his responsibility—was determined from the beginning to engage all employees in the turnaround at Scripps Health. In 2002, within months of his arrival, he launched a company-wide survey which indicated that only a little over half (58 percent) of its employees considered Scripps a great place to work. Using benchmarks of the Great Place to Work Institute—a company devoted to the development of high-trust workplace cultures around the world[2]—the HR team was able to focus on the highest-gain areas at each site as well as in the system overall. Each year employee satisfaction was methodically measured and steadily improved, and by 2004 the figure climbed to 78% (and has continued climbing every year) despite the sudden arrival of a nurses' union at Scripps Encinitas at the end of 2003, and a struggle over union certification and decertification which simmered there for over three years.

Chief Executive of Scripps Memorial Hospital Encinitas Carl Etter is overseeing the expansion of the Encinitas campus.

courtesy of Scripps Health

The primary "spark" at Encinitas was the one at the heart of all employee disputes, lack of trust—in this case, a reaction against a revolving door of administrators at the chief executive level (five in five years). Ironically, Carl Etter, the chief executive who would earn a level of trust at Scripps Encinitas beyond any seen for years, had arrived there ten days before the union vote and too late to head off the action. Carl said:

> I had worked at hospitals with unions and hospitals without unions, and tried not to alter my approach. However, Scripps was the first organization I worked for that believed in its values and respected the rights of every staff person to the extent

that it didn't just give in and learn to live with an exterior entity that would have inserted itself between management and caregivers.

> I stayed out of negotiations and focused on turning around the hospital, improving patient care and engaging our employees. Nursing is the heart of every hospital, and it was very awkward to have an ongoing disagreement with the very "heart" of patient care.[21]

Vic Buzachero's major at the University of Alabama was Industrial Relations (including unions) and he said, "I lived those negotiations."

> I spent a lot of time with the board and a lot of time with senior management making sure we all understood what was at stake and what we had to do to change it. And it wasn't about fighting the union. It was about creating a different environment and different relationship with the people. But to give that time, you couldn't agree to give the union certain things that you didn't give the rest of the organization. The one union contract of 2006 contained absolutely nothing beyond what our nurses on every other campus received.

Jan Zachry, BSN, with a new MBA from the University of Phoenix, took over as chief nurse executive at Encinitas in 2006. She said:

> The union was finally decertified in 2008 and by that time things were much better. There was much higher morale among staff in the hospital in general and nurses were part of that. I think leaders had learned a great deal about communicating to their staff. Carl Etter made a huge difference.[22]

In that same year, 2008, 88 percent of employees rated Scripps Health a Great Place to Work, and the company was first named to *Fortune* Magazine's national "100 Best Companies to Work For"—only the second San Diego company after Qualcomm to make the list ever – and the acclaim has been sustained five years in a row. The "Culture Audit Application" that Vic's team submits for this award is 147 pages of *personal stories* on hiring and welcoming, inspiring, speaking, listening, thanking, developing, caring, celebrating and sharing. In 2011, the Great Place to Work Institute published A Case Study of Scripps Health called "Transforming Into a Great Workplace." Now Scripps Health is rated one of the "100 Best Companies for Working Mothers"[23] and *the* single "Best Employer for Workers Over 50" nationwide.[24] Vic Buzachero says:

> We consider Scripps to be a career destination company and design our human resources program to appeal to people in every stage of life. Over a third of our workforce is age 50 or older and we work to retain them because the knowledge they pass down ultimately results in better outcomes for our patients.

> Scripps understands that its brand comes, not from its buildings, but from the talent and know-how of its people and how they care for patients.

In 2004, a profound change occurred at Scripps Mercy and Chula Vista when the two hospitals and their two medical staffs reinvented themselves, with great trepidation, as one hospital and one medical staff on two campuses. The "merging of licenses" was a strategy directly aimed at saving the mission of the two members of the Scripps family providing a "disproportionate share" of care to low-income and uninsured patients. The Chula Vista campus, especially, was in financial straits; and although Chris Van Gorder had closed the East County campus in 2000 on account of low occupancy, this was an entirely different situation with a high-needs community streaming in for care. However, paying patients were going elsewhere. Mercy Chief Executive Tom Gammiere said:

> Scripps Chula Vista had lost market share when the prior administration canceled contracts. Local patients with insurance who arrived in the Emergency Department were regularly transferred to Sharp under existing contracts with payors.[25]

The merger was designed to consolidate resources, make operations more efficient, re-establish contracts and demonstrate to the financial markets that Scripps was dealing responsibly with a piece of the system that was losing money. But Chris Van Gorder said:

> I would not make the change without the approval of the two medical staffs.

> We talked; and they had meetings and forums and discussions. I went back to Chula Vista again and had a second Q and A with the medical staff. And they were quite polite to me in the room. But it was controversial.

> In the end both medical staffs held a vote and both agreed to the merger.

But merging the two cultures was not easy. It helped that Tom Gammiere had started his Scripps administrative career at Chula Vista and actually served there twice as long as he'd been at Mercy. (Tom began his career at Chula Vista in 1987 and was transferred to Mercy in 1999 by Sister Mary Jo Anderson, while she was chief operating officer of Scripps Health.) The process was immensely helped by the committed chief of staff at Chula Vista, nephrologist Diogo Belo, originally from Peru, and by the chief and vice-chief at Mercy, Eugene Rumsey, Jr. and Jerry Glassman. It also helped that both cultures were predominantly Catholic so that the *Ethical and Religious Directives* were not a serious stumbling block. But still, according to Mercy Chula Vista emergency department physician Dr. Juan Tovar:

Seven years ago, there was huge strife, fear, animosity. Now: markedly decreased animosity, more collaboration. We realize that Mercy Hospital has two campuses and that each campus has positives and negatives and we're working more as one.[26]

Juan Tovar himself may be the best indicator of how far the two "Mercies" have come along the path toward a truly blended culture. He is the first chief of staff elect – or, in the new parlance, chair-elect of the medical executive committee–from Scripps Mercy Chula Vista. Born in 1966 in Colombia to a medical student father getting death threats for political protest, Juan was raised in New York City from the age of five. He went on to graduate from UC San Diego School of Medicine in 1996, tried returning to New York for emergency medicine residency at Bellevue, but missed San Diego and moved back in 2000 after calling Dr. Don Vance every week for eight months for a job in the Scripps Chula Vista ED.

Juan Tovar likes multiculturalism and speaks three languages himself, including Portuguese. About working in the ED at Chula Vista, he says:

> It's such an interesting place to work. There's never a dull moment. And the pathology! Everybody has diabetes, hypertension, end stage renal disease. We have a huge amount of pathology. And because people are underinsured, they let things go a little longer. So, if you like medicine, if you like treating disease, you'll find everything here.
>
> And you serve a population that is value based, hardworking, and grateful for what you have given them.

More than 200 community members, Scripps employees, friends, and dignitaries attended the dedication and blessing of Scripps Mercy Hospital, Chula Vista in January 2005, which marked the reinvention of Scripps Memorial Hospital Chula Vista and Scripps Mercy Hospital as one hospital, Scripps Mercy Hospital, on two campuses. Left to right, Tom Gammiere, chief executive of the newly merged Scripps Mercy Hospital; Sister Mary Jo Anderson; Bishop Gilbert Chavez; and CEO Chris Van Gorder attended the event. Right, Scripps was presented with proclamations marking January 12 as Scripps Mercy Chula Vista Day.

courtesy of Scripps Health

Mercy Hospital led the way in the transformation of the emergency departments throughout the Scripps system. Patients are seen within thirty minutes by a team that follows them from triage to discharge.

courtesy of Scripps Health

As for what Mercy brings to the rest of the Scripps Health system:

> The Mercies are known for their leanness. They're lean. We operate really close to a hundred percent productivity and we've been doing that for quite some time. We've had to, because of financial constraints working with this population. You have to be really efficient.

And as to the state of medical staff integration now, not only within Mercy, but throughout the system:

> As a system, we have a great opportunity because we've started changing things. We've started having interaction, collaboration between groups now where they're starting to realize the difficulties of working at each place. And they're starting to walk in those people's shoes. So they're developing empathy.

A huge increase in empathy among the "silos" of Scripps Health was one surprising gift of the hurricane that drowned New Orleans in the early morning of August 29, 2005. When Katrina broke down the levees, preconceived notions about colleagues on other campuses broke down as well. At the request of the head of the Public Health Service, U. S. Surgeon-General Richard Carmona—who was a trauma surgeon and colleague of Brent Eastman—Chris Van Gorder sent out a system wide call for volunteers for a Scripps Medical Response Team (SMRT) to go to the medical aid of survivors pressed into the George R. Brown Convention Center in Houston

In 2005, U.S. Surgeon-General Richard Carmona asked Scripps CEO Chris Van Gorder to send out a team to aid the victims of Hurricane Katrina. Left to right, Dr. Brent Eastman, Chris Van Gorder, and Dr. Carmona meet to discuss the logistics of preparing and mobilizing a disaster relief team.

courtesy of Scripps Health

and relieve an exhausted team from the University of Texas. Within twenty-four hours, more than 200 physicians and employees from every site in the system offered to put their lives on hold in order to staff a temporary clinic for the great mass of evacuees from Louisiana welcomed to Houston by the compassionate Mayor Bill White. On September 12, 2005, Scripps deployed a thirty-seven-member medical response team and then another twenty-one members to Houston for a two-week assignment. What they found were 5,000 displaced persons on one side of a great hall, with a comprehensive clinic set up by the University of Texas on the other; the unit was fully equipped to serve general medicine, minor surgery, pediatrics, and psychiatry, with a full pharmacy and even an optical dispensary for glasses washed away

Above, this child's drawing was left on the convention center floor in Houston, where evacuees from Hurricane Katrina fled in 2005. Disaster relief teams from Scripps provided care for the frightened victims.

in the flood. In order to practice medicine legally in Texas, all members of the Scripps team were deputized as "Disaster Service Workers" under the Public Health Service. Chris and Brent attended morning report daily with the mayor, while nurses Patty Skoglund and Kelly Hardiman organized assignments and operations.

The teams treated an average 500 patients a day until Houston itself was evacuated September 23 ahead of Hurricane Rita, and Chris found himself directing his own people to safety among the vast throngs fleeing the city to Dallas and points north. A month later, Mayor White and the US Public Health Service asked Scripps to return to Houston to staff community clinics for survivors of both storms, and another nine-person team deployed for a week."[27]

The entire Scripps family back home was riveted by Chris Van Gorder's daily *Notes from the Field* – his late night dispatches from Houston on his very first BlackBerry, with words and pictures of the highlights of the day - including the child's drawing picked up by Rob Sills from the convention center floor with the big crayon letters: *Have Hope. Help is on the Way.*

Chris later said:

> Our cultural shift really picked up steam when we did the blogs back then. You know, I think a lot of our employees didn't think anybody at corporate had any compassion for patients in the system. I think they saw us only as the "business" people and thought we actually didn't care about others. But there seemed to be a 180 degree turnaround when they realized that not only do we care, we actually went out and took care of patients ourselves and then communicated back to them.[28]

In 2005, Scripps sent medical teams to help survivors of Hurricane Katrina who were evacuated to Houston. The teams treated an average 500 patients a day until Houston was evacuated ahead of Hurricane Rita.

courtesy of Scripps Health

The first Hospital Administrative Support Unit to support mobile field hospitals, Scripps is a leader in disaster preparedness in California. Right, Mary Lou Carraher, chief executive of Scripps Home Health Care, and Ken Leake, RN, chart patient conditions and bed availability in the mobile field hospital command center.

courtesy of Scripps Health

It was four years earlier on the morning of 9/11 when Chris Van Gorder turned to his chief medical officer and asked, "Are we prepared?" Chris said, "We both knew the answer was no." But the terrorist attacks led directly to the Scripps Disaster Preparedness Office under Patty Skoglund, and from there to the SMRT team designed to identify and train physicians, nurses, disaster managers/ administrators and support staff to deploy into the community—originally thought of as the community of San Diego—during a disaster. It just happened to be the people of the Gulf Coast who needed the SMRT team first. Next would be San Diegans fleeing the Cedar Fire of October 2003 which burned a quarter of a million acres of the county, setting a record which lasted a mere four years; then the hellish Witch Creek firestorms of October 2007 when half a million acres burned in a "raging fire that was visible from space"[29] and caused the evacuation of 1,000,000 people from their homes, the largest in California history. That week, the disaster team set up an outpatient medical clinic in Rancho Bernardo at the blackened verge of 800 burned-out homes, and were thanked there in person by President George W. Bush.

The disaster team set up an outpatient medical clinic in Rancho Bernardo to help the victims of the Witch Creek firestorms of 2007. Left, President George W. Bush thanks Scripps CEO Chris Van Gorder.

courtesy of Scripps Health

Nearly 2,000 Scripps employees and physicians volunteered to go to Haiti after the devastating earthquake in 2010. Only a few were able to enter the country and provide disaster relief and help the victims

courtesy of Scripps Health

But then, on January 12, 2010, came the killing earthquake in Haiti. And the misery the team encountered in Port au Prince resembled nothing they'd seen so far.

For this mission, nearly 2,000 employees and physicians volunteered, although the chaos in Haiti and destruction at all points of entry allowed only a handful in. From January 22, the two-man advance team of Chris Van Gorder and Brent Eastman made their way in stages by commercial and private plane,[30] and then by careening car with diplomatic plates, arriving January 24 at the grossly damaged Hospital Saint Francois de Sales. Through the intercession of former Scripps La Jolla trauma surgeon Dr. Edward Gamboa, they were housed above the shattered city in the compound of Archbishop Bernardito Auza, the Vatican *nuncio*,[31] and so had beds and safe water at night. As for the scene at the hospital, Chris wrote, "Not sure even how to describe today, but I will never forget it." Half the hospital had collapsed; one surgical room still standing was unbearable with the smell of death; the operating room available had no working anesthesia machine and insufficient light. Still Chris pulled out his search and rescue headlamp and put it on Brent's head, they washed their hands under a naked pipe outside, and the two of them, surgeon and scrub nurse, worked to repair crushed limbs and gaping wounds.

The concept of horizontal integration came to CEO Chris Van Gorder as he was standing on a hilltop in Haiti after the devastating earthquake of 2010.

courtesy of Scripps Health

The reconnaissance mission ended on January 26 with contacts made for return; and later that same week, Brent and Chris led combined medical and administrative teams totaling 11 people[32] back to Haiti along with crates, boxes, and bags of supplies. All team members were experienced in disaster and able to integrate quickly into an operating team with five counterparts from the University of Maryland. Once again, day after day, the *Notes from the Field* inspired everyone waiting at home. One physician reading in her Scripps Clinic office wrote in reply:

> The journal is so moving that my eyes tear up every time I read it. I have to catch my breath before I can go to see my next patient. I read your experiences to my family and friends, and my children are so inspired they too want to be on the next plane to Haiti.[33]

Later, Chris would say that his concept of *horizontal integration* of the entire Scripps Health system came to him in Haiti—that he was standing at the rim of the *nuncio's* compound on the hill overlooking a city that appeared, from that distant perspective, quite tranquil and even beautiful stretching to the sea; and that it was only at ground level that the disorder could be seen and set right by a network of determined people working together.

But it was an earthquake in California that led in serpentine fashion to an announcement in 2006 by Chris Van Gorder of plans for a system wide Cardiovascular Institute to be built on the campus of Scripps Memorial La Jolla. In the Northridge earthquake of 1994:

> Eleven hospitals…were damaged or unusable…Not only were they unable to serve their local neighborhoods, they had to transfer out their inpatient populations, which further increased the burden on nearby hospitals that were still operational. As a result, the state legislature passed a law [SB 1953] requiring all California hospitals to [be] earthquake-proof by January 1, 2005. Most were unable to make that deadline…[34]

Projected costs of the "retrofit" statewide were astronomical and deadlines pushed out year after year. Perhaps surprisingly, of all the Scripps hospitals, the one with the most expensive "fix" was La Jolla – with projected costs in the hundreds of millions of dollars. Meanwhile, the number one "clinical care line" in the system was cardiology, with Scripps the largest provider of cardiovascular care in San Diego County, including a long and productive partnership with Kaiser Permanente. Interventional cardiologist Dr. Richard Fortuna of Kaiser has been based at La Jolla permanently for over 15 years—and the arrangement is that Kaiser patients requiring electrophysiology, pacemaker, implantable defibrillator, cardiac catheterization, and intervention, as well as surgery for coronary artery bypass graft (CABG) and replacement of damaged valves are all treated at Scripps.[35] So, Chris Van Gorder decided on a plan to build out a new campus at La Jolla, ultimately razing the existing towers, and he began with the Scripps Cardiovascular Institute (SCI).

2006 was still early in the horizontal integration process; the famous words "to turn the organization on its side" had not yet been heard. The staffs at the Mercy campuses were still struggling to rub along together without friction, and now Chris was suggesting that all cardiologists, cardiac surgeons, nurses, support personnel and researchers come together in a system wide care line with its nucleus at La Jolla. This was especially hard for Scripps Clinic and Green with their already-excellent Heart Lung and Vascular Center—not to mention the philanthropic arm of the Scripps Green Cardiovascular Advisory Board. Negotiations over the next five years were extremely delicate.

Ultimately, the SCI was embraced by most. The genius was that all medical leaders were selected by the Physician Leadership Cabinet – and a critical component was the pledge of a new medical office building connected to the SCI for the Scripps Clinic Medical Group. The fully-committed SCI Steering Committee going forward in 2011 included: Medical Director Paul Teirstein (Green), Chair Jerry Glassman (Mercy), Richard Fortuna (Kaiser), Donald Buehler (La Jolla) and Martin Charlat (Encinitas).

The next great thing would be changing the name.

In 2006, CEO Chris Van Gorder announced plans to create a new campus at Scripps Memorial Hospital La Jolla, which would include demolishing the existing towers and building a new cardiovascular institute.

courtesy of Scripps Health

Dr. Eric Topol, right, is in the vanguard of genomics and individualized medicine. Dr. Topol discusses the results of his genetic scan with Rashaad Forehand.

courtesy of Scripps Health

By 2006, Scripps Health was strong enough as an institution to take a bold step into the future: not only to deliver health care that was the standard of the time, but to recruit one of the most renowned physician-scientists in the nation to lead the search for discoveries which could change the future of medicine.

Dr. Eric Topol[36] is an interventional cardiologist who came to San Diego to create the Scripps Translational Science Institute, of which he is Director. He is also Chief Academic Officer of Scripps Health, senior consultant cardiologist at Scripps Clinic, and professor of translational genomics at The Scripps Research Institute (TSRI) – which is one of the first new connections Scripps Health has to that institution since its drawn-out divorce from SIMS in the 1990s.

Eric Topol has "always been interested in genetics" and his senior thesis at the University of Virginia in 1975 was

> about the idea that you could have genetic *therapy* – you could already sense that's where the field would head to someday, that we were going to be able to insert genes and manipulate DNA to cure disease.

He had not intended at first to go into medicine—being more into math and biology and genetics – but happened to put himself through college working nights as a respiratory therapist in a hospital ICU. He saw patients he thought were going to die, and then "they were turned around and their lives were saved. And I wanted to be part of that." Eric graduated from the University of Rochester School of Medicine in 1979 and in May of 2011 returned to his alma mater to give the commencement lecture and receive the University's Hutchinson Medal in recognition of all the remarkable achievements which had brought him to Scripps.[37]

Eric Topol, like Richard Schatz and Mimi Guarneri before him, first came to Scripps because of Paul Teirstein. The two men were interventional cardiologists trained at about the same time in the 1980s and often found themselves on panels at cardiology conferences debating the merits of such things as angioplasty—Eric more conservative and Paul the liberal. But what really cemented the friendship was the coincidence of sitting in adjacent seats on a flight home from Stockholm in 1990 when both had presented at the 12th Congress of the European Society of Cardiology (an international event which is the largest cardiology conference in the world.) And Eric said:

> We had a chance to talk for eight hours straight and we had lots to talk about—a lot of similar experiences with the old guard who didn't want to let this field change and all this intervention take hold. But we also had a lot of laughs. I used to tell Paul he was the Jerry Seinfeld of medicine.

And Paul said:

> It taught me that if one wants to get to know a colleague (or anyone for that matter) take a trans-Atlantic flight.[38]

In 2006 Eric Topol was Professor of Genetics at Case Western Reserve University, a mile away from the Cleveland Clinic where he had chaired the department of cardiovascular medicine for fifteen years, a period during which *US News and World Report* ranked it number one in the nation for eleven consecutive years. He was also founder and provost of a medical school, the Cleveland Clinic Lerner College of Medicine. But Eric was ready for a move, and he called his friend Paul Teirstein at Scripps Clinic. By the summer of 2006, Eric was in the office of Chris Van Gorder who understood immediately the case for translational medicine and began a quick digital recruitment on his BlackBerry of a physician who would emerge at the forefront of the digital revolution. And at the turn of the new year 2007, Eric Topol began work in his first laboratories at Scripps.

Within ten months, he completed a masterful application for the most prestigious grant in the National Institutes of Health, the Clinical and Translational Science Awards (CTSA)—a process which required staggering feats of persuasion to get unlikely scientific and clinical bedfellows together. Eric said:

Left to right, Dr. Darryl D'Lima; Pam Pulido, RN; and Dr. Clifford Colwell of the Shiley Center for Orthopaedic Research and Education (SCORE) at Scripps are in the forefront of orthopaedic research. In 2004, Dr. Colwell made history when he implanted the world's first electronic knee, or e-knee, into a Scripps patient. The unique prosthesis contains a computer chip that measures forces in the joint while the patient participates in various activities, such as walking, climbing stairs and exercising. The newest e-knees also measure forces in the knee experienced during the rehabilitation process. The Scripps research has garnered numerous accolades and awards since its inception.

courtesy of Scripps Health

> In order to be awarded this flagship grant, perhaps the most competitive grant in all the NIH, you have to convincingly demonstrate that you can fully execute the whole continuum, at the highest quality and impact, of *basic* to *translational* to *clinical* research.
>
> And you had to make a case of how, by getting one of these grants, you would change the future of medicine.

When alliances engineered by Eric threatened to break apart because of politics, Chris Van Gorder stepped in with full support; and ultimately, with Chris's intervention, the key alliances held and the application was submitted on time on Halloween day 2007.

The coveted CTSA was won in May 2008—the first for any of the myriad medical and scientific institutes in San Diego, and the first in the nation not linked to a university. The initial grant was $20 million over five years, plus an additional $10 million in grants only accessible to winners of CTSA—essentially creating at Scripps a "mini-NIH, where we ourselves award funds for exciting studies."[39] Now in the CTSA network, Eric Topol says, Scripps is known for three things:

> Number one is our emphasis on *genomics* –applying the techniques of genetics and molecular biology to mapping sets of genes, organizing the results in databases, and applying the data in medicine;
>
> Second is our establishment of an unparalleled number of *collaborations with the life science industry*. We collaborate with every worthy entity in San Diego, which has the largest number of such companies outside of Silicon Valley;
>
> And third is that we are the only hub of *wireless biosensors*. We have established our wireless medicine presence.

Because of Eric's relationship with patients Gary and Mary West, in 2008 Scripps Health became founding clinical sponsor of the West Wireless Health Institute, along with Qualcomm as technical affiliate. Now Eric holds the Gary and Mary West Chair of Innovative Medicine at Scripps Health, endowed with a $5 million gift – and also chairs the newly formed Wireless Technology Committee designed to channel the most important of the world's zettabyte[40] of digital information out of the "cloud" and home to patients at Scripps Health.

Left to right, Mary West, Dr. Eric Topol, and Gary West. The Wests committed $45 million to launch the West Wireless Health Institute in 2009 as one of the world's first medical research organizations dedicated to advancing health and well-being through the use of wireless technologies.

courtesy of Scripps Health

President and CEO Chris Van Gorder established the Physician Leadership Cabinet in 2001. Left to right, front row, Tom Gammiere, Dr. Brent Eastman, and Chris Van Gorder, Middle row, Dr. James LaBelle, Dr. Scott Eisman, Dr. Kent Diveley, Dr. Jon Worsey, Mary Ellen Doyle, Robin Brown, and Gary Fybel. Back row, Dr. Donald Vance, Dr. Juan Tovar, Dr. Shawn Evans, and Dr. Thomas Chippendale. Not pictured, Carl Etter, Larry Harrison, Dr. Jason Mason, George Perez, and Dr. Ricardo Soltero. *courtesy of Scripps Health*

When Chris Van Gorder decided in 2010 to "turn the organization on its side," talented people at local sites found themselves suddenly promoted to jobs with system wide responsibility. One key innovation was to take operating officers out of the four hospitals[41] and make them corporate vice-presidents under the leadership of Barbara Price, John Armstrong, and Dr. Brent Eastman, to facilitate horizontal integration. Chris was supported in this by a strong collaboration of physicians, hospital executives and nursing through the Physician Leadership Cabinet (PLC). In the nine years of its existence, the PLC chaired by Chris and Brent had created a gratifying revolution in how system decisions are made; and in 2010 the newest member of PLC became Mary Ellen Doyle, BSN, MBA, as Corporate Vice President of Nursing Operations. Mary Ellen had come to Scripps from a position as Systems CNE at St. Luke's Health, Kansas City and was hired as nurse executive at La Jolla by Gary Fybel in 2008. She was willing then to take a step back from her high-powered position at St. Luke's in order to enjoy a more relaxed southern California lifestyle. But when the call came from Chris, she was fully-qualified to lead shared governance by nurses with Scripps physicians and executives. And Mary Ellen said:

> When patients in the San Diego Community enter a Scripps facility, they're entering a Scripps facility. And we should be providing a consistent standard of care – regardless of which door the patient enters first.[42]

Similarly, Richard Neale, LLB, MBA, had been recruited by Eric Topol in 2008 as Chief Business Officer for the Scripps Translational Medicine Institute. With years of business and operational experience within the pharmaceutical industry, Rick quickly made the connections with San Diego life science companies that are such a strong feature of the Institute today.[43] But then he was called to a system wide role as Corporate VP for Research Operations.

And now the stakes were raised by the federal government with the concept of the *accountable care organization* (ACO)—a whole new economic model. Imperative in this model is a collaboration of the health system with physician business leaders (meaning heads of organized medical groups). Chris recognized the need for a physician leader with both proven credibility and business skills to meet this challenge, and—following his own preference to search from within - appointed Dr. James LaBelle in the spring of 2011 to the new position of Corporate VP of Quality, Medical Management and Physician Co-Management within the newly-constituted medical division. Jim LaBelle was perfectly positioned to assume this job with a background of MBA from UC Irvine, chief of staff at Encinitas for two terms in the rocky years 2000-2004, and management of the Encinitas emergency department and hospitalists. Regarding the concept of an ACO led by administrators and physicians working together, Dr. LaBelle agreed that the structure was crucial. "Otherwise," he said:

> the answer to the question, 'Who is going to lead accountable care organizations, physicians or hospitals?' will produce an inevitable result—a winner and a loser."[44]

And Chris Van Gorder was several moves ahead with the creation of the Physician *Business* Leaders Cabinet (PBLC), as a vehicle to fill the gap of information and to prepare for the coming of accountable care and health reform. Formed in 2009, the PBLC now brings together the presidents of seven primary and specialty care medical groups spanning San Diego County. [45] In July 2011, the Scripps Health Board of Trustees and physician leaders voted to convert the PBLC from an advisory board to a "non-profit mutual benefit corporation"[46] called *ScrippsCare* under the elected chair, Dr. James LaBelle.

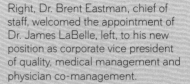

Right, Dr. Brent Eastman, chief of staff, welcomed the appointment of Dr. James LaBelle, left, to his new position as corporate vice president of quality, medical management and physician co-management.

courtesy of Scripps Health

The Scripps Mercy Hospital Internal Medicine Residency Program has prepared generations of physician leaders like Dr. Kevin Hirsch, president of Scripps Coastal Medical Group (seated). Dr. Hirsch graduated from the program—the longest established graduate medical education provider in San Diego—in 1989.

courtesy of Scripps Health

As of this writing there is a continuous migration of private practice physicians into the foundation, which has been expanded to include primary care as key to the new health care model. Historically, as chief executive of Scripps Clinic, Larry Harrison directed business for two medical groups: the multi-specialty SCMG; and the forty or so primary care physicians of Scripps Mercy Medical Group (SMMG) under the "homegrown leader" and graduate of Mercy's internal medicine program, Dr. Kevin Hirsch. In 2008, Dr. Hirsch's group merged with the sixty physicians of Sharp Mission Park Medical Group (SMPMG), led by Dr. Lou Hogrefe, bringing together as "Scripps Coastal" two of the county's top-rated medical groups for quality and patient satisfaction.[47]

Expanding relationships with physicians is so critical to future success that a new position has been created—Corporate VP of Physician Services—as a single point of contact for doctors who desire a relationship with the organization. Again Chris looked within and chose Shiraz Fagan, with a Harvard MBA, strong background in finance and ten years of service in multiple roles, as the ideal person to lead any good and committed doctor to the best home within Scripps Health.

On the morning of the summer solstice 2011, ground was broken at Scripps La Jolla for the Scripps Cardiovascular Institute. What allowed the groundbreaking to go forward was a major gift by newspaper businessman Robert Howard, a longtime patient and friend of both Dr. John Carson and Dr. Hugh Greenway. A big white tent shaded rows of dignitaries including the new SCI advisory committee of community leaders and cardiovascular physicians. There were speeches, and a trumpet fanfare as a crane raised an enormous banner in the air.

As Chief Executive of Scripps Clinic, Larry Harrison oversees Scripps Medical Foundation, formed in 2000 to replace Scripps Clinic and Research Foundation as a vehicle for physicians to become part of the Scripps Health system.

courtesy of Scripps Health

Top, Hundreds of community leaders, physicians, and Scripps employees attended the groundbreaking for the Scripps Cardiovascular Institute in 2011. Left, Dr. John Carson worked at Scripps Memorial Hospital La Jolla with Dr. David Carmichael in the 1960s. Top right, CEO Chris Van Gorder; San Diego Mayor Jerry Sanders; and Garry Fybel, chief executive at Scripps Memorial Hospital La Jolla, spoke to the crowd. Bottom right, trumpets sounded as a banner depicting the center was raised to commemorate the beginning of construction.

courtesy of Scripps Health

Five weeks later the name was expanded to the Prebys Cardiovascular Institute in honor of the donation by philanthropist Conrad Prebys of $45 million, the largest single gift in Scripps Health history. On July 27, 2011 the announcement and celebration took place before a standing-room only crowd in the Schaetzel Center Great Hall. Mr. Prebys, who made his fortune in real estate development and management, had previously donated $10 million to Scripps Mercy for its new emergency and trauma center in a tribute to Dr. Michael Sise—about which, Dr. Jerry Glassman, Chair of the SPCI Physician Steering Committee, said, "The Scripps Prebys Emergency Department serves 150-200 patients a day who have nowhere else to go, making it an epicenter of charitable care for the county." Mr. Prebys had also been treated at Scripps Mercy for a serious illness. He told the crowd:

> I was treated for cancer a few months ago at Mercy by Dr. Bill Stanton. It turned out to be a rewarding experience (though my sweetheart didn't like me saying that.)
>
> Like Scrooge waking up on Christmas Day, I found out "it's not too late."

Engineer of the elegant celebration and instrumental in securing the naming gift, was Chief Development Officer John Engle. John was among the most inspired of Chris Van Gorder's promotions of talent from within. Not quite thirty years old when he first arrived at Scripps, John was hired by James Bowers in 1990 as development director for the Whittier Institute. And he was so astute and original in his approach to funding, especially with the original donor family, that in 1994 he was made president and CEO of the Whittier (which was then a separate company, although a subsidiary of Scripps Health) and continued in that role for a decade—until ascending to the office of development director in 2004. John, and his Senior Director of Development Mary Braunwarth, understood the basic truth that philanthropy in health care derives from the physician-patient relationship.

Left to right, Chris Van Gorder, Dr. Jerrold Glassman, Conrad Prebys, Dr. Eric Topol, San Diego Mayor Jerry Sanders, Dr. Paul Teirstein, and Robert Tjosvold celebrate at the 2011 event announcing the naming of the Prebys Cardiovascular Institute. The cake was designed as a replica of the institute.

courtesy of Scripps Health

Top, Conrad Prebys donated $45 million for the Conrad Prebys Cardiovascular Institute. A celebration marked the announcement of the historic gift and the naming of the new center. Private patient rooms are designed to promote health and healing in the seven-story center. Bottom, left to right, Chief Development Officer John Engle, Conrad Prebys, Senior Development Director Mary Braunwarth, and CEO Chris Van Gorder at the naming event.

courtesy of Scripps Health

Construction continues on the Prebys Cardiovascular
Institute, scheduled to open for patient care in 2015.
Located on the campus of Scripps Memorial La Jolla, the
385,000-square-foot building will offer world-class heart
care to patients throughout San Diego and beyond.

courtesy of Scripps Health and Chris Van Gorder

Mayor of San Diego Jerry Sanders proclaimed "Conrad Prebys Day" and Dr. Paul
Teirstein spoke of the intention of all concerned that the new SPCI become "a heart
hospital with a heart, both high-tech and high-touch." Mr. Prebys said that his gift
was about participating in what he sees as an exciting time in health care—that he was
fascinated by a lecture by Dr. Eric Topol and that:

> I'm especially hooked on the Buck Rogers stuff—genomics and
> wireless technology—and also about the potential to treat more
> people at lower cost.

And of Chris Van Gorder and the physicians and teams he has assembled to lead
Scripps Health onward into the 21st century, Mr. Prebys said, "These are giants
of the health care world.

ScrippsCare Board 2011-2012, left to right, Dr. Michael Karp, Dr. Davis Cracroft, Miranda Klassen, Dr. James LaBelle, Dr. Kevin Hirsch, Dr. Stewart Frank, Chris Van Gorder, Dr. Robert Sarnoff, Marc Reynolds, Richard Vortmann, Dr. Marc Sedwitz, Dr. Scott Eisman. *courtesy of Scripps Health*

CHAPTER FOURTEEN

The Value Proposition

THIS HAS BEEN THE STORY OF TWO INTREPID WOMEN who set out to better the health care of their neighbors and to do it in a sustainable way. They were large-hearted, but also clear in their expectation that what they and the citizens of San Diego invested in this great venture would not be lost.

It has also been the story of their successors, the legion of men and women following after through twelve decades of change in health care so deep and so wide that the only constant is change. Even the visionary Miss Ellen might have been surprised by Scripps Health in 2012. But would she, and Mother Mary Michael, be pleased?

On a brilliant La Jolla winter day in 2012, three Scripps Health executives arrived at Central Hall of the University of California San Diego to address an upper division class on The U.S. Health Care System. Chris Van Gorder and Drs. Brent Eastman and James LaBelle came to present "A Fresh Look at Health Care Delivery" to ninety or so students seeking health careers who had so far heard from other speakers that news from the front was grim. But this day they were hearing news with a different tone and the room was at attention.

In an era of claims and counterclaims about what ails our "broken" national health system and how to cure it, what the Scripps Health leaders were presenting was both a blueprint and a manifesto for a health care system that works. Such a system, they said:

is first of all a system—an organization co-managed by physicians and administrators, and linking hospitals, outpatient clinics, doctors' offices and home health. It is an integrated health care delivery network.

It is focused on health—and has moved from being a "sick" company with the hospital at the center, to one invested in keeping people well. It works to keep patients, especially with chronic disease, out of the hospital and skillfully managed in the outpatient setting.

It is centered on the patient—with policies designed for the comfort and satisfaction of patients rather than providers. Hours and locations of service are adjusted to the realities of modern life. Wait times in emergency departments are drastically reduced or eliminated. Patients are treated always with respect and attentive concern.

It is based on the value proposition: Value = Quality/Cost—where value is what the patient receives. The surprise in this proposition is that increasing quality *decreases* cost, as internal best procedures are promulgated across the system. So-called "non-value-added" variation—inappropriate variation that is waste—is eliminated; the system does more with less. True innovation – which increases quality, by definition—is not stifled; but medicine is "evidence-based rather than eminence-based."

What the leaders were describing to the class, of course, is everything Scripps Health is, believes in, and is working toward today. The mood everywhere in the system is more open and more collaborative, extending from site to site and even to erstwhile family on Torrey Pines mesa. The new President and CEO of The Scripps Research Institute (TSRI), Dr. Michael Marletta, has this to say:

The focus of TSRI has been and will continue to be on discovery—discovery focused on understanding human biology and turning that knowledge gained toward treating and curing disease. What problems need to be solved? What discoveries need to be made?

The answers to those questions lie with clinical medicine. The history of TSRI began with the Scripps Metabolic Clinic and that very Clinic is still next door. The opportunity for collaboration and shared learning is one we plan to recapture in building a productive relationship of discovery and translation that will lead to new treatments for the most difficult of human diseases.

Our past history from our common founding will serve as the foundation for a new beginning, an era of research that will be exciting and unique.[1]

As the story of Scripps Health comes to a close it seems important to address two special questions about a tax-exempt organization: Where do all the profits from good stewardship go? And who is really responsible at the top? Who bears the ultimate burden of ensuring that patients are safe and well-served?

California law requires that community not-for-profit hospitals answer the first question every year, describing and documenting the full range of community benefits they provide. The latest report shows that Scripps Health provided nearly $338 million ($337,784,350) to community benefit programs and services in fiscal year 2010. The largest single category was *Under-Reimbursed Care* (68 percent), not including *Charity Care* (13 percent), *Bad Debt* (4 percent) and *Subsidized Health Services (2 percent)*. The remaining 13 percent was divided between *Professional Education and Health Research* and *Community Health Services.*[2] Not included in these figures is the uncompensated follow-up care provided by Scripps physicians. Nor is there an accounting of medical outreach at home and abroad, in times of disaster and of ordinary desperation.[3]

As to who is responsible at the top, the Scripps system is governed by a single, fourteen-member volunteer Board of Trustees—in recent times, roughly one-third are members who may focus on mission (often Sisters of Mercy); one-third are leaders in business; and a third are from the wider community. They work extremely hard, for thousands of hours, in terms stretching multiples of years. They are paid nothing and receive nothing, except thanks and a sense of giving back to the 13,000 employees of Scripps Health, the physicians, and the people of San Diego.

It seems likely the founders would be pleased.

From left to right, Vice Chair Judy Churchill, PhD; Abby Weiss; Marty J. Levin; Chairman Maureen Stapleton; Douglas A. Bingham, Esq.; Jeff Bowman; Chris Van Gorder; Mary Jo Anderson, CHS; Jan Caldwell; Robert Tjosvold; Richard C. Bigelow; Katherine A. Lauer; and Gordon R. Clark. Not pictured: Virginia Gillis, RSM, EdD.[4]   *courtesy of Scripps Health*

Endnotes

PREFACE

1   George Macaulay Trevelyan, *Illustrated English Social History 1*, (New York 1949), xxi-xiii.

2   Molly McCalin, "The Scripps Family's San Diego Experiment/Why the Scripps Family Came to San Diego," *The Journal of San Diego History* 56, nos. 1 and 2 (Winter/Spring 2010).

CHAPTER ONE — BEGINNINGS 1890 AND BEFORE

1   Molly McClain, "The Scripps Family's San Diego Experiment,"
    The Journal of San Diego History 56, nos. 1 and 2 (Winter/Spring 2010): 1-23.

2   William E. Smythe, "San Diego's First Boom," *History of San Diego 1542-1908,* 3.

3   Sister Mary Athanasius Sheridan, *…And Some Fell on Good Ground: A History of the Sisters of Mercy of California and Arizona* (New York: Carlton Press, 1982), 201-202.

4   McClain, "Scripps Family Experiment," 5. Cousins Hans and Fanny Bagby; Fanny had worked on several Scripps papers and in 1890 was a journalist for the *San Diego Sun.*

5   http://www.hoteldel-coronado.com/history.aspx.

6   *History of Tijuana, Mexico,* http://www.tijuanamexicoinsdier.com/tijuana-history.asp. Tijuana was founded 1889 and developers were very interested in tourists from the start.

7   McClain, "Scripps Family Experiment," 6.

8   Albert Britt, *Ellen Browning Scripps, Journalist and Idealist* (Oxford: Scripps College University Press, 1960), 1-2.

9   McClain, email message to author, 5 September 2011.

10 William Armiger Scripps had seven children: Mary, William Washington, Virginia, James Mogg, John, Thomas and Anne.

11 Edward Dessau Clarkson, *Ellen Browning Scripps: A Biography* (La Jolla: Self-published, 1958), 9.

12 Chester Foust, *…about this name, SCRIPPS,* (San Diego: Friends of Research of Scripps Clinic and Research Foundation, 1962), 2.

13 Patricia A. Schaelchlin, *The Newspaper Barons: A Biography of the Scripps Family* (San Diego: San Diego Historical Society and Kales Press, 2003), 179.

14 Ibid., 35.

15 Britt, *Ellen Browning Scripps,* 31.

16 Ibid., 18.

17 Schaelchlin, *Newspaper Barons,* 47. Two Scripps brothers fought in the Civil War: John Mogg, who died October 1863 at Blue Springs, Tennessee, and George, who was "permanently disabled with a scrofulous abscess in the groin." Their brother-in-law, Thomas Sharp, Elizabeth's husband, died at Andersonville.

18 Britt, *Ellen Browning Scripps*, 31.

19 Clarkson, *A Biography*, 51.

20 Britt, *Ellen Browning Scripps*, 83. Her original investment in the stock of the *Detroit News* in 1873 probably included the small bequest that came to her through the will of her grandfather, less than a thousand dollars. The rest of her contribution to the founding of the first Scripps newspaper was the savings from her small wage as a schoolteacher in Rushville. The case of the *News* was typical of the pyramiding of newspaper profits in that time of fabulous growth. When the paper was incorporated in 1877, fifty shares were issued, of which Ellen received two. Her share of dividends was increased correspondingly. By 1927 (fifty years) the profits of the paper were fifty million dollars, of which Ellen earned two million dollars, and soon more than four million.

21 Schaelchlin, *Newspaper Barons*, 145. By the terms of George Scripps' will, admitted to probate July 2, 1900, his twenty-three shares of the Scripps Publishing Company were bequeathed to Ellen.

22 Clarkson, *A Biography*, 51-52.

23 Ibid., 93. E.W. Scripps, thirty-one, finally married nineteen-year-old Nackie Holtsinger in 1885, two years after returning from his European adventure.

24 Ibid., 82-85.

25 Adam Begley, "A Quiet Corner of Italy," *The New York Times*, May 2011. Trieste has been part of Italy since the end of WWI, but in 1881 was still a corner of the Austro-Hungarian Empire and its most important port. *Completed in 1860, [it was] the princely residence of the Archduke Maximilian, younger brother of the Hapsburg emperor. Miramare has a melancholy history that its brave white dazzle can't erase: the Archduke had barely finished building his castle when he was shipped across the ocean to become Maximilian I of Mexico, a brief adventure that ended in execution by firing squad.*

26 We are indebted to historians Molly McClain and Patricia Schaelchlin for details of the long illness of Ellen Browning Scripps.

27 Schaelchlin, *Newspaper Barons*, 231.

28 McClain, "Scripps Family's Experiment," 4-5.

29 Schaelchlin, Newspaper Barons, 110.

30 Gerald Imber, Genius on the Edge (New York: Kaplan Publishing, 2010), 155.

CHAPTER TWO — THE SISTERS OF MERCY IN SAN DIEGO 1890-1924

1   Sisters of Mercy, San Diego Chapter, *Annals of the Sisters of Mercy, San Diego,* as quoted in Sister Mary Rose McArdle, Sisters of Mercy in San Diego, 1969, Scripps Mercy Hospital San Diego, San Diego, Calif.

2   H.B., *Memoirs of Mother Mary Michael Cummings of San Diego, California,* (after 1922).

3   Sister Mary Athanasius Sheridan, *...And Some Fell on Good Ground: A History of the Sisters of Mercy of California and Arizona* (New York: Carlton Press, 1982), 201-202.

4   J.P. Levre, L.H. Estes, "First Annual Report of the San Diego County Hospital and Poor Farm to the Board of Supervisors, For the Year Ending June 30, 1889," *The Journal of San Diego* 48:4 (Fall 2002) (http://www.sandiegohistory.org/journal/).

5   John Walton Caughey, *California,* as quoted in Sheridan, *Some Fell on Good Ground,* 167.

6   Michael Kelly, "Introduction: San Diego's Health 1888-1889," *The Journal of San Diego History, San Diego Historical Society Quarterly,* Fall 2002, Volume 48, Number (http://www.sandiegohistory.org/journal/).

7   J.P. Lever, L.H. Estes, "First Annual Report of the San Diego County Hospital and Poor Farm."

8   Ibid.

9   McArdle, Sisters of Mercy in San Diego.

10 Bill Finley, A History of Mercy Hospital ... and its century of service to San Diego, 1990, Scripps Mercy Hospital, San Diego, Calif., 8.

11 Not to be confused with Sister Alphonsus Cox, who served a ministry elsewhere. See Sheridan and McArdle.

12 "Sisters of Mercy," *The San Diego Weekly Union,* 10 July 1890.

13 Charles E. Rosenberg, "Social Class and Medical Care in 19th Century America: The Rise and Fall of the Dispensary," *Sickness & Health in America: readings in the history of medicine and public health,* eds. Judith Walzer Leavitt and Ronald L. Numbers (Madison: University of Wisconsin Press, 1997), 309.

14 "A Century of Caring for San Diego," *MercyShield Centennial Edition* (Winter 25: 1990), Mercy Hospital and Medical Center, San Diego: 3.

15 *San Diego Sun,* 9 July 1890, as quoted in Finley, *A History of Mercy Hospital.*

16 Finley, History of Mercy Hospital, 7.

17 *St. Joseph's Log—July 9, 1890-Dec. 1913,* Scripps Mercy Library, Scripps Mercy Hospital, San Diego, Calif. Twenty-three years of patient admissions in a single volume. Careful perusal of the entries suggests that "Pagans" were patients with Japanese surnames, "Heathens" were Chinese, and "Infidels" were Europeans who had presumably lapsed and denied their Christian faith.

18 San Diego History Center, Timeline of San Diego History, http://www.sandiegohistory.org/timeline/timeline1.htm.

19 Sioban Nelson, *Say Little, Do Much: Nursing Nuns and Hospitals in the Nineteenth Century* (Philadelphia: University of Pennsylvania Press, 2001), 32-33.

20 Finley, History of Mercy Hospital, 1.

21 *Rome of the West,* http://www.romeofthewest.com/2006/02/photos-of-immaculate-conception-church.html.

22 H.B, *Memoirs,* 4.

23 Finley, History of Mercy Hospital, 10.

24 Sister Mary Beata Bauman, *A Way of Mercy: Catherine McAuley's Contribution to Nursing* (New York: Vantage Press, 1958), 20-21. Catherine McAuley's birth date has been disputed by various biographers; evidence seems to favor 1778.

25 *Who We Are,* http://www.sistersofmercy.org/index.php?option=com_content&task=view&id=109&Itemid=164.

26 Bauman, *A Way of Mercy,* 53-54.

27 Mother Teresa Austin Carroll, as quoted in Bauman, *A Way of Mercy,* 72.

28 *Familiar Instructions of Rev. Mother McAuley.* ed. Sisters of Mercy of St. Louis, Missouri (St Louis: Ev. E. Carrerras, 1888), 21, as cited in Bauman:76.

29 Sister M. Josephine Gately, *The Sisters of Mercy: Historical Sketches 1831-1931* (New York: Macmillan, 1931), 303.

30 *Annals,* 105, as cited in McArdle, 6-7.

31 *Annals,* as cited in McArdle.

32 Rev. Henry Brinkmeyer, *Memoirs of Mother Mary Michael Cummings* (n.d., n.p.), 12, as cited by McArdle, Sister Rose, Sisters of Mercy in San Diego.

33 *San Diego Union,* January 1 1895. The resident physician was a Dr. Stephen Cleary, Ph.G., from San Francisco. His two-year "Pharmacy Graduate" degree reflects the lack of standardization in medical training of the day.

34   McArdle, Sisters of Mercy.

35 John Northrup, *A Short History of Carmel Valley & McGonigle Canyon Del Mar CA.* *(np, nd).*

36 Chris White, *Historic Architectural Survey Report* for *Caltrans Architectural Inventory/ Evaluation Form on Mt. Carmel Ranch*, State of California, Business Transportation and Housing Agency, 1988.

37 Sheridan, *Some Fell on Good Ground, 213.*

38 "History of Sisters of Mercy Includes Farming" *Mercy Shield* Vol 12, No. 5, May 1977: pp 1 & 8.

39 McArdle.

40 *MercyShield Centennial: 4.*

41 Sheridan, *Some Fell on Good Ground*, 214.

42 Ibid., 212-13.

43 Barbara Palmer, Ph.D., "Angel in Black," *San Diego Reader,* 27 Sept 27 2001: 50-51. Death Certificate of Mother Mary Michael Cummings lists cause of death as "angina pectoris and myocarditis."

44 HB, Memoirs, 30. Among a cascade of public tributes was a poetic one in *The Bulletin of the San Diego County Medical Society* that said, "…at the very hour of her death the architect was on his way to her bedside in response to her calling. Little did the architect dream that the Angel of Death was to frustrate his bedside consultation."

45 Mercedes Graf, "Band of Angels: Sister Nurses in the Spanish-American War, Parts 1 and 2," *Prologue* 34: 3 (Fall 2002) www.archives.gov/publications/ prologue/2002/fall/band-of-angels-2.html#net50, www.archives.gov/ publications/prologue/2002/fall/band-of-angels-1/html. Sister Liguori McNamara nursed Army soldiers at Matanzas, Cuba, during the Spanish-American War.

46 *Annals of the Sisters of Mercy in San Diego*, as quoted in Palmer, "Angels in Black," 51.

47 *John D. Spreckels (1853-1926),* San Diego History Center. www.sandiegohistory.org/bio/spreckels.htm.

48 The Factual History of Mercy Hospital, San Diego (1890-1956), 4, Scripps Mercy Hospital San Diego.

CHAPTER THREE — MISS ELLEN AND HER FAMILY SCRIPPS MEMORIAL HOSPITAL 1890-1924

1   *The Streetcar Companies vs. Mayor Pingree (1890-1900)*,
    http://www.detroittransithistory.info/ThePingreeYears.html.

2   Molly McClain, "The Scripps Family's San Diego Experiment,"
    The Journal of San Diego History 56, nos. 1 and 2 (Winter/Spring 2010): 3.

3   http://en.wikipedia.org/wiki/Looking_Backward.

4   Erich Fromm, forward to *Looking Backward 2000-1887* (New York: Signet, 1960).

5   McClain, "Scripps Family's Experiment," 3.

6   Ibid., 27.

7   Vance Trimble, *The Astonishing Mr. Scripps* (Ames, Iowa: Iowa State University Press, 1992), 163.

8   Charles Preece, *E. W. and Ellen Browning Scripps: An Unmatched Pair* (Chelsea, Michigan: Bookcrafters, 1990), 70.

9   Cori Van Noy, *Scripps Miramar Ranch, San Diego, California: Country Living Within City Limits* (Yale University, 1995), 2.

10 Robert L. Santos, "California, Here I Come," *The Eucalyptus of California. Section One: The Early Years* (Denair, California: Alley-Cass Publications, 1997), http://library.csustan.edu/bsantos/section1.htm#FROM DOWN UNDER IT.

11 Ibid.

12 Patricia A. Schaelchlin, *The Newspaper Barons: A Biography of the Scripps Family* (San Diego, California: San Diego Historical Society and Kales Press, 2003), 141.

13 Albert Britt, *Ellen Browning Scripps, Journalist and Idealist* (Oxford, Scripps College University Press, 1960), 18.

14 Preece, *E. W. and Ellen Browning*, 109.

15 Trimble, *The Astonishing Mr. Scripps*, 163.

16 Second Lieutenant F.A. Wilcox, First Infantry, Military Map of the United States (Sheet No. 127), Department of California, circa 1900, San Diego Historical Society, San Diego, California. This map identifies both "Scripps Ranch" and "Miramar" in about 1900 and shows the road to La Jolla.

    Also, Schaelchlin, *Newspaper Barons*, 15. E.W began building roads with "a full gang of men and my own road grader and teams now at work…"including Miramar Ranch to La Jolla, to Del Mar, and from La Jolla to Torrey Pines State Reserve."

17 Richard Sullivan, "Judge Approves Transfer of Scripps Hospital Site," *San Diego Evening Tribune,* 21 April 21 1964. The article states the address of the new hospital.

18 Patricia Daley-Lipe and Barbara Dawson, "Ellen Browning Scripps 1836-1932, "*La Jolla: A Celebration of Its Past* (San Diego: Sunbelt Publications, 2002), 35-42. Both versions of the house on Prospect Street were called South Molton (or Moulton) Villa, after the London street in Mayfair on which Ellen Browning Scripps was born.

19 Schaelchlin, *Newspaper Barons,* 183.

20 Oliver C. Thornton, "Crisis," *La Jolla Light,* 14 January 1960. Oliver Thornton was the president of the Scripps Memorial Hospital Board of Directors.

21 Patricia A. Schaelchlin, "The La Jolla Medical Community," *La Jolla: The Story of a Community, 1887-1987* (La Jolla, California: The Friends of the La Jolla Library, 1988), 116.

22 Ibid, 116-117.

23 Ellen Browning Scripps (EBS) to J.C. Harper, 14 June 1917, Drawer 13/Folder 25, Scripps Memorial Hospital La Jolla 1916-1917, Ellen Browning Scripps Collection (EBSC), Ella Strong Denison Library, Scripps College, Claremont, Calif. (EDL).

24 J.C. Harper to EBS, 1 April 1918, Drawer 13/Folder 26, Scripps Memorial Hospital La Jolla 1918, EBSC, EDL. Courtesy of Dr. Molly McClain.

25 Bruce Kammerling, "Hebbard & Gill, Architects," *The Journal of San Diego History* 36, nos. 1 and 2 (Summer 1990), http://www.sandiegohistory.org/journal/90summer/hebbard.htm.

26 Patricia Schaelchlin, *La Jolla,* 117.

27 Ibid.

28 Ada K. Gillispie to J.C. Harper, 6 March 1918, Drawer 13/Folder 26, Scripps Memorial Hospital La Jolla 1918, EBSC, EDL.

29 Ibid., J.C. Harper to Mrs. S.T. Gillispie, 14 Mar 1918.

30 Ibid., J.C. Harper to Mrs. Ada K. Gillispie, 15 Mar 1918.

31 Ibid., Ada K. Gillispie to J.C. Harper, 11 April 1918.

32 Ibid., EBS to J.C. Harper, 14 June 1918.

33 Grant creating trust between Ellen Browning Scripps, grantor, and Jacob Chandler Harper, grantee, for the foundation, endowment and maintenance of a hospital and school for nurses. Placed in the trust was the property on which the Sanitarium was built. 23 October 1918, Scripps Health.

34　Handwritten history, c. 1948, Historical Papers, Scripps Health. *L.J. Sanitarium was situated on Lots 43, 44 & 45. Blk 17, L. J. Park (present site of Clinic). It was constructed by Miss E. B. Scripps and was completed Dec. 1, 1918 – gross value $30,588.82. Equipment cost totaled $3,788.30. Had facilities for 10 adult patients and 2 infants. Leased and operated by Ada K. & Dr. Samuel T. Gillispie until Feb 19 1921.*

35　"The Great Pandemic: The United States in 1918-19," United States Department of Health and Human Services, http://1918.pandemicflu.gov/ By the summer of 1919, 675,000 Americans were dead of influenza.

　　Also: "Timeline of San Diego History," http://www.sandiegohistory.org/timeline/ timeline.htm, Approximately 368 people died in San Diego of Spanish influenza.

36　EBS to J.C. Harper, La Jolla, 23 March 1918, Drawer 13/Folder 26, Scripps Memorial Hospital La Jolla 1918, EBSC, EDL.

37　EBS to E.W. Scripps (EWS), 23 February 1919, Drawer 3/Folder 19, EBSL, EDL.

38　Western Union Telegram to EBS, 23 January 1922, Drawer 1/Folder 31 Hip Fracture 1922, EDSC, EDL. The telegram referred to the fact that "you had a fall yesterday in which you sustained a fracture of the hip."

39　Molly McClain, email to author, September 2011. The Pierce-Arrow became an ambulance in 1923 when E.W. Scripps bought his sister a new limousine.

40　Robert Smith, "Life with Miss Ellen Browning Scripps, An oral history by Mr. Fred Higgins transcribed October 1974," *The History of Scripps Clinic and Those Who Created It* (San Diego: Personal Files of author, 1999), 20.

41　Britt, *Ellen Browning Scripps*, 18.

42　Ibid.

43　Drawer 1 / Folder 31, Hip Fracture 1922, EBSC, EDL.

44　Dr. Clifford Colwell, email orthopedic consultation with author, 2 October 2011.

45　Molly McClain, email to author, September 2011.

46　EBS to EWS, 24 June 1922, Drawer 3/Folder 3, Scripps Memorial Hospital La Jolla, EBSC, EDL.

47　Kathleen A. Crawford, "The Promise Fulfilled: A History of the Scripps Institutions of Medicine and Science, 1924-1999" (San Diego: Personal files of author, 1999), 22-23.

48　"The Hospital Betterment Movement in California," *California State Journal of Medicine,* 29 January 1920.

49　Ibid. July 1921: 1.

50 J.C. Harper to C.F. Mosher (banker to EBS), 24 April 1923, Drawer 13/Folder 28, Scripps Memorial Hospital, La Jolla 1919-28, EBSC, EDL.

51 Ibid., 21 November 1923.

52 Kyle Lewis, email to author, 13 June 2011.

53 Deborah Day, "Ellen Browning Scripps, her Life and Philanthropy," talk presented to Ellen's Circle 18 October 2000, http://scilib.ucsd.edu/sio/hist/day_ellen_browning_scripps.pdf.

54 Jacob C. Harper, "Memorandum New Hospital Building," 17 November 1923, Scripps Health.

55 Minutes of the First Meeting of the Board of Directors of Scripps Memorial Hospital, 6 October 1924.

56 EBS to C.P. Mosher May 10, 1924, Drawer 13 / Folder 28, Scripps Memorial Hospital La Jolla, EBSC, EDL.

57 *La Jolla Journal, 19* September 1924, quoted in Schaelchlin, *Newspaper Barons*, 117.

58 Historical Site Board, 1989.

59 Ada Gillispie continued on as superintendent of Scripps Memorial Hospital until Aug 1, 1929, when she resigned and was succeeded by Jessie A. Horn, RN. Mrs. Gillispie had a forceful personality and spoke her mind, which sometimes created trouble with attending physicians [Minutes of the Board of Directors Meeting of Scripps Hospital, 9 January 1928]. When she resigned her post after five years at Scripps Hospital, Ada Gillispie turned her attention and energies to child care, and "in 1937 founded Gillispie Cottage, named after her husband, as a daycare center for children of working parents." ["Funeral services held for Mrs. Ada Gillispie," *La Jolla Light*, 3 December 1970, 1].

CHAPTER FOUR — SCRIPPS METABOLIC CLINIC 1924-1955

1   "Medicine: Physiatric Hospital," Time, December 16, 1929.

2   The American Heritage Dictionary of the English Language (Houghton Mifflin Harcourt Publishing Co., 2010). Physiatrics: Physical medicine. The branch of medicine that deals with disease and injury by physical means, including manipulation, massage and exercise, often with mechanical devices, and the application of heat, cold, electricity, radiation, and water.

3   "Diabetes," California State Journal of Medicine. November 1916. "The Influence of Metabolism on Tooth Structure," April 1923. "Hyperchlorydria," January 1923. "The Slowly Elaborating Stomach," September 1915.

4   Thea Cooper and Arthur Ainsberg, Breakthrough: Elizabeth Hughes, the Discovery of Insulin, and the Making of a Medical Miracle (New York: St. Martin's Press, 2010).

5   Jacob C. Harper, Memorandum, "Metabolic Clinic in Connection with the La Jolla Sanitarium," 25 January 1924, Scripps Health.

6   Ibid.

7   Ibid.

8   Ibid.

9   Cooper and Ainsberg, Breakthrough," 23. "[At Frederick M. Allen's private sanitarium for diabetic patients in a mansion in New York City on Fifty-first Street] His three assistants, Drs. James W. Sherrill, J. West Mitchell, and Henry J. John, were all competent doctors from reputable medical schools." The book does not mention Dr. Sherrill going to Toronto with Banting and Best.

10 Ibid., 50.

11 Dr. James W. Sherrill, Jr. interview by Dr. Clifford Colwell and author, taped recording, 6 January 2011. Other physicians were also considered. Drs. Elliott P. Joslin of Boston and Rollin T. Woodyatt, of Chicago sent out promising young physicians for consideration by Miss Scripps and her advisors.

12 J.C. Harper, "Metabolic Clinic," 22-27 June 1924, Scripps Health.

13 Ibid, 28 June.

14 Dr. Sherrill, Jr., interview.

15 Lucy H. Sherrill to Miss Hutchinson, 13 October 1960.

16 La Jolla Journal, 5 December 1924, as quoted in Patricia Schaelchlin, La Jolla, The Story of a Community 1887-1987. (La Jolla, La Jolla Friends of the Library, 1988), 118, 137.

17 Dennis Blakeslee, "Scripps Clinic: An Overview 1924-1986," ed. Robert Smith, The History of Scripps Clinic (La Jolla, 1999), 4.

18 Ellen Browning Scripps to E.W. Scripps, 21 January 1925, as quoted in Molly McClain, "The Scripps Family's San Diego Experiment," The Journal of San Diego History 56 (Winter/Spring 2010): 24.

19 Building Agreement for Nurses Home between Ellen B. Scripps, owner, and Thomas M. Russell, contractor, 9 April 1925, Scripps Health. The agreed–upon price of construction was $55,960.

20 Verna Brooks, "Verna Brooks, 4th Prize," 1936, La Jolla Historical Society.

21 Articles of Incorporation of Scripps Memorial Hospital, 25 September 1924, Scripps Health, San Diego, Calif.

22 William VanderLaan, (remarks following a lecture at the La Jolla Historical Society by Charles Cochrane and Michael Oldstone, "From Metabolic Clinic to The Scripps Research Institute"), 17 March 2009.

23 Robert Smith, The History of Scripps Clinic and Those Who Created It (San Diego: Personal Files of author, 1999), 4.

24 Historical Site Board for the City of San Diego, "Historical Significance," Historical Site Board Report, (San Diego, 1989).

25 Smith. History of Scripps Clinic, 5.

26 Joyce B. Tullis, Scripps Memorial Hospital Women's Auxiliary, 1929 Sampler 10 2004, Scripps Memorial Hospital Library (San Diego, Calif.).

27 Minutes of the meeting of Scripps Memorial Hospital, a corporation, 24 October 1946, Scripps Health, San Diego, Calif.

28 James W. Sherrill (La Jolla, California), M. D., Johns Hopkins University. Practice limited to Diseases of Metabolism. Hospital connections: Director, Scripps Metabolic Clinic, La Jolla, California. J Sherrill, James W. and Copp, E.F.F. "Changes in Blood Serum Calcium Following the Administration of Parathyroid Extract. Journal of California and Western Medicine Feb 1926 ,Vol 24, No 2: 183.

Publications: "Chemical Studies of Edema," with F. M. Allen (Jr. Ass'n Amer. Phys. 1920); "Clinical Observations Concerning Progressiveness of Diabetes" (Jr. Metabolic Research, vol. I, 5; 667, 1922); "The Diagnosis of Latent or Incipient Diabetes" (J. A. M. A., 77, 1779, Dec., 1921); "The Treatment of Combined Diabetes and Nephritis," with F. M. Allen (J. A. M. A., 75, 444, 1920); "Experiments on Carbohydrate Metabolism and Diabetes," with Henry J. John (Jour. Metab. Resch., I, 109, 1920); "Clinical Observations on Treatment and Progress in Diabetes," James W. Sherrill and F. M. Allen (Jr. Metab. Resch.,2, 803, 1922); "The Influence of Carbohydrate and Protein on Diabetes and the Insulin Requirement" (Jour. Metab.Resch., 3, 13, 1923); "The Treatment of Arterial Hypertension," with

Frederick M. Allen (Jour. Metab. Resch., 2, 429, 1922); "Progress of Potentially Diabetic Persons in Relation to Dietary Control" (Med. Clinics N. Amer., 6, 465, 1922);"Metabolic Observations in Psychiatric Conditions," James W. Sherrill (Jr. Metab. Resch., 5, 128, 1924).

29 E. F. F. Copp (La Jolla, California), M. B. from University of Toronto, 1923. Associated with Banting in early experiments with insulin: Christie Street Military Hospital, Toronto; with F. M. Allen one year. Practice limited to research and diseases of metabolism. Hospital connections: Scripps Metabolic Clinic. Appointments: Resident physician Scripps Metabolic Clinic.

Publications: "Restoration of Hydropically Degenerated Cells of the Pancreatic Islands in Dogs Under Insulin Treatment" (Journal of Metabolic Research, vol. 4, Nos. 3-4. From "Changes in Blood Serum Calcium Following the Administration of Parathyroid Extract" in California and Western Medicine, Feb 1926, p. 183. First presented Dec 9 1925.

30 Smith, History of Scripps Clinic, 27.

31 Dr. Sherrill, Jr., interview.

32 Dr. Henry J. John to Lucy H. Sherrill, 10 Jan 1955.

33 "Dr. James Winn Sherrill, Scripps Metabolic Clinic Director, Dies; Rites Set Tomorrow," La Jolla Light, 6 January 1955, front page.

34 http://www.ljbtc.com/History?ssid=212856.

35 E. Ludlow Keeney, Jr. (b. 1939), interview by Dr. Clifford Colwell and author, tape recording, Scripps Clinic, San Diego, Calif., 20 April 2011. The younger Mr. Keeney is a real estate attorney in La Jolla who grew up in Baltimore, spending six weeks every summer in La Jolla with his father.

36 E. Ludlow Keeney Jr., interview.

CHAPTER FIVE — SCRIPPS MEMORIAL HOSPITAL 1924-1964

1   Scripps Memorial Hospital Women's Auxiliary, *1929 Sampler to 2004; May '29-1936; 1939-1949. 1950-1954*, Scripps Memorial Hospital La Jolla (San Diego, Calif.).

2   Scripps Memorial Hospital Women's Auxiliary, *Scripps Auxiliary History Reviews & Summaries*, Scripps Memorial Hospital La Jolla (San Diego, Calif). As I note in this paragraph there is a collection of all sorts of ephemera, most of it without careful notations about source.

3   *Casa de Manana Retirement Community Our Story,* http://www.casademanana.org/our-story.asp.

4   Auxiliary, *History Reviews & Summaries.*

5   "13th Annual Charity Ball," *San Diego Union,* 8 Feb 1942.

6   "Women," *The San Diego Union,* 29 November 1969. Section D showed preparations for Candlelight Ball at Miramar Ranch on December 6. Clippings from December 8 describe the ball itself.

7   *La Jolla Journal.* September 1927. As collected in *Ellen Browning Scripps 1836-1932* – a compilation of tributes to Ellen Browning Scripps in her last years as well as excerpts from her will. La Jolla California, 1936. "Ninety-First Birthday" page 25.

8   Patricia A. Schaelchlin, *The Newspaper Barons: A Biography of the Scripps Family* (San Diego: San Diego Historical Society and Kales Press, 2003), 194.

9   Ibid., 194.

10   Ibid., 195.

11   The author was one of the children.

12   Dr. Willliam J. Doyle, "The Medical Future of San Diego: An Exciting Prospect" (San Diego: Personal Files of author, 1 March 1965).

13   Dr. William J. Doyle, personal essay (San Diego: Personal Files of author).

14   Major General Joseph Henry Pendleton (1860-1942) was a Marine Corps officer for more than forty years and the Mayor of Coronado from 1928-30. http://en.wikipedia.org/wiki/Joseph Henry_Pendleton.

15   *California State Military Museum. California and the Second World War San Diego Metropolitan Area during World War II,* http://www.militarymuseum.org/SDWW2.html.

16   David Carmichael, MD, with William J. Kuzman MD, "Cardiology in San Diego, California WWII to 2006," lecture San Diego County Medical Society; and http://en.wikipedia.org/wiki/Werner_Forssmann#cite_note-NobelBio-0.

17   http://www.centennialofflight.gov/essay/Aerospace/convair/Aero36.html.

18   Audrey Stone Dimond, later Audrey Geisel, wife of Theodor Geisel, Dr. Seuss.

19   Dr. John C. Carson (b. 1927), interview by author, taped recording, 10 November 2010.

20   Ibid.

21   Ibid.

22   Ibid.

23   Carson, John MD. "San Diego Cardiology 1955-2011." Lecture recorded by San Diego County Medical Society and Ralph Ocampo, MD, Feb 23, 2011.

24   Dr. Herbert L. Fred, "Maxwell Myer Wintrobe: New History and a New Appreciation," *Tex Heart Inst J.* (2007): 34 (3) 328-335.

25   Three members of Specialty Medical Associates–so far–have won a Lifetime Achievement Award from Scripps Memorial Hospital: Drs. John Carson (2008), John Trombold (2010), and Ernest Pund (2011).

26   John C. Carson, MD, "Medicine in La Jolla and Locally – 1960s and on," 14 November 2010.

27   Other physicians in the tight-knit group were generalist Joe McLaughlin; OB/GYNs Chuck Weber, Charles "Bun" Wright and Bernie Hark; pediatrician John Welsh; urologists Bob Boughton and James Whisenand; in ENT, Robert Movius and his young associate Howard Doty; and in anesthesia, Keith Jeffery, Gordon Langsdorf, John Blankenship, Paul Thomas, Robert Andrews and Gil Kinyon (whose wife Jessie Kinyon, RN, was the first chair of the Doctors Wives' Unit and championed the Scripps La Jolla Medical Library, which was named for her after her tragic early death in 1963.) The specialists still linking Hospital and Clinic were radiologists (John Wells, Rex Uncapher and Charles Campbell); and surgeons, beginning with elder statesman Hall Holder, who established the department of surgery on Prospect Street in 1930; oncologist Anita Figueredo; surgeon-historian Clifford Graves, who grew up in Holland and wrote graceful English prose for the *San Diego Historical Society Quarterly* and the *Journal of the American Medical Association*, among others; Dick Jones, Walt Merdinger, and Richard Tullis.

28   Alan J. Berkenfield, MD (b. 1926), interview by author, telephone, 16 September 2011. All information in the following two paragraphs is from Dr. Berkenfield.

29   The Flying Samaritans had their beginnings in 1961 when two aviators landed in the remote town of El Rosario on the Baja Peninsula to avoid strong winds and dust storms… The people of El Rosario were extremely cordial, sharing their food and offering accommodations for the night. They were treated with such kindness that the aviators asked what they could do in return… One month later the

aviators returned with clothing and gifts for families. Among those who made the return trip was a Medical doctor who brought his medical bag and asked if anyone needed attention. http://flyingsamaritans.com/history.htm.

30   Rosita was subsequently adopted by Dr. Berkenfield and his wife.

31   *Scripps Hospital News* 1, no. 4 (June 1952).

32   Kathleen A. Crawford, "The Promise Fulfilled: A History of the Scripps Institutions of Medicine and Science 1924-1999," (San Diego: Personal Files of author), 47.

33   Crawford, "The Promise," 50.

34   Sarita Eastman, *A Trail of Light: The Very Full Life of Dr. Anita Figueredo* (Bloomington, Indiana: Wordclay, 2009), 217.

35   San Diego's first regional shopping center, *Mission Valley Center*, opened in 1961. http://en.wikipedia.org/wiki/Mission_Valley,_San_Diego.

36   La Jolla Community Hospital Foundation, Inc., "La Jolla's Hospital Dilemma: How Did It Come About?" c. 1963, (San Diego: Personal files of author).

37   Ibid.

38   The names of the 1964 Board of Directors, Scripps Memorial Hospital were engraved on a silver platter. They included: Willis Allen, Robert B. Conway, James S. Copley, William S. Dwinnell, Bernard Hark, MD, William Scripps Kellogg, Arthur H. Keyes, Burl Mackenzie, Nackey Meanley, Ruth Harper Munger, Harold Radatz, Sallie C. Richard, Everette M. Rogers, MD, William Schofield, David M. Scoville, Richard N. Smith, Oliver C. Thornton, Norton S. Walbridge. The platter was inscribed to Burl H. Mackenzie as a token of esteem for her service as a Director of Scripps Memorial Hospital 1958-1964.

39   Burl H. Mackenzie, interview by Dr. Clifford Cowell and author, tape recording, in her home at White Sands in La Jolla, Calif., 22 October 2010.

40   Case No 278623, in the matter of Stanley Mosk, Attorney General of the State of California vs. Scripps Memorail Hospital, a California nonprofit corporation, Attorney Superior Court of the State of California for the County of San Diego. 21 April 1964 Judgment in Favor of Scripps Memorial Hospital.

41   "Judge Okays Shift for Scripps Hospital," San Diego *Evening Tribune*, 21 April 1964.

42   "Scripps Hospital ale backed by Ruling of Court," *San Diego Union,* 22 April 1964.

43   Louis Peelyon to Dr. William J. Doyle, San Diego, November 1964 (San Diego: Personal Files of author).

CHAPTER SIX — SCRIPPS CLINIC AND RESEARCH FOUNDATION 1955-1977

1 Dennis Blakeslee, "Scripps Clinic: An Overview 1924-1986," ed. Robert Smith, *The History of Scripps Clinic and Those Who Created It* (San Diego: Personal files of author, 1999), 4. Blakeslee was a member of the development office staff. Smith was the vice president for development at Scripps Clinic from 1977 to 1989.

2 William F. Black (b. 1933), interview by author, tape recording, 31 October 2011.

3 James W. Sherrill Jr., MD (b. 1933), interview by Dr. Clifford Colwell and author, tape recording, 6 January 2011.

4 Amendment of Articles of Incorporation of Scripps Metabolic Clinic, 26 October 26 1955.

5 Halvor N. Christensen, *Albert Baird Hastings 1895-1987: A Biographical Memoir* (Washington, D.C.: National Academy of Sciences, 1994), 192-196.

6 Charles G. Cochrane, MD, "Emergence of Pioneering Scientific Institutions in La Jolla: From Metabolic Clinic to Scripps Research Institute," (lecture presented at the La Jolla Historical Society, 17 Mar 2009).

7 "In Memoriam: Frank Dixon, 1920-2008," *News & Views, Online weekly of The Scripps Research Institute* 8 (11 February 2008).

8 Charles G. Cochrane, MD (b. 1930), interview by Dr. Clifford Colwell and author, 6 January 2011. The quotes in this chapter, unless otherwise noted, are from Dr. Cochrane.

9 Donald Harrison, "Family Stories about Admiral Baker of wartime and golfing fame." *San Diego Sightseeing Examiner.* 1 January 2010. Admiral Wilder Baker (1890-1975) was among the senior officers in the theatre at the time of Japan's surrender in 1945. He retired with the rank of vice admiral in 1952 and joined senior management of Solar Aircraft for several years thereafter, as well as the board of Scripps Clinic.

10 Edmund Ludlow Keeney, MD, "Scripps Clinic and Research Foundation History, Scripps Clinic from 1924-1977," in *The History of Scripps Clinic and Those Who Created It,* ed. Robert H. Smith (Scripps Health, 1999).

11 Valerie Timken Sturgis Whitney was treated by Dr. Willard VanderLaan, as he commented at the La Jolla Historical Society, 17 March 2009.

12 Bettye Hobbs Pruitt, "Famous Automotive Brothers, The Formative Years," *Timken: from Missouri to Mars: a century of leadership in manufacturing* (Boston: Harvard Business School Press, 1998), note 4. And "*History, Timken Museum of Art,*" http://www.timkenmuseum.org/about/history.

13   Hans Müller-Eberhard was the recipient of the Green Chair in Immunology, endowed by Dr. and Mrs. Cecil Green on July 23, 1970. A huge furor erupted some years later when Frank Dixon inexplicably decided on his own to rescind the chair, infuriating Dr. Müller-Eberhard, who left the Clinic in 1988 and returned to Hamburg, Germany.

14   Michael Oldstone, "Emergence of Pioneering Scientific Institutions in La Jolla: From Metabolic Clinic to Scripps Research Institute," (lecture given at La Jolla Historical Society, 17 Mar 2009).

15   The Unicorn began in 1964 at the back of a bookstore across from the Bishop's School on La Jolla Blvd, and the Cove opened decades earlier on Girard Avenue, across from the Catholic church. http://cinematreasures.org.

16   Dr. Keeney, "Scripps Clinic from 1924-1977," 26-34.

17   James L. Bowers (b. 1928), interview by author, taped recording, 9 November 2011.

18   Bowers, interview.

19   Smith, *The History of Scripps Clinic,* 32.

20   Dr. Keeney speaks of the "dismal, cutting sadness" when James Copley died at 57 of cancer at the old clinic in October 1973. Dr. Keeney and a private nurse had accompanied Copley to Europe in May 1973, when the publisher "left his sickbed for over two weeks to receive the Gold Medal of the City of Paris in recognition of his contributions to Franco-American relations and leadership in promoting freedom of the press and international understanding." Richard Reilly and Timothy Biel, *A Promise Kept: The Story of the James S. Copley Library in La Jolla* (La Jolla, Calif.: Copley Books 1983).

21   Black, interview.

22   "Edward Durrell Stone (1902-1978)," *The Encyclopedia of Arkansas History and Culture. http://encyclopediaofarkansas.net/encyclopedia/entry-detail.aspx?entryID=1776.* Also, "Edward Durrell Stone (1902-1978)," *Modern San Diego, http://www. modernsandiego.com/EdDurrellStone.html.* The Beckman Center for Clinical Sciences appears to occupy the same original building, but was added on in 1996.

23   "In 1974, the Attorney General of California ruled that, as salaried employees of the Foundation, Scripps physicians were under the control of non-physicians – a lay Board of Trustees – and that this was illegal under California law. He demanded that the Clinic reorganize." Blakeslee, "Scripps Clinic: An Overview 1924-1986." 8.

24   *Survey of State Laws Regarding the Corporate Practice of Medicine: California.* http://www.dobbinslaw.com/cpmarticle.html.

25   James O. Boylan, director of public affairs, SCRF, "The SCMI, YESTERDAY, TODAY...AND BEYOND," June 1976.

26   Ida and Cecil H. Green Cancer Center: After Ida Green succumbed to cancer in 1986, Scripps Clinic found that it had been named as one of the primary beneficiaries under her will, with the largest bequest ever received by the organization. Half of the annual income from this endowment was used to establish the Ida M. Green Cancer Center, later modified to include Cecil's name.

27   Robert H. Smith, email message to author, 17 August 2011.

28   Charles Cochrane, "Scientific Growth of The Scripps Research Institute Since 1961," email to author, 12 September 2011.

29   All details of dates, appointments of personnel, and the order of acquisition of buildings are taken from Smith, *The History of Scripps Clinic.*

30   Charles C. Edwards, MD, and Mina Ono Benedyk, *Tough Choices: My Extraordinary Journey at the Heart of American Politics and Medicine* (Private printing, c. 2005).

CHAPTER SEVEN — SCRIPPS MEMORIAL HOSPITAL 1964-1991

1   The Hospital Survey and Construction Act (1946), http://www.nvcc.edu/home/bhays/dogwood/hillburtonact.htm.

2   Ames S. Early (b. 1937), interview by author, taped recording, Rancho Santa Fe, CA, 29 July 2010.

3   Kathleen Crawford, "Scripps Memorial Hospital 1964-1991," *The Promise Fulfilled: A History of the Scripps Institutions of Medicine and Science 1924-1999* (San Diego: Personal files of author, 1999).

4   Burl H. Mackenzie, interview by author and Dr. Clifford Colwell, taped recording, La Jolla, Calif., 22 October 2010.

5   William E. "Bill" Nelson, J.D., Ph.D., (b. 1925), interview by author, taped recording, La Jolla, Calif., 5 August 2010.

6   Dr. John C. Carson (b. 1927), interview by author and Dr. Clifford Colwell, taped recording, San Diego, Calif., 18 November 2010.

    Dr. John C. Carson, "A Georgia Angel-Fish Revisited," *Mark Twain Journal* 36, no. 1 (Spring 1998), 16-18. Frances Winzer went on to make "contributions to Scripps Memorial totaling some $5 million."

7   "PSRO: Update 1974," *Western Journal of Medicine,* Feb 1974, 155-56.

8   http://www.scribd.com/doc/52222832/AAPS-Newsletters-from-1974.

9   Ames, interview.

10 Mercy Hospital Miami was founded and staffed by the Sisters of St. Joseph of St. Augustine, Florida.

11 Louis Peelyon died of lung cancer within a year of leaving Scripps; Ames Early attended his funeral in Julian.

12 Dr. Charles C. Edwards and Mika Ono Benedyl, *Tough Choices: My Extraordinary Journey at the Heart of American Politics and Medicine* (San Diego: Self-published, c. 2005), 124.

13 Dr. Alan Blank, NCOG, (San Diego: Personal files of author, 1999), 1-2.

14 North Coast Surgeons who came later were: Dana Launer (Chief of Staff 2006-07), James Peck, Marc Sedwitz (Chief of Staff 2010-11) and Mary Wilde.

15 Dr. A. Brent Eastman (b. 1940), interview by author, taped recording, Wilson, Wyoming, 29 December 2010 and 11 January 2011.

16 Dr. Donley McReynolds (b. 1937), interview by author, phone and email, 13 September 2011.

17 Edna "Bunny" Carroll (1927-2010)
Louise Favor (b. 1936), Marla Hess (b. 1938), Joan M. "Joni" Lee (b. 1940), interviews by author, telephone, email. All biographical information about the nurses comes from these interviews.

18 http://earthquake.usgs.gov/earthquakes/states/events/1959_08_18.php. The so-called Hebgen Lake earthquake registered 7.3 on the Richter scale and was the largest earthquake ever in Montana with 28 dead. Many of the injured were transported the 93 miles to Bozeman Deaconess Hospital where new nurse Louise Favor would start on duty Monday morning.

19 Dr. Eastman, interview.

20 Dr. Clifford Colwell (b. 1937), interview by author at his office at the Shiley Center for Orthopedic Research and Education (SCORE), La Jolla, Calif., 16 September 2010.

21 That is, they did not want residents on the campus of Scripps Hospital. Many Scripps Hospital physicians had clinical teaching appointments at UCSD and devoted considerable time to students and house staff there.

22 SCORE, The Shiley Center for Orthopaedic Research and Education, investigates the safety and efficacy of new technologies and therapies designed for the treatment of musculoskeletal diseases and disorders. SCORE was established in 1983 by Dr. Clifford Colwell.

23 "Professional grandma loves job, helps young," *The Milwaukee Sentinel*, 13 October 1980. In this article, written early in her twenty-year career at Scripps, Mrs. Carter was quoted as saying, "I've had more than 6,000 babies since I started working at the hospital and I'm on call 24 hours a day for the parents after they've taken their baby home." Her formal title at the hospital was "new family coordinator."

24 Lanie Carter, *Congratulations, You're going to be a Grandmother* (La Jolla, Calif.: Oak Tree Publications, Inc., 1980). Introduction by author.

25 "Appendix B: Historical Overview of Trauma System Development," http://www.nhtsa.gov/people/injury/ems/emstraumasystem03/appendices-b.htm. The EMS Systems Act of 1973 was perhaps the single most important piece of legislation affecting the development of regional emergency and trauma care systems. The act called for the creation of a lead agency under the Department of Health, Education and Welfare and identified fifteen components (one being trauma systems) to assist system planners in establishing area-wide or regional EMS programs. A substantial amount of federal funds was devoted to the establishment of an EMS infrastructure in more than 300 EMS regions nationwide.

26 http://medicine.yale.edu/emergencymed/whatis.aspx. In 1979, Emergency Medicine

was recognized as the 23rd medical specialty by the American Board of Medical Specialties. The American Board of Emergency Medicine, the independent certifying body for the specialty, was established, and the first certification examination was given in 1980.

27   County of San Diego Health and Human Services Agency, Emergency Medical Services, "San Diego County Trauma System 20 Year Report" (December 2004), 21. http://www.sdcounty.ca.gov/hhsa/programs/phs/documents/EMS-Trauma20yrReport1984-2003.pdf.

28   Ibid., 1.

29   Dr. Richard Virgilio (b. 1937), interview by author, taped recording, 13 October 2011.

30   Sister Mary Jo Anderson, b. 1939, interview by author, taped recording, 21 January 2011. Sister Joanne De Vicente was the last Sister of Mercy to run Mercy Hospital; she was chief executive in the late 70s and early 80s.

31   Dr. Virgilio, interview.

32   Steven Shackford, email to author, 22 September 2011. Dr. Bill Long left early on and was followed by Dr. Tom Wachtel as "acting division head of trauma" until replaced by Steve Shackford in July 1983.

33   Dr. David Butler Hoyt went on to become chair of the American College of Surgeons (ACS) Committee on Trauma (1998-2002) and ultimately executive director of ACS (2010-present.) In his early San Diego days, Dr. Hoyt was also a postdoctoral fellow in immunology at Scripps Clinic Research Institute under Dr. Charles Cochrane, 1980-82.

34   The Medical Audit Committee has continued to meet uninterrupted, still including representatives from UCSD, Sharp, Palomar, and Scripps Mercy, as well as La Jolla, for twenty-seven years at Scripps La Jolla.

35   The original trauma surgeons at Scripps La Jolla included: Drs. David Baker, Alan Berkenfield, Joe Capozzi, John Cherry, Brent Eastman, Paul Hyde, Dana Launer, Donley McReynolds, Louis Powers, Rick Tullis, and Steve Wilson. Dr. Brent Eastman was appointed trauma director.

      Mary Middleton, MSN, was director of Nursing; Patricia Berkenfield, RN, paramedic coordinator; and Barbara Friend, MSN, associate director of trauma services. This information came from the records of Cheryl Wooten, MSN, current director, trauma service (September 2011) and from a spiral-bound book called "Scripps Memorial Hospital La Jolla – Trauma Center – March 18, 1985," produced in-house.

36   John G. West , Donald D. Trunkey, Robert C. Lim, "Systems of trauma care. Study of Two Counties," *Archives of Surgery* (April 1979), 114: 455-60.

37   In 1982, the Hospital Council of San Diego and Imperial Counties undertook an assessment to determine whether San Diego County would benefit from a regionalized trauma system. The study represented the first comprehensive concurrent

and retrospective audit of trauma care in the nation ("Trauma Care Needs Assessment Study" by Amherst and Associates). The findings and recommendations of this report, released in November 1982, led to the development of a joint hospital council and medical society plan for care of trauma patients in San Diego County. From "County of San Diego Emergency Medical Services – Trauma System," http://www.sdcounty. ca.gov/hhsa/programs/phs/emergency_medical_services/trauma_system.html.

The Amherst Study showed a 21.2 percent preventable death rate with 46.9 percent of the trauma patients receiving suboptimal care. Gail Cooper, former Chief of SDC-EMS, email to author, 21 September 2011.

"Helen Woodward—Deaths Elsewhere," *The Blade: Toledo Ohio,* 14 November 1984: 26 http://news.google.com/newspapers?id=ClBPAAAAIBAJ&sjid=wQIEAAAAIBAJ&pg=5967%2C6900908.

38 Dr. Eastman, interview.

39 County of San Diego Health and Human Services Agency Emergency Medical Services, *San Diego County Trauma System 20-Year Report,* December 2004), http://www.sdcounty.ca.gov/hhsa/programs/phs/documents/EMS-Trauma20yrReport1984-2003.pdf.

40 Ibid.

41 Whittier Trust Company, "A Tradition of Service.", http://www.whittiertrust.com/why_f.html.

42 SMW Bass, "Diabetes: The Whittier Approach," *San Diego Magazine,* September 1986.

43 Molly McClain, "The Scripps Family's San Diego Experiment," *The Journal of San Diego History* 56, nos. 1 and 2 (Winter/Spring 2010): 25, endnote 17.

44 John Engle (b. 1960), interview by author, taped recording, 17 October 2011. A second triangle was attached in the 1990s to complete the insitutute in a more typical shape.

John Engle, now chief development officer at Scripps Health, was development director at the Whittier Institute from 1990-94, and president and CEO from 1994–2004, during which time the Whittier changed focus from collateral research to an outpatient program promoting optimal diabetes care and education, called the Scripps Whittier Diabetes Institute, under director Dr. Athena Philis-Tsimikas.

45 "Whittier Time Capsule Preserves History," *Inside Scripps,* May 2010.

46 "Helen Woodward," *The Blade: Toledo Ohio,* 14 November 1984: 26 http://news.google.com/newspapers?id=ClBPAAAAIBAJ&sjid=wQIEAAAAIBAJ&pg=5967%2C6900908.

47 "Philanthropist Paul Whittier Dies," *Los Angeles Times, 23* August 1991 http://articles.latimes.com/1991-08-23/local/me-890_1_paul-whittier.

CHAPTER 8 — THE GROWING FAMILY
SCRIPPS ENCINITAS

1   R.W. Brackett, *The History of San Diego County Ranchos*. 4th Ed. (San Diego: Union Title Insurance and Trust Company, 1951).

2   Except for part of 1925 when a Dr. D.B. Wegensen practiced briefly in an Encinitas hotel. *Coast Dispatch,* 4 March 1961.

3   Dr. Charles V. Lindsay Jr. (b. 1931), interview by author, taped recording, Encinitas, Calif, 15 October 2010. The younger Dr. Lindsay is a retired ansesthesiologist.

4   *Paul Ecke Poinsettias: The Ecke Ranch Story, 1923—The Move to Encinitas,* www.pauleckepoisettias.com/history.

5   Jan Day, *The History of Lima Bean Plants,* http://www.ehow.com/print/about_6499118_history-lima-bean-plants.html.

6   *Olivenhain: A History,* http://www.encinitaslive.com/olivenhain/.

7   Mac Hartley, *Encinitas History and Heritage,* (Virginia Beach: The Donning Company, 1999), 95.

8   Ibid., 106-108.

9   CHARLES FREDERICK BRASS 1920-2002, Mustang Memories The Official Website of the San Dieguito High School Academy Alumni. http://sdafoundation.com/alumni/contact/remembering-alumni/class-of-1937/.

10 Dr. Dwight Euvon Cook (b. 1928), interview by author, taped recording, Leucadia, Calif., 5 November 2010. See note 12 below.

11 Robert Hall (b. 1926), interview by author, telephone, 13 October 2011. Mr. Hall said his father, Bruce T. Hall, in partnership with a man named Young, owned the property bordered by Santa Fe Drive and Devonshire on the southwest, and Requeza St and Regal Road on the northeast, which is now bisected on the diagonal by I-5.

12 Joyce Mizock, interview by author, Carlsbad, Calif., 5 October 2011. Ms. Mizock owns Memento Arts & Design and created the "Dwight E. Cook Memory Book 1959-2009" from memorabilia of Dr. Cook's 50-year career. The Memory Book is kept at Dr. Cook's home in Leucadia; DVD in possession of Dr. Eastman.

The first tenants of the Encinitas Medical-Dental Center were: Dr. Lawrence Townsend; Ray Kieffer, DDS; and Charles Thompson, DDS. Included in the memory book are progress notes and an invitation to the open house at the Encinitas Medical-Dental Building on March 4, 1961, with photos of all tenants.

13 Adam Kaye, "Demolition of St. Mark Lutheran begins," *North County Times,* 24 June 2006. http://www.nctimes.com/news/local/article_36a22548-1470-5716-8e45-066d48f96749.html.

14 Dr. James LaBelle (b. 1957), interview by author, taped recording, Encinitas, Calif., 15 October 2010.

15 *Coast Dispatch,* 17 October 1963 as reprinted in Mizock, Joyce under architect's' drawing of Encinitas Community Hospital.

16 Joyce Mizock, "Scripps Project: Dwight Cook," 20 April 2009, 2. Also, Maura Wiegand, "The Wiegands: Early Settlers," *San Dieguito Heritage* (Encinitas: San Dieguito Heritage Museum, 1993), 63-69.

17 Wiegand. *San Dieguito Heritage,* 65.

18 Dr. J. Byron Wood (b. 1947), interview by author, telephone, Encinitas, Calif., 23 September 2011.

19 Eva Kilgore, "Remembering architect Don Hartfelder 1924-2007," *Orange County Register,* 21 February 2007, http://articles.ocregister.com/2007-02-21/cities/246959861huntington-harbour-mother-design#.

20 Dr. Ronald Summers (b. 1931), interview by author and Joyce Mizock, telephone, Colorado, 18 2011.

21 *The Citizen "a weekly serving the beach communities south of Oceanside,"* 16 July 1964.

22 Eric Davis (born 1928), interview by author, taped recording, Encinitas, Calif., 9 September 2011. Mr. Davis, retired from a career with Pacific Telephone, was a son-in-law of Harry Lorang. His wife Barbara Lorang Davis, RN, was employed at Scripps Memorial Hospital La Jolla; she later worked to get accreditation for the change from Encinitas Convalescent to San Dieguito Hospital. Mr. Davis drew a site map on a yellow pad as he spoke.

23 Dr. Cook, interview.

24 *Insight 1979.* a publication of Scripps Memorial Hospitals containing the Annual Report 1978.

25 News clipping, undated, but with surrounding material dated Oct 12, 1975. From scrapbook compiled by Dwight Cook's mother, Ruth Cook.

26 Mizock, "Scripps Project: Dwight Cook," 3.

27 Lew Scarr, "Scripps Buys Hospital in Encinitas," *San Diego Union,* 9 February 1978.

28 "Hospital buys hospital," *La Jolla Light,* Thursday, 9 February 1978. Also unidentified newspaper clipping, "Scripps Memorial: Encinitas hospital purchase finalized, " no date.

29 Samuel David Winner, MD (1941-2010) was Chief of Surgery at Scripps Encinitas 1979-80 and Chief of Staff 1981-82. *North County Times* Nov 3, 2010 "Remembering Samuel David Winner: North County surgeon played key role in Scripps Encinitas": B6.

30 Leland Housman, MD. Currently a member of Scripps Clinic Medical Group, since 2000.

31 Ronald MacCormick MD (1948-). Interview at Scripps Encinitas Chief of Staff's office by Sarita Eastman, August 19, 2010.

32 Mizock, Joyce. Dwight Cook Memory Book. "Progress Notes 1978-1990" and photograph: "1987: Dr. Clark takes over the reins at the official hospital ground breaking for the new East Wing addition."

33 Perry, Anthony. *Los Angeles Times*, Aug 25, 1989. http://articles.latimes.com/1989-08-25/local/me-1089_1_kentucky-fried.

34 Masciola, Carol. "Hospital shows off new wing" in un-named newspaper clipping, n.d.; and Mizock, Joyce, "Progress Notes 1978-1990", Dwight Cook Memory Book; and Stacey, Tom. *Los Angeles Times* May 29, 1990, "For Many Businesses, North County is Now the Place to Be". http://articles.latimes.com/1990-05-29/business/fi-1181north-county.

35 Michael Lobatz MD , Chief of Staff 2007-09 / Vice-President for Medical Affairs 2010 / System-Wide Director of Rehabilitation 2011.

36 Thomas Chippendale MD, Chief of Staff 2011 / Medical Director Neuroscience Care Line 2011.

37 Brainline.org – preventing, treating and living with traumatic brain injury. http://www.brainline.org/resources/local_resource.php?id=453; and "Scripps Returns Teacher to the Head of the Class" http://www.scripps.org/news_items/3980-scripps-returns-teacher-to-head-of-class.

38 James LaBelle interview.

CHAPTER 9 — THE GROWING FAMILY SCRIPPS CHULA VISTA

1   "The Orchard Period," *Local History*, http://www.chulavistaca.gov/City_Services/ Community_Services/Library/LocalHistoryMuseum/LocalHistRmHistOfCV.asp.

2   http://www.sharp.com/video/transcripts/vision-from-the-hill-transcript.cfm.

3   "World War II," *Local History* http://www.chulavistaca.gov/City_Services/ Community_Services/Library/LocalHistoryMuseum/LocalHistRmHistOfCV.asp.

4   Founding physicians Drs. Anthony Pierangelo (b. 1923), Lewis Palmer (b. 1923), George Cave (b. 1930), Leroy Miller (b. 1931), Charles Camarata (b. 1932), group interview by author, Scripps Mercy Chula Vista, email and telephone, 5 August 2010. A number of follow-up emails and phone conversations ensued.

5   http://www.sharp.com/about/history-of-sharp-healthcare.cfm.

6   Lewis Palmer, email to author, 8 August 2010.

7   *Chula Vista Star-News,* 8 August 1963, A1. All references to articles in the *Chula Vista Star-News* are from the microfilm collection by that name in the Chula Vista Public Library, Civic Center Branch, 365 F Street @ 4th Avenue, Chula Vista CA 91910. Search date 4 November 2010.

8   Physician Interview.

9   *Chula Vista Star-News*, 12 January 1969, A:1:5.

10 Anthony Pierangelo, interview by author, 7 August 2010, email to author.

11 "The Voice of our Chaldean Nation," http://www.kaldaya.net/DailyNews_April/ News_April272006_StDeddeh.html. The Chaldeans are Christians from "the land of the Tigris and Euphrates", i.e., Iraq. Wadie Deddeh had a 26-year career in the California Assembly and Senate 1967-1993. http://www.oac.cdlib.org/findaid/ ark:/13030/kt6n39r0xg/   He was the subject of the 2009 documentary film, *The Lion's Journey*. http://www.filmbaby.com/films/4079.

12 Bay General Hospital newsletter and invitations to open house for staff and auxiliary, 13 May 1971, invitation to general public, May 16.

13 "Special Section paid for by Bay General Hospital and devoted to the grand opening of the hospital's new wing," *Chula Vista Star-News*, 16 May 1971, D1-D8. Paper given to author by Dr. Anthony Pierangelo along with invitations to Open House for New Hospital Wing, 13 and 16 May 1971.

14 Bay General Hospital newsletter, December 1970.

15 *Bay General Hospital News,* "Expansion Continues. New Medical-Service Center on Schedule," n. d.

16 Pierangelo, interview.

17 1984: Bay General Community Hospital changed its name to Bay Hospital Medical Center. http://sduptownnews.com/critical-care-as-scripps-mercy-hospital-celebrates-120-years-its-connection-to-patients-remains-vital/ p 5.

18 Keith Owens, Financial Problems Cited: Chula Vista to Consider Private Firm for Hospital," *Los Angeles Times* 28 January 1986. "http://articles.latimes.com/1986-01-28/local/me-885_1_bay-hospital.

19 Cave, interview.

20 Ames Early (b. 1937), interview by author, taped recording, Rancho Santa Fe, Calif., 29 July 2010.

21 Tom Gammiere (b. 1960), interview by author, taped recording, Scripps Mercy San Diego, 28 January 2011.

22 Francisco Gracia, MD (b. 1939), interview by author, taped recording, South Bay Surgical Associates, Chula Vista, Calif., 27 September 2011.

23 *STAT – the newsletter of Scripps Memorial Hospital Chula Vista*, September 1992, 1.

24 Gracia, interview.

25 http://www.thestarnews.com/health/a-century-plus-of-giving-to-the-community/.

26 *Update Summer 1999*, Mike Godfrey email to author, 18 October, 2011.

27 Carla Stayboldt, MD (b. 1955), Interview by author, taped recording, 12 October 2011.

28 Dr. Stayboldt, interview.

29 Dr. Stayboldt says that when the deadline for submitting an alternate candidate passed, a group of twenty-twenty-five physicians began meeting at a restaurant called *Casa Salsa*, and eventually circulated among the entire medical staff a petition to have her removed as Chief of Staff Elect. Since the only legitimate grounds for such an action were failure to perform, the petition fizzled. Other physicians were chagrined by the actions of their colleagues and apologized; one said, "I'm really sorry, but it's because you're a woman and you have blue eyes."

30 Marianne McKennett, MD, interview by author, telephone, 20 October 2011. Email to author followed, 21 October 2011.

CHAPTER TEN — SCRIPPS CLINIC MEDICAL INSTITUTIONS 1977-1991

1   Frank Dixon was CEO of SCRF from 1974-1977, but was not president; that title was retained by Dr. Edmund Keeney.

2   William Faulkner Black (b. 1933), interview by author, taped recording, 31 October 2011. Dr. Edwards was the unanimous choice of the board, and trustee Bill Black said, "In my sixteen years on the board, my greatest legacy to Scripps Clinic was Charlie Edwards."

3   Dr. Charles Cornell Edwards (1923-2011), interview by author and Dr. Clifford Colwell, taped recording, 18 November 2010.

4   Charles Edwards and Mika Ono Benedyk, *Tough Choices* (Self-published: 2003), 59-123. Chronology prepared by author.

5   Early, interview.

6   Edwards and Benedyk, *Tough Choices*, 123.

7   Ibid., 123-24.

8   Ibid., 125.

9   Linda Gonzalez, Scripps Health Foundation, "Naming Around Green and Clinic." Anderson Outpatient Pavilion: In 1981 construction began on a new medical office building, located north of Green Hospital. The support of George M. and Thelma B. Anderson facilitated the completion of the building. Thelma Baker Anderson's father, Rueben Carlton Baker, founded Baker Oil Tools, Inc., in 1913 in Coalinga, California. Thelma Baker's husband, George Anderson, joined Baker in 1919 as a machinist. At the time of his retirement, he was a vice president and a member of the board of directors.

10 Ibid., 125.

11 In 2011, there are ten Scripps Clinic locations outside of Torrey Pines, plus ten affiliated Scripps Coastal Medical Center locations. Scripps Health flyer: "Finding the Right Doctor is Easy at Scripps." The Clinic at Borrego Springs closed in 1990. http://www.borregomedical.org/about-us/foundation-history.

12 Hospital Corporation of America website. "Our History" http://hcahealthcare.com/about/our-history.dot.

13 Edwards and Benedyk, *Tough Choices*, 127-128.

14 David Carmichael, MD, "Cardiology in San Diego, California WWII to 2006," lecture San Diego County Medical Society, 2006, video disc.

15 William Faulkner Black (B. 1933), interview by author, taped recording, Fairbanks Ranch, 31 October 2011.

16 Allen "Skip" Johnson, MD (b. 1941), interview by author, taped recording, Scripps Green Hospital, 2 November 2011.

17 Guy Curtis, MD (b. 1938), interview by author, taped recording, Scripps Green Hospital, 2 November 2011.

18 The Kaiser Permanente Excellence in Teaching Award, UCSD Medical School, given annually on nomination by the medical students. Skip Johnson and Guy Curtis each won the Kaiser Award, two years apart.

19 Robert Sarnoff, MD (b. 1948), interview by author, taped recording, Scripps Green Hospital, 12 September 2011.

20 Richard A. Schatz, MD (b. 1952), interview by author, taped recording, Scripps Green Hospital, 19 October 2011.

21 "The Burning Genius of Andreas Gruentzig," *Cardiology* (Journal), September 2007. "Some flames burst so hot and bright that they consume themselves. Perhaps that was the case with Andreas Gruentzig, the father of interventional cardiology, who died in 1985 at the age of 46 in a plane that he was flying…Gruentzig performed the first coronary angioplasty on an awake human patient." http://www.cardiosource.com/Sep07_Cardio_Gruentzig_Article2.pdf.

22 Dr. Schatz, interview.

23 Ibid.

24 http://www.medhelp.org/general/stent.htm, Craig Walker, MD. Cardiovascular Institute of the South. "Device to prop open arteries may be major heart treatment advance."

25 Paul Teirstein, MD, email to author, 4 October 2011, follow-up interview by author, taped recording, 5 October, La Jolla.

26 St. Vincent College, Latrobe, PA, conference on the 10th Anniversary of Mother Teresa's death. 6 October 2007. http://www.post-gazette.com/pg/07280/823536-51.stm?cmpid=localstate.xml.

27 "Dr. Philip Arthur Higginbottom Obituary." *San Diego Union-Tribune*, 6 January 2010. http://www.legacy.com/obituaries/signonsandiego/obituary.aspx?n=philip-arthur-higginbottom&pid=138206201.

28 Erminia "Mimi" Guarneri, MD (b.1959), interview by author, taped recording, Scripps Center for Integrative Medicine, 31 October 2011.

29 Edwards and Benedyk, *Tough Choices*, 129.

30 Dr. Edwards, interview.

31 Edwards and Benedyk, *Tough Choices*, 131.

32 Dr.Cochrane, interview.

33 Richard A. Lerner and Frank Dixon. "Transfer of Ovine Experimental Allergic Glomerulonephritis (EAG) with Serum," *The Journal of Experimental Medicine* Vol 124 No 3, 1 September 1966: 431–442.

34 William H. Beers, Ph.D, "The Scripps Research Institute," *Molecular Medicine* 3, no. 12, December 1977: 793-98 The Picower Institute Press, 1977. http://www.ncbi. nlm.nih.gov/pmc/articles/PMC2230281/pdf/molmed00036-0007.pdf.

35 Dr.Cochrane, interview.

36 Major donors to the campaign for the "Lusk Research Campus" and the "Lita Annenberg Hazen Science Center" were John and William Lusk and Ms. Hazen. "Scripps Clinic Buys 21 Acres to Develop Biotech, Research Facility," *Los Angeles Times*, 18 January 1989.

37 Edwards and Benedyk, *Tough Choices*, 128.

CHAPTER ELEVEN — MERCY HOSPITAL 1924-1985

1 Marilyn Gouailhardou, RSM, Sisters of Mercy of the Americas Burlingame Regional Community, *List of Sister Administrators, Mercy Hospital San Diego*, email to author, 28 November 2011.

2 Sioban Nelson, *Say Little, Do Much: Nursing, Nuns, and Hospitals in the Nineteenth Century* (University of Pennsylvania Press, Philadelphia: 2001).

3 *San Diego Union,* 23 August 1923, as quoted in Sr. Rose McArdle, Thermofax, 15.

4 "Hillquest – Medical Community History" compiled by QHome. http://www. hillquest.com/history/timeline_medical.html and "Mediterranean Revival" http://www.historicpreservationmiami.com/mediterranean.html.

5 Stan Amundson, MD (b. 1947), interview by author, taped recording, Scripps Mercy San Diego, 29 November 2011. Dr. Amundson and his wife, also a physician, lived in "the Manor" for three years in the mid-70s and "were able to take ward call from the Manor, surrounded by friends and peers."

6 Sister Rose McArdle (Sister Mary Aurelia), Thermofax on the History of Mercy San Diego (Scripps Mercy San Diego: n.p., 1960-69), 15.

7 Gouailhardou, emails to author, 1 December and 6 December 2011.

8 Ralph Ocampo, MD (b. 1931), surgeon and long-time medical historian for San Diego, interview by author, taped recording, San Diego, Calif., 29 November 2011.

9 Sister Mary Jo Anderson CHS (b. 1939), interview by author, taped recording, 26 November 2011.

10 Anita V. Figueredo, MD, "Breaking In," *San Diego Physician, Women in Medicine* (September 1992): 15. Official Publication of the San Diego County Medical Society.

11 Anderson, interview.

12 Gouailhardou, email to author, 28 November 2011.

13 "Hillquest – Medical Community History" compiled by QHome. http://www. hillquest.com/history/timeline_medical.html.

14 Sister Rose McArdle (Sister Mary Aurelia), Thermofax on the History of Mercy San Diego (Scripps Mercy San Diego: n.p., 1960-69), 9-10.

15 Bill Finley, *A History of Mercy Hospital…and its century of service to San Diego* (Scripps Mercy San Diego: n.p., June 1990), 17.

16 McArdle, Thermofax.

17 McArdle, Thermofax.

18 David Shaw, MD (b.1942), "History of Internal Medicine Associates," attachment in email to author, 4 December 2011.

19 Dr. David Shaw and Stan Amundson, MD (b. 1947), interview by author, San Diego, Calif. 29 November2011.

20 Ibid.

21 Matthew T. and Donald H. Estes, "Hot Enough to Melt Iron: The San Diego Nikkei Experience 1942-1946," *The Journal of San Diego History* 42, no. 3 (Summer 1996): 1-2, http://www.sandiegohistory.org/journal/96summer/nikkei. htm.

22 Laurence Tanaka, MD, emails to author, 15 and 16 December 2011.

23 Ibid.,citing Roy Kiyoshi Tanaka, MD, interview by Donald H. Estes, taped recording, San Diego, 21 February 1979, San Diego Nikkei History Project.

24 "The Sisters of Mercy Clinic," framed history, basement lobby wall near west auditorium, Scripps Mercy Hospital, San Diego campus.

25 Stan Amundson, MD, interview.

26 Drs. David Shaw, Stan Amundson and Jerrold Glassman. Drs. Shaw, Amundson and Glassman arrived at Mercy in 1973, '73 and '76 respectively.

27 Anderson, interview.

28 Gouailhardou, email to author, 30 November 2011, Dr. Peter McDermott, as quoted in the *Community Obituary*, September 1998.

29 "Mercy Hospital Expansion Program to Cost Millions," *San Diego Union*, 8 July 1957.

30 Daniel Mulvihill (b.1927), interview by author, taped recording, San Diego, 18 November 2011.

31 Anderson interview.

32 Dr. Eugene Rumsey Jr. (b. 1947), interview by author, telephone, 8 December 2011. According to Eugene Rumsey Jr., the new Mercy Medical Building on 4060 Fourth Ave. opened in late 1979, just after he arrived to join his father in practice. By that time, Sister Mary Placida had been replaced as administrator by Sister Mary Joanne De Vincenti.

33 Anderson interview.

34 Ibid.

35 Jerrold Glassman, MD (b. 1950), interview by author, Scripps Mercy San Diego, 29 November 2011.

36 Cliff Smith, "Rare Heart Surgery Saves Girl," 30 March 1966.

37 "John H. Mazur, MD, medical director of Cardiology, 1963-1996, recognition wall in the Heart Care Center, Scripps Mercy Hospital, San Diego campus.

38 Rumsey, Jr. MD, interview. George Zorn, Jr. MD (b. 1948), interview by author, telephone, 9 December 2011.

39 Dr. Steven R. Shackford succeeded Dr. Dick Virgilio as head of the Navy Trauma Unit, was then Division Head of Trauma at UCSD from 1983-89, and a founder of the San Diego Trauma System, and professor and chair of the Department of Surgery at the University of Vermont from 1989-2007, and was recruited by Dr. Sise to Scripps Mercy in 2007.

40 Dr. Michael Sise (b. 1950), interview with author, 21 January 2012.

41 Mulvihill, interview.

42 "Our Lady of La Salette," http://en.wikipedia.org/wiki/Our_Lady_of_La_Salette.

CHAPTER TWELVE — Change and Unrest 1990-2000

1   Barbara Marsh, "San Diego in Lead of HMO Revolution," 30 August 1995. http://articles.latimes.com/1995-08-31/news/mn-40821_1_san-diego.

2   Ames Early, interview by author, taped recording, 29 July 2010.

3   Charles Edwards, MD, and Mika Ono Benedyk, *Tough Choices* (Self-published: 2003), 142.

4   Catholic Healthcare West: About Us. http://www.careerbuilder.com/Jobs/ Company/C8M4DP65YG1SP8RQRSV/Catholic-Healthcare-West/

5   Sister Mary Jo Anderson, interview by author, taped recording, 21 January 2011.

6   Linda Roach, "Scripps Clinic, Sharp Are Discussing a Merger," *Los Angeles Times*, 9 June 1990. http://articles.latimes.com/print/1990-06-09/local/me-426_1_ biomedical-research-facilities.

7   Early. interview.

8   Ibid.

9   Bill Nelson (b. 1925), interview by author, taped recording, 5 August 2010.

10 Linda Roach Monroe, "Spurned by Scripps Clinic, Sharp Now Seeks Grossmont Merger." *Los Angeles Times*, 6 October 1990. http://articles.latimes.com/1990-10- 06/local/me-1422_1_hospital-district.

11 Greg Johnson, "Scripps Speeds Plans to Merge Clinic, Hospital," *Los Angeles Times*. Date printed on-line as December 17, 1992, but text indicates 1990. http:// articles.latimes.com/print/1992-12-17/local/me-2675_1_health-care-services.

12 Nelson, interview.

13 Richard A. Lerner, MD (b. 1938), interview by author, taped recording, 3 October 2011.

14 Four Winds Enterprises 1985-87: Household Goods Shipping/Warehousing. Filed for bankruptcy 1987. *94 B.R. 694 (1988)* In re FOUR WINDS ENTERPRISES, INC., a Virginia corporation, and its affiliates, Debtor. United States Bankruptcy Court, S.D. California. December 13, 1988.

15 Adapted from Edwards and Ono Benedyk, 143, corrections made by Richard Sheridan, general counsel at Scripps Health, email to author, 16 December 2011.

16 Ames Early, interview by author, telephone, 17 December 2011.

17 PR Newswire Corporation, "ScrippsHealth to Acquire Valley Medical Center in El Cajon," 19 February 1993. http://www.thefreelibrary.com/SCRIPPSHEALT H+TO+ACQUIRE+VALLEY+MEDICAL+CENTER+IN+EL+CAJON -a013117413

18 Robin Brown (b. 1951), interview by author, taped recording, 7 September 2011.

19 Ibid.

20 PR Newswire Corporation.

21 Ibid.

22 Pr Newswire Corporation, "Charles C. Edwards MD Announces Retirement as President of Scripps Institutions of Medicine and Science," 10 May 1993. http://www.thefreelibrary.com/CHARLES+C.+EDWARDS,+M.D., +ANNOUNCES+RETIREMENT+AS+PRESIDENT+OF-a013154257.

23 Dr. Lerner, interview.

24 Richard Sheridan, emails to author, 16 December 2011.

25 Files, "Search Committee for CEO of SIMS/SH 1993-94," "Search Committee for Chair, Office of Presidents 1995," (Scripps Health).

26 Richard V. Allen, "The Day Reagan was Shot," *Hoover Digest,* 30 July 2001, Hoover Institution, Stanford University. http://www.hoover.org/publications/hoover-digest/article/6281.

27 Early, interview, December.

28 Mrs. William McCormick (Deeda) Blair, Jr to members of the SIMS Search Committee, 15 November 1995.

29 SIMS ceased to be the statutory voting member of Scripps Health on May 7, 1999. *Articles of Incorporation Certificate of Amendment* to Scripps Health's Articles of Incorporation.

30 Robert Sarnoff, MD (b. 1948), interview by author, taped recording, 12 September 2011.

31 Ibid.

32 Richard Sheridan (b. 1957), interview by author, 11 November 2011, email to author, 19 December 2011.

33 Sister Mary Jo Anderson, interview by author, 26 November 2011.

34 *Indult,* from the Latin *indultum* meaning "concession." A faculty granted by the Pope to deviate from the common law of the Church. http://www.thefreedictionary.com/indult The Indult was given at Rome, 21 April 1995.

35 Andrew Santos III (b. 1971), administrative director of Mission Integration for Scripps Mercy Hospital, interview by author, taped recording, 20 April 2011. "The *Ethical and Religious Directives of Catholic Healthcare Services 5*[th] *Ed, 2009*, issued by the United States Conference of Catholic Bishops are spelled out in a six-part document. Part of it, I term the 'thou shall nots'. We cannot, for example, participate in elective abortions, sterilizations, physician assisted suicides or euthanasia. It also lays out the 'thou shalls', what we should do [for instance, respecting] patient privacy, and the relationship between physician and patients, the rights of physicians, the rights of employees, the rights of patients."

36 Anderson, interview.

37 Early, interview, July.

38 Pappelbaum, Turner and Associates–Strategic Healthcare Consultants. http://pappelbaum-turner.com/about.htm.

39 A. Brent Eastman, MD (b. 1940), interview by author, taped recording, 29 December 2010.

40 Sheridan, interview.

41 Dr. Eastman, interview.

42 Ibid.

43 "Aetna Names Sebastianelli President," 6 March 1997; and "Sebastianelli Resigns As President of Aetna," 16 May 1997. http://www.aetna.com/news/1997/pr_19970306.htm; http://www.aetna.com/news/1997/pr_19970516.htm.

44 After the retirement of Ames Early in 1999, the name ScrippsHealth began to be written as two words: Scripps Health, and the two-word spelling of the name became the preferred form.

45 "Metropolitan Movers," *San Diego Metropolitan Uptown Examiner & Daily Business Report,* April 1999. *http://sandiegometro.archives.whsites.net/1999/apr/metro.html.*

46 Kevin Glynn, MD, "Preventing Civil War: A case study for physician CEOs," *The Physician Executive*, March-April 2002: 44-45.

47 Early, interview, 29 July 2010.

48 Chris Van Gorder had first been president and CEO of Anaheim Memorial Medical Center, which then merged with Memorial Health Services (MHS). After the merger, Mr. Van Gorder was made executive vice president of MHS and CEO of Long Beach Memorial Medical Center.

49 Chris Van Gorder (b. 1952), interview by author, taped recording, 9 September 2010.

50 Glynn, "Preventing Civil War," 44.

51 Brown, interview.

52 Alan Schulman, chairman of the Mercy Foundation to Stanley Pappelbaum MD, president and CEO of Scripps Health and Stewart Frank, MD, president of the Mercy Physicians Medical Group, 28 March 2000.

53 Van Gorder, interview.

54 Frank Panarisi (b. 1933), interview by author, telephone, 22 December 2011. Scripps Health Board of Trustees 1999–2000: Frank Panarisi (Chair), Ames Early, Dr. Francisco Gracia, Sister Phyllis Hughes, Arnold LaGuardia, Donald Mitchell, Bruce Moore, Daniel Mulvihill, David Nuffer, Janet Rodgers, Abby Silverman, Leonard Stephens.

55 Tony Fong, "Despite physicians' unrest, Scripps board backs CEO," *San Diego Union-Tribune,* 4 May 2000.

56 Cheryl Clark, "Scripps Health quality under fire," *San Diego Union-Tribune,* 15 May 2000.

57 James Grisolia, MD, chief of Neurology at Scripps-Mercy, to Donald Mitchell, Scripps Health Board of Directors, 17 May 2000.

58 Cheryl Clark. "Scripps CEO says he's not quitting," *San Diego Union-Tribune,* 19 May 2000.

CHAPTER THIRTEEN — THE NEW MILLENNIUM
2000-2012

1 "Open Letter to the Residents of San Diego County from the Physicians of Scripps Hospitals," *San Diego Union Tribune,* 19 June 2000. Signed by Chiefs of Staff Drs. Carla Stayboldt (Scripps Chula Vista), Michael Skyhar (Scripps Encinitas), Giacomo DeLaria (Scripps Green), David Roseman (Scripps La Jolla), and Kevin Glynn (Scripps Mercy).

   In an email to author 31 December 2011, Dr. Kevin Glynn remarked: "The medical staffs wanted the public to know that the doctors were going to work with the trustees and administrators… Chris came on with a willingness to listen that reassured me and the other chiefs. The ad was a result of this."

2 "The child life profession …improves healthcare experiences for children by providing play, preparation and educational programs…[encouraging] emotional stability and healthy development of hospitalized children while mitigating the fear and pain associated with treatment….and also advocates for frequent family visits and parental participation in care." Child Life Council, History of the Profession. http://www.childlife.org/the%20child%20life%20profession/historyoftheprofession.cfm.

3 "Scripps Closure: A Matter of Life and Death," *The Jacob Journal: a newsletter from Supervisor Dianne Jacob*, May 2000. http://www.diannejacob.com/journal/2000/may2000. The sixth Scripps Hospital, East County, closed for good June 5, 2000. Jobs were found on other Scripps campuses for virtually all employees who requested them. Subsequently, the land was purchased by Kaiser Permanente, the hospital torn down and an outpatient clinic erected on the other end of the property.

4 Richard Sheridan, emails to author, taped recording, 16 January 2012.

5 Bob Erra., interview with author, taped recording, 19 January 2012.

6 Chris Van Gorder, interview with author, taped recording, 23 January 2012.

7 Richard Sheridan (b. 1957), interview by author, taped recording, 11 November 2011, and email to author 19 December 2011.

8 Dr. Robert Sarnoff (b. 1948), interview by author, taped recording, 12 September 2011.

9 Dr. Hugh Greenway served as CEO of Scripps Clinic from August 1, 2000 through late February 2003, when he transitioned to the position of Executive Vice President for Institutional Advancement in the Scripps Foundation. Email to author from Dr. Greenway 20 Jan 2012.

10   Elliot Kushell, Ph.D, Consultant, Office of the President, email to author, 16 January 2012.

11   Johan Otter, System Wide Senior Director of Occupational Health, email to author, 11 January 2012.

12   Gary Fybel, email to author, 25 January 2012.

13   Wolfstein Sculpture Park was established in 1998 by donors Ralyn and Nathan Wolfstein; to date, the park has grown to include more than thirty affecting pieces on the green lawns and hardscape of Scripps La Jolla, and patients and visitors are often seen strolling among them.

14   Richard Sheridan, interview.

15   Vic Buzachero (b. 1951), interview with author, taped recording, 4 January 2012.

16   Richard Rothberger (b. 1950), interview with author, taped recording, 18 January 2012.

17   Vic Buzachero, interview.

18   Mary Lou Carraher, interview with author, 10 November 2011.

19   Larry Harrison, interview with author, 7 September 2011.

20   "Great Place to Work: About Us," http://www.greatplacetowork.com/about-us.

21   Carl Etter, email to author, 20 January 2012. Carl Etter arrived as Chief Executive at Scripps Encinitas on 8 December 2003.

22   Jan Zachry (b. 1955), Chief Nurse Operating Executive, Scripps Encinitas, interview with author, taped recording, 10 January 2012.

23   "2011 Working Mother 100 Best Companies," *Working Mother*, http://www.workingmother.com/best-company-list/116542.

24   "2011 Winners: AARP Best Employers For Workers Over 50 Award," September 2011. #1 = Scripps Health. http://www.aarp.org/work/on-the-job/info-09-2011/aarp-best-employers-winners-2011.html.

25   Tom Gammiere (b. 1960), interview with author, taped recording, 28 January 2011.

26   Juan Tovar MD (b. 1966), interview with author, taped recording, 10 October 2011. All quotations in this section about the merger of the two Mercy campuses are taken from Dr. Tovar.

27   Patty Skoglund, RN, email to author, 27 January 2012.

28 Chris Van Gorder, interview with author, taped recording, 23 January 2012.

29 "October 2007 Wildfires," http://en.wikipedia.org/wiki/October_2007_California_wildfires.

30 Two seats were donated by John Bardis, President and CEO of MedAssets, in his private plane, which was already flying to Haiti.

31 A papal nuncio is a permanent diplomatic head of mission of the Vatican to another state, and has the rank of ambassador plenipotentiary. The term comes from the Latin word *nuntius,* meaning envoy. http://en.wikipedia.org/wiki/Nuncio.

32 The second Haiti team included: Chris Van Gorder; trauma surgeons Brent Eastman and Steven Shackford (Mercy San Diego); anesthesiologists Michael Capozza (Scripps Clinic) and Todd Austin (Mercy San Diego and Green); orthopedist Drew Peterson (Mercy Chula Vista); nurses Patty Skoglund (Dir. Disaster Preparedness), Kelly Hardiman (Dir. Policy), Deb McQuillen (Mercy San Diego, Dir. Cardiac and Critical Care), Maureen Shackford (Mercy San Diego), Rob Sills (Dir. Support Services).

33 Dr. Dayna Arnstein, Scripps Clinic.

34 "1994 Northridge Earthquake" http://en.wikipedia.org/wiki/1994_Northridge_earthquake.

Also "California's Hospital Seismic Retrofit Program" http://mceer.buffalo.edu/Nonstructural_Components/presentatiions/02Tokas.pdf.

35 Richard Fortuna, MD, email to author, 27 January 2012.

36 Eric Topol, MD (b. 1954), interview by author, taped recording, 5 January 2012. All quotations in this section, unless otherwise noted, are from Dr. Topol.

37 University of Rochester Commencement 2011 Awards and Honorary Degrees http://www.rochester.edu/commencement/2011/honorees.html As a clinician and a researcher, Topol has helped advance medicine throughout his career. His work in the genomics of heart attack led to the discovery of two key genes recognized by the American Heart Association as one of the top ten research advances and by *Time* magazine as a "Top 10 Medical Breakthrough in 2010." He administered recombinant tissue plasminogen activator to the first patient in 1984 and pioneered the clinical development of clopidogrel, known as Plavix; bivalirudin, known as Angiomax; and abciximab, known as ReoPro. Topol was the first physician to publish concerns about the safety and cardiovascular risk of the drug known as Vioxx, which eventually was withdrawn from the market. He has been a prodigious author with more than 1,000 original peer-reviewed publications. He has edited more than thirty books, including major textbooks on interventional cardiology and cardiovascular medicine. In 2012, he published a new book for consumers, *The Creative Destruction of Medicine: How the Digital*

Revolution Will Create Better Health Care. He is the founder and vice-chairman of West Wireless Health Institute which supports the development of wireless health technology.

38   Paul Teirstein, MD, email to author, 9 January 2012.

39   According to Dr. Topol: A Science Committee made up of National Academy of Science people from TSRI and leading physician researchers from Scripps come together to select the most deserving projects. Each application gets $50,000 of direct funds and approximately that much indirect, so close to $100,000; and well over seventy of these grants have been awarded to date. Also funded are two-year salaries of four *clinician scholars,* MDs who have finished their training; and of six *translational scholars,* PhDs, all of whom wish to bring cutting-edge science to the bedside.

40   Zettabyte=a unit of information equal to one sextillion bytes. From a lecture by Dr. Eric Topol called "The Creative Destruction of Medicine, 2 February 2012, Hyatt Regency, La Jolla.

41   The former chief operating officers and their hospitals: Todd Hoff (Mercy); Lisa Thakur (La Jolla); Tim Collins (Green); Rebecca Cofinas (Encinitas).

42   Mary Ellen Doyle (b. 1951), interview by author, taped recording, 10 January 2012.

43   Scripps Translational Science Intsitute. http://www.stsiweb.org/index.php/about/bio/neale

44   James LaBelle, "Physicians and Hospitals Must Partner to Survive," *San Diego Union Tribune,* 3 March 2011; and *Inside Scripps,* March 2011, 6-7.

45   Robert Sarnoff (Scripps Clinic Medical Group); Kevin Hirsch (Scripps Coastal Medical Group); Davis Cracroft (Scripps Mercy Physician Partners); Scott Eisman (Connect the Docs); Stewart Frank (Mercy Physicians Medical Group); Michael Karp (Primary Care Associates Medical Group); Mark Sedwitz (XiMED Medical Group). James LaBelle MD, email to author, 4 February 2012.

46   Richard Sheridan, general counsel Scripps Health, email to author, 9 February 2012.

47   A third (specialty) group joined the foundation in May 2009: Scripps Cardiovascular and Thoracic Surgeons, who do more such surgery than any other group in the county. Current members are: Drs. Scot Brewster, Donald Buehler, Richard Stahl, James Hemp, John Tyner, Sam Baradarian, and Douglas Mellinger.

CHAPTER FOURTEEN — THE VALUE PROPOSITION

1   Michael A. Marletta, Ph.D. President and CEO, Cecil and Ida M. Green Professor of Chemistry, The Scripps Research Institute. Email to author 31 Jan 2012.

2   "2011 Community Benefit Plan and Report, Scripps Health. Report submitted to the Office of Statewide Health Planning and Development (OHSPD) May 2011 in accordance with SB697. Section 1 Fulfilling the Scripps Mission: 1–3.

3   A partial list of ongoing relief efforts with Scripps personnel and others includes: Mercy Outreach Surgical Team (M.O.S.T.) to the interior of Mexico; Committee for the Rural Development of Milot (CRUDEM) in Haiti; and Loloma Foundation serving island nations of the South Pacific.

4.   Sister Virginia Gillis (24 Oct 1933–9 Mar 2012) brought her humor and wisdom to the Scripps Health Board of Trustees from 2008 until her death in 2012. Sister Virginia spent thirty years fulfilling her ministry in the health care field, including service on the Board of Directors at [then] Mercy Hospital during the 1980s.

Appendix

TIMELINE

1890	Sisters of Mercy open St. Joseph's Dispensary.
1891	St. Joseph's Sanitarium opens in Hillcrest.
1918	Ellen Scripps' first hospital, La Jolla Sanitarium, opens on Prospect Street.
1922	Mother Mary Michael Cummings dies.
1924	(September) Scripps Memorial Hospital opens on Prospect Street.
1924	(December) Scripps Metabolic Clinic opens on Prospect Street.
1924	Hospital and Clinic function as one unit, becoming the second such medical research institution in the United States.
1924	St. Joseph's Sanitarium is renamed Mercy Hospital and moves to 5th and Washington.
1932	Ellen Browning Scripps dies.
1946	American Medical Association approves Mercy Hospital's new Graduate Medical Education program.
1947	Scripps Metabolic Clinic spins-off as separate corporation.
1955	Scripps Metabolic Clinic becomes Scripps Clinic and Research Foundation.
1964	Scripps Memorial Hospital relocates to Miramar Road (later Genesee Avenue).
1966	Mercy Hospital opens a new eleven-story facility.
1970	Dow Chemical Company donates twelve acres of land on Torrey Pines Mesa to Scripps Clinic and Research Foundation.
1974	Scripps Clinic and Research Foundation groundbreaking at Torrey Pines Mesa location.
1974	Scripps Clinic and Research Foundation re-organizes into three corporations: Scripps Clinic and Research Foundation; Hospital of Scripps Clinic; Scripps Clinic Medical Group.

1975	Hospital of Scripps Clinic renamed Green Hospital.
1977	Scripps Clinic and Research Foundation moves to its Torrey Pines Mesa location.
1978	San Dieguito Hospital in Encinitas is acquired and renamed Scripps Memorial Hospital Encinitas.
1980	Satellite clinics operated by Scripps Clinic Medical Group are opened across San Diego County, beginning with Borrego Springs and Rancho Bernardo.
1981	The Whittier Institute for Diabetes and Endocrinology opens at Scripps Memorial Hospital La Jolla.
1981	The Scripps Mende Well Being Center, the first storefront health education center of its kind in the United States, opens at the University Town Center in La Jolla. Well Being Centers are later expanded to Encinitas and Chula Vista.
1983	Scripps Clinic opens the Anderson Outpatient Pavilion, a 164,000 square foot facility, to provide preventative medicine and outpatient care to Scripps Clinic patients.
1984	Scripps Memorial Hospital La Jolla joins other facilities in San Diego, including Mercy Hospital, to create a countywide trauma system.
1986	Bay Hospital Medical Center in Chula Vista is acquired and renamed Scripps Memorial Hospital Chula Vista.
1986	Scripps creates Home Health Care Services to provide specialty home care services.
1989	The Donald B. and Darlene V. Shiley Sports and Health Center opens on Torrey Pines Mesa next to Scripps Clinic.
	After a 44-year separation, Scripps Memorial Hospitals and Scripps Clinic and Research Foundation reaffiliate as operating divisions of Scripps Institutions of Medicine and Science. The Scripps Research Institute separates from SCRF and is a third operating division of SIMS.
1991	The name Scripps Health first comes into use for all entities. By 1995, the name Scripps Institutions of Medicine and Science is no longer used.
1995	Mercy Hospital joins Scripps as Scripps Mercy Hospital. Scripps Mercy Hospital remains San Diego's only Catholic hospital.

1996	Scripps Clinic and Scripps Health once again separate; Scripps Green Hospital continues as part of Scripps Health.
1999	Scripps Center for Integrative Medicine is established, providing complementary therapies to traditional medical care.
1999	Scripps Health, Scripps Clinic and The Scripps Research Institute join forces to create the Scripps Cancer Center, integrating basic research, clinical research , cancer care and community outreach.
2000	Scripps Health and Scripps Clinic unite for the third time.
2000	Scripps CEO Chris Van Gorder establishes the Physician Leadership Cabinet, composed of elected medical staff leadership from each Scripps hospital.
2001	Scripps Leadership Academy is launched.
2002	Scripps provides its first "Great Place to Work Survey" on a voluntary basis to all employees.
2004	Scripps opened Scripps Clinic Carmel Valley ambulatory center. Scripps would expand the number of ambulatory sites to 24 centers across the county.
2004	Scripps Mercy Hospital consolidates operating licenses with Scripps Memorial Hospital Chula Vista. The two become Scripps Mercy Hospital, San Diego and Scripps Mercy Hospital, Chula Vista.
2005	Scripps Medical Response Team (SMRT) is created and deployed to Houston, Texas at the request of the federal government to care for patients displaced by Hurricanes Katrina and Rita.
2006	(May) Scripps Health announces plans to build a comprehensive Cardiovascular Institute as part of a $360 million first phase replacement of Scripps Memorial Hospital La Jolla.
2006	Scripps Health announces a new Translational Science Institute and Genomic Medicine program to support basic research and clinical programs.
2006	Philanthropist Conrad T. Prebys donates $10 million to Scripps Mercy Hospital in support of its emergency department and trauma services. The new Conrad Prebys Emergency and Trauma Center opens 2012.
2007	The Success Shares program is established.
2007	Scripps Health receives a $30 million gift from The Howard Charitable Foundation—the largest in its 83-year history—to support development of a new cardiovascular institute on the Scripps Memorial Hospital La Jolla campus.

2008	Scripps Health makes its first appearance on Fortune magazine's list of America's "100 Best Companies to Work For." This is the first time a San Diego health care provider is included in the list.
2008	Scripps Health opens the Scripps Clinical Research Center to support researchers, improve communication and help create new partnerships with drug and device companies.
2008	The Whittier Institute for Diabetes is fully integrated with Scripps Health, becoming the Scripps Whittier Diabetes Institute.
2008	Scripps Health purchases Sharp Mission Park Medical Group and joins it with Scripps Mercy Medical Group, creating Scripps Coastal Medical Center.
2008	Scripps Cancer Center becomes the first accredited cancer center network in California and one of only 28 to receive the designation nationally by the American College of Surgeon's Commission on Cancer.
2009	Scripps Health commits to further development of wireless health care technology through a unique working relationship with the West Wireless Health Institute.
2009	Scripps Health creates the Physician Business Leadership Cabinet (PBLC). The members include the leaders of Scripps affiliated medical groups.
2010	Scripps Medical Response Team (SMRT) is deployed to Haiti to aid victims of devastating earthquake.
2010	Scripps Health announces a 25-year master plan to create a comprehensive regional medical campus at Scripps Memorial Hospital La Jolla.
2011	Philanthropist Conrad T. Prebys donates $45 million to support and name a regional cardiovascular institute on the Scripps Memorial Hospital La Jolla campus. It is the largest gift in Scripps history.
2011	Scripps Health breaks ground on three new facilities: Scripps Prebys Cardiovascular Institute, Scripps Proton Therapy Center, and the Scripps Radiation Therapy Center.
2011	ScrippsCare is formed as a new not-for-profit corporation that is governed by Scripps and seven physician groups. The PBLC board becomes the ScrippsCare board.

GOVERNING BOARD LEADERSHIP

Scripps Memorial Hospital/Scripps Health Past Board Chairs

Maureen Stapleton	2012–present	Robert Conway	1974
Robert Tjosvold	2010	Robert M. Boughton, MD	1972
Richard Vortmann	2008	William E. Ferguson	1970
Jeff Bowman	2006	Preston H. Kelsey	1969
Abby Silverman Weiss	2004	Richard N. Smith	1966
Janet Rodgers	2002	William Schofield	1965
Frank Panarisi	2000	Oliver Thornton	1959
Don Mitchell	1998	Louis F. Overgard	1958
Charles Scribner	1997	Oliver Thornton	1956
Gordon C. Luce	1996	Robert C. Watts	1955
J. Frank Mahoney	1993	Oliver Thornton	1953
Fred Shean, MD	1991	Kary Canatsey	1951
Ed Danenhauer	1989	Gerald Crary	1950
Richard McMahon	1987	John Scripps	1949
Lee Taylor	1986	Erskine Sandys	1948
William Hillyer	1983	Robert B. Watts	1947
Robert Gotfredson	1982	Donald Glazebrook	1946
David H. Hill	1982	Curtis Hillyer	1940
Ames S. Early	1980	W. L. Vanschaick	1939
H.M. Poole, Jr.	1978	Jacob C. Harper	1924
Harry Collins	1977		
Richard Hibbard	1975		

Founding Scripps Memorial Hospital/Scripps Health Board of Directors: 1924

Ellen B. Scripps
Jacob C. Harper
Albert W. Bennett
Wesley G. Crandall
Grace Kimball
Eleanore McG. Mills
Milton A. McRae

Scripps Metabolic Clinic/Scripps Clinic & Research Foundation Board Chairs

William E. Nelson	1991
Gordon. C. Luce	1987
V. Dewitt Shuck	1983
Donald Roon	1978
William Black	1972
Edgar J. Marston	1968
Hiram G. Dillin	1965
Admiral Wilder D. Baker	1958
William S. Kellogg	1951
Harry L. Smithton	1950
Curtis Hillyer	1946

MEDICAL STAFF LEADERSHIP

Scripps Memorial Hospital–La Jolla
Chiefs of Staff

Shawn D. Evans, MD	2012–present	George Hartley Jr., MD	1959
Marc M. Sedwitz, MD	2010	Thomas Mitchell, MD	1958
John C. Spinosa, MD	2008	Edward Weigle, MD	1957
Dana Launer, MD	2006	Ernest Neber, MD	1956
Sabina Wallach, MD	2004	Clifford Graves, MD	1955
Martin Griglak, MD	2002	C.R. Hyde, MD	1954
David M. Roseman, MD	2000	G.C. Langsdorf, MD	1953
Harold Shively, MD	1998	Damon E. Corbin, MD	1952
Adrian Jaffer, MD	1996	Fred Ullrich, MD	1951
Richard Fosburg, MD	1994	Rex Ucapher, MD	1950
John Steel, MD	1992	O.C. Helming, Jr., MD	1949
Clyde Beck, MD	1990	Ross Paull, MD	1948
John Cherry, MD	1988	J.W. Calloway, MD	1947
Fredric Shean, MD	1986	J.T. Lipe, MD	1946
Donald Ritt, MD	1985	Edward Copp, MD	1945
Glen Gibbons, MD	1983	James Chalmers. MD	1944
Phillip Gausewitz, MD	1981	W.L. Garth, MD	1943
Robert Reid, MD	1979	Arthur Marlow, MD	1942
Charles Campbell, MD	1978	Francis Smith, MD	1941
F. Bruce Kimball, MD	1977	W.E. Diefenbach, MD	1940
Thomas Elias, MD	1976	Eaton MacKay, MD	1939
John C. Carson, MD	1975	Ralph Kaysen, MD	1938
Ernest Pund, MD	1974	Ross Paull, MD	1937
Charles Wright, MD	1973	Hall Holder, MD	1936
Richard Jones, MD	1972	Francis Smith, MD	1935
David Carmichael, MD	1971	B.F. Eager, MD	1934
James Whisenand, MD	1970	W.L. Garth, MD	1933
James Kiely, MD	1969	Ray Lounsberry, MD	1932
J.W. Johnson, MD	1968	W.E. Diefenbach, MD	1931
Robert Boughton, MD	1967	A. B. Smith, MD	1930
Edward Mitchell, MD	1966	W.R. Eastman, MD	1929
Richard Tullis, MD	1965	Horace Lazelle, MD	1928
William J. Doyle, MD	1964	J.W. Sherrill, MD	1927
John J. Wells, MD	1963	W.C. Oatman, MD	1926
Bernard Hark, MD	1962	Truman Parker, MD	1925
Ralph Mullenix, MD	1961		
Everette Rogers, MD	1960		

MEDICAL STAFF LEADERSHIP

Scripps Mercy
Chiefs of Staff

Kent Diveley, MD	2011–present	Maurice J. Brown, MD	1962
Theodore S. Thomas, MD	2009	Winston Hall, MD	1960
Jerrold Glassman, MD	2005	Purvis Martin, MD	1959
Eugene W. Rumsey Jr., MD	2003	E. Minton Fetter, MD	1957
David J. Shaw, MD	2001	J.J. O'Hara, MD	1949
Kevin P. Glynn, MD	1999	Elmo Crabtree, MD	1948
Davis Cracroft, MD	1997	Clarence E. Rees, MD	1945
William Davidson, MD	1995	Bryan R. Simpson, MD	1944
Josephine Von Herzen, MD	1993	H.K. Graham, MD	1943
J. Robert Jacobs, MD	1991	T.O. Burger, MD	1942
Ralph P. George, MD	1989	Bryan R. Simpson, MD	1941
John Riley, MD	1988	E.F. Chamberlain, MD	1940
Stephen A. Pye, MD	1987	Samuel J. McClendon, MD	1939
John Morse, MD	1986	Lyell C. Kinney, MD	1938
Leo J. Murphy, MD	1985	A.J. Thornton, MD	1937
Richard L. Doyle, MD	1984	W.O. Weiskotten, MD	1936
Gordon Sproul, MD	1983	T. Wier, MD	1934
David K. Subin, MD	1982	L.H. Redelings, MD	1933
Stanley A. Moore, MD	1981	Clarence E. Rees, MD	1931
George G. Zorn, MD	1980	Lyell C. Kinney, MD	1930
Douglas P. Mooney, MD	1979	Charles Fox, MD	1929
Michael J. Feeney, MD	1978	L.H. Redelings, MD	1927
Harney M. Cordua Jr., MD	1977	Thomas Burger, MD	1926
William S. Mowrey, MD	1976	James Churchill, MD	1925
Jerome L. Heard, MD	1975	Lyell C. Kinney, MD	1923
Hugh Buff, MD	1974	Homer Oatman, MD	1922
Howell E. Wiggins, MD	1973	B.J. O'Neill, MD	1920
James C. MacLaggan, MD	1972		
Edwin L. Glazener, MD	1971		
Walter F. Carpenter, MD	1969		
David E. Wile, MD	1968		
Harold M. Messenger, MD	1965		
Robert M. Kimble, MD	1964		
Homer Peabody, MD	1963		

MEDICAL STAFF LEADERSHIP

Scripps Mercy–Chula Vista
Chiefs of Staff

Donald Vance, MD	2011–present	Douglas D. Hill, MD	1984
Rueben M. Farris, MD	2009	R. Edward Sanchez, MD	1983
Carlos F. Jimenez, MD	2007	Roger D. Stoike, MD	1982
Luis F. Sanchez, MD	2005	Charles F. Bower, MD	1981
Diogo Belo, MD	2003	Leroy A. Miller, MD	1980
Kousay Al-Kourainy, MD	2001	Charles Umansky, MD	1979
Carla Stayboldt, MD	1999	Robert M. Dimmette, MD	1978
Edgardo Gracia, MD	1997	Raymon E. Lawton, MD	1977
Henry A. Krumholz, MD	1995	Benjamin Layton, MD	1976
Edward Friedman, MD	1994	Louis Lurie, MD	1975
Vernon White, MD	1993	Carl Von Pohle, MD	1974
Francisco O. Gracia, MD	1991	Wendell F. Lienhard, MD	1973
Donald A. Sandweiss, MD	1990	James Collins, MD	1972
Tomas Romero, MD	1989	Donald F. Smith, MD	1971
Thomas Martinez, MD	1988	Charles A. Camarata, MD	1968
Leonard Kornreich, MD	1987	Anthony Pierangelo, MD	1965
George Cave, MD	1986		

Scripps Memorial Hospital–Encinitas
Chiefs of Staff

Thomas Chippendale, MD	2011–present	Michael Kimball, MD	1988
Ronald MacCormick, MD	2009	Vincent M. Ricchiuti, MD	1986
Michael Lobatz, MD	2007	James T. Hay, MD	1985
Ed Cohen, MD	2005	Thomas J. Rueben, MD	1983
Jim LaBelle, MD	2001	Samuel D. Winner, MD	1981
Michael Skyhar, MD	1998	Peter E. Pool, MD	1978
Joseph Traube, MD	1997	Joseph A. Bonano, MD	1977
Richard Gross, MD	1995	Dwight E. Cook, MD	1973
Robert F. Brunst, MD	1993	Charles E. Clark, MD	1968
Antone F. Salel, MD	1991		
Michael Lundberg, MD	1990		

MEDICAL STAFF LEADERSHIP

Scripps Green Hospital
Chiefs of Staff

James Mason, MD	2011–present	John G. Curd, MD	1987
Paul Pockros, MD	2009	Stanley Freedman, MD	1985
Prabhakar Tripuraneni, MD	2007	Gary W. Williams, MD	1983
John S. Romine, MD	2005	Roger C. Cornell, MD	1982
Peter C. Walther, MD	2003	Melvin A. Block, MD	1981
David S. Rubenson, MD	2001	Stanley G. Seats, MD	1979
Giacomo A. DeLaria, MD	1999	David A. Mathison, MD	1978
Robert B. Sarnoff, MD	1997	Donald J. Dalessio, MD	1977
Richard H. Walker, MD	1995		
Shirley M. Otis, MD	1993		
Guy P. Curtis, MD	1991		
Ralph B. Dilley, MD	1989		

ADMINISTRATIVE LEADERSHIP

Scripps Memorial Hospital-La Jolla

Gary Fybel, FACHE	2000-present
Tom Gagen	1998
Glenn Chong	1994
Jeff Bills	1992
Martin Buser	1983
Lauren Blagg	1978
Ames S. Early	1976
Louis Peelyon	1961
Fred W. Trader	1958
Gerald Crary	1953
Frank Guchereau	1948
Robert B. Witham	1947
H.B. Hatfield	1944
Jessie A. Horn	1930
Ada Gillispie	1924

Scripps Green Hospital (1977)

Robin Brown, FACHE	2000-present
Tom Gagen	1998
Glenn Chong	1994
Richard Bracken (HCA)	1982
Charles Edwards, MD	1977

Scripps Memorial Hospital-Encinitas (1978)

Carl Etter, FACHE	2003-present
John Schleif	2002
Barbara Mitchell	2001
Rebecca Ropchan	1997
Gerald Bracht	1993
Steve Goe	1986
Donald Zuercher	1979
Paul O'Neill	1978

Scripps Mercy-Chula Vista (1986)

Tom Gammiere, FACHE	2004
Todd Hoff	2004
John Grah	2001
Tom Gammiere	1992
Jeff Bills	1986

ADMINISTRATIVE LEADERSHIP

Scripps Mercy–San Diego (1995)

Tom Gammiere, FACHE	1999-present
Nancy Wilson	1996
Ralph George, MD	1995
Mary Yarbrough	1992
Richard Keyser	1983
Sister Mary Joanne De Vincenti	1977
Sister Mary Placida Conant	1965
Sister Mary Eucharia Malone	1956
Sister Mary Leonard Fahey	1944
Sister Mary Beatrice Malone	1938
Sister Mary Thomas Shanley	1932
Sister Mary Angela Cooney	1929
Sister Mary Liguori McNamara	1923
Sister Mary Angela Cooney	1922
Mother Mary Michael Cummings	1890

Scripps Clinic

Larry Harrison	2003-present (Scripps Medical Foundation)
Hugh Greenway, MD	2000 (Scripps Medical Foundation)
Thomas Waltz, MD	1991 (Scripps Clinic and Research Foundation)
Charles Edwards, MD	1977 (Scripps Clinic and Research Foundation)
Frank Dixon, MD	1974 (Scripps Clinic and Research Foundation)
Edmund Keeney, MD	1955 (Scripps Clinic and Research Foundation)
James Sherrill, MD	1924 (Scripps Metabolic Clinic)

CORPORATE LEADERSHIP

Scripps Chief Executive Officer

Chris Van Gorder, FACHE	2000-present
Stan Pappelbaum, MD	1999
Ames S. Early	1994
William Nelson	1993
Charles Edwards, MD	1991
Ames S. Early	1976

Scripps Chief Medical Officers

Brent Eastman, MD	1999-present
Clyde H. "Bud" Beck, MD	1997

PHILANTHROPIC LEADERSHIP

Development Committee, Scripps Health Board of Trustees

Judy Churchill, PhD	2009–present
Robert Tjosvold	2007
Sister Mary Jo Anderson	2005

Scripps Foundation for Medicine and Science Board Chairs

David Nuffer	2003
Daniel Mulvihill	2001
Martin C. Dickinson	1997
Thomas P. Nickell, Jr.	1995
Michael S. Cavanaugh	1993

Scripps Memorial Hospitals Foundation Board Chairs

Gail Stoorza-Gill	1991
Michael S. Cavanaugh	1990
Betsy Manchester	1989
Vincent Benstead	1987
Arthur J. Benvenuto	1986
Fred C. Stabler	1983
John Weld	1980
Ewart H. Wyle, DD	1979
Helen Nix	1978

PHILANTHROPIC LEADERSHIP

Scripps Mercy Hospital Foundation Board Chairs

Maureen King	2009-present
Robert Horsman	2007
Judy Churchill, PhD	2005
Gerald Davee	2003
Richard Woltman	2001
Alan Schulman	1999
Sister Mary Jo Anderson	1997
Bruce Moore	1996
Lynn Silva	1995
Norman Seltzer	1993
William Beamer	1991
James Mulvaney	1989
Daniel Mulvihill	1985

SCRIPPS HEALTH CORPORATE LEADERSHIP 2012

Scripps Health Board of Trustees

Maureen Stapleton, Chairman
Judy Churchill, PhD, Vice Chair

Mary Jo Anderson, CHS
Richard C. Bigelow
Douglas A. Bingham, Esq.
Jeff Bowman
Jan Caldwell
Gordon R. Clark
Virginia Gillis, RSM, EdD
Katherine A. Lauer
Marty J. Levin

Robert Tjosvold
Chris Van Gorder, FACHE
Abby Weiss

Scripps Executive & Leadership Teams

Chris Van Gorder, FACHE
President & CEO

Robin Brown, FACHE
Victor Buzachero
Mary Lou Carraher
Brent Eastman, MD
John Engle
Carl Etter, FACHE
Gary Fybel, FACHE
Tom Gammiere, FACHE
Larry Harrison
June Komar
Richard Rothberger
Richard Sheridan

John Armstrong
David Cohn
Mary Ellen Doyle
Shiraz Fagan
James LaBelle, MD
Glen Mueller
Richard Neale
Athena Philis-Tsimikas, MD
Barbara Price
Marc Reynolds
Don Stanziano
Patric Thomas
Eric Topol, MD

SCRIPPS HEALTH CORPORATE LEADERSHIP 2012

Physician Leadership Cabinet

Chris Van Gorder, FACHE, President & CEO
Brent Eastman, MD, Chief Medical Officer

Robin Brown, FACHE

Tom Chippendale, MD

Kent Diveley, MD

Mary Ellen Doyle

Scott Eisman, MD

Carl Etter, FACHE

Shawn Evans, MD

Gary Fybel, FACHE

Tom Gammiere, FACHE

Larry Harrison

James LaBelle, MD

James Mason, MD

Ricardo Soltero, MD

Juan Tovar, MD

Don Vance, MD

Jon Worsey, MD

ScrippsCare Board and Directors

Marc Reynolds, CEO

James LaBelle, MD, President

Stewart Frank, MD, Vice Chair

Scott Eisman, MD, Treasurer

Robert Sarnoff, MD, Secretary

Davis Cracroft, MD

Kevin Hirsch, MD

Michael Karp, MD

Miranda Klassen

Marc Sedwitz, MD

Chris Van Gorder

Richard Vortmann

SCRIPPS DISASTER RESPONSE TEAMS

Haiti – 2010

Chris Van Gorder, FACHE, President & CEO
Brent Eastman, MD, Chief Medical Officer

John Armstrong
Todd Austin, MD
Michael Capozza, MD
Kelly Hardiman, RN
Katrina Kelly, MD
Debra McQuillen, RN
Drew Peterson, MD

Maureen Shackford
Steven Shackford, MD
Robert Sills
Charles Simmons, MD
Patty Skoglund, RN
David Smith, MD
Michael Sykes

Katrina – 2005

Chris Van Gorder, FACHE, President & CEO
Brent Eastman, MD, Chief Medical Officer

Nursing Staff

Gayle Allen, RN
Grace Baldo, RN
Darlene Bourdon, RN
Anna Coons, RN
Sarah Davis, RN
Stephanie Decker, RN
Elizabeth Dodson, RN
Elizabeth Embry, RN
Cathy Faulkner, RN
Mary Ann Garcia, LVN
Susanna Gonzales, RN
Kelly Hardiman, RN
Debra Harris, RN
Angela Hudson, RN
Deb Kosak, RN
Christine Kowalski, RN
Ken Leake, RN
Regina Long, RN

Patricia McAuliffe, RN
Joseph McGinnis, RN
Deb McQuillen, RN
Steve Miller, RN
Sheryl Nespor, NP
Terry Newman, RN
Clela Patterson, RN
Mary Prehoden, RN
Luanna Quirk, RN
Peggy Quiroz, RN
Sara Ruff, RN
James Russel, RN
Peter Schultz, NP
Sara Shoop, RN
Patty Skoglund, RN
Jeanette Stiles, RN
Chris Vasquez, RN
Jeanne Williams, RN

SCRIPPS DISASTER RESPONSE TEAMS

Katrina – 2005

Physicians

Peter Aldrich, MD

Ken Antons, MD

Juliet Bleha, MD

Joseph Bonanno, MD

Erin Castelloe, MD

Davis Cracroft, MD

Dan Dworsky, MD

Brent Eastman, MD

Alissa Gilles, MD

Kevin Glynn, MD

Billie Green, MD

Holly Hauser, MD

Elan Hekier, MD

Mark Kalina, MD

Jonathan Lee, MD

Vimal Nanavati, MD

Valerie Norton, MD

Paul Pockros, MD

George Rodriguez, MD

Robert Sarnoff, MD

Lynne Scannell, MD

Jennifer Steeper, MD

Greg Teregis, MD

Stefan Willging, MD

Amy Witman, MD

Physician Assistants

Margaret Diliberto, PA

Zarin Kahn, PA

Christy Kerr, PA

Administration/Support Staff

Robin Brown, FACHE

Larry Harrison

Mike Morris

Ana Reibstein

Rob Sills

Don Stanziano

Mike Urquhart

Administrative/Support Staff at home

Kay Alexander

Vic Buzachero

Mary Lou Carraher

Debbie Gac

June Komar

Virginia Leary

Samantha Saunders

Meg Ulrich

Index

A

E

F

G

L

N

O

R

T

W

Sarita Eastman is a physician and poet whose first non-fiction book, *A Trail of Light: The Very Full Life of Dr. Anita Figueredo*, won the San Diego Book Award for biography in 2010. She was a long-time Scripps pediatrician with a specialty in development and behavior until her retirement from the practice of medicine in 2011 to devote herself to writing full time. She lives with her husband in Rancho Santa Fe, California.

sarita.eastman@gmail.com • PO Box 1248, Rancho Santa Fe, CA 92067